FEDERAL FURNITURE

FEDERAL FURNITURE

Michael Dunbar

The Taunton Press

**Cover and text photos by Andrew Edgar,
except where noted.**

Photos, pp. 8 and 10, by John Corcoran.

First printing: May 1986
International Standard Book Number: 0-918804-48-5
Library of Congress Catalog Card Number: 85-52239
Printed in Denmark

A Fine Woodworking Book

Fine Woodworking® is a trademark of The Taunton Press, Inc.,
registered in the U.S. Patent and Trademark Office.

The Taunton Press, Inc.
63 South Main Street
Box 355
Newtown, Connecticut 06470

Acknowledgments

My wife, Carol, and I dedicate this book to our good friend Dr. Dorothy Vaughan. During World War I, when she was a teenager, Dorothy began her lifelong love affair with Portsmouth, New Hampshire. Throughout most of this century, when few others cared or were able to understand why, she struggled to protect this old city by the sea from the wrecker's ball. The special character and architectural heritage that Portsmouth has only lately learned to cherish were in large part saved for us all by Dorothy.

She stands as a bridge between Portsmouth's past and its future. She has read and committed to memory the city's written history. And before each recent generation of older citizens slipped away, she befriended them, keeping alive in the process two centuries of oral history for this generation.

Dorothy shares her knowledge liberally. She has always willingly helped me with my research, and in so doing she has also shared her unique gift with you, the readers of this book.

I would also like to acknowledge the contribution to this book of Andy Edgar, whose patience and good humor helped us both survive many hours of photography. Jack and Diane McGee's generosity brought the Lord box home. Fellow craftsmen and woodworkers Pat Edwards, Al Breed and Tom Hinckley contributed their special knowledge and information. Much of the wood used in the projects fell to Eddy Tremblay's chainsaw. Through Charlie LeBlanc at the Portsmouth Public Library, resources were only a phone call away. And since this book contains no index, Ed Hyder has yielded his place.

Contents

AN INTRODUCTION TO FEDERAL FURNITURE 1

THE PARLOR 8

  1 *Card Table* 10
    Project: String inlay

  2 *Mirror* 20
    Project: Rope turning

  3 *Sofa* 30
    Project: Reeding by hand

  4 *Candlestand* 38
    Project: Sliding dovetails

  5 *Lord Box* 44
    Project: Jointed lid and ''matched'' veneers

  6 *Tip-Top Table* 50
    Project: Hinge block

  7 *Secretary* 58
    Project: Muntins

THE DINING ROOM 72

  8 *Tray* 74
    Project: Edge banding

  9 *Hepplewhite Chair* 80
    Project: Angled mortise-and-tenons

  10 *Gateleg Table* 90
    Project: Wooden hinge

  11 *Fancy Chair* 100
    Project: Reeding with a plane

  12 *Bellows* 108
    Project: Front-board decoration

THE KITCHEN 116

  13 *Windsor Chair* 118
    Project: Shaping the seat

  14 *Display Shelf* 126
    Project: Stop dadoes

  15 *Candle Box* 132
    Project: Sliding lid

  16 *Desk on Frame* 138
    Project: Simulated four-way miter joints

THE BEDROOM 146

  17 *High-Post Bed* 148
    Project: Roping the frame

  18 *Pembroke Table* 156
    Project: Rule joints

  19 *Bracket-Base Blanket Chest* 164
    Project: Rabbeted lid moldings

  20 *Chest of Drawers* 170
    Project: Simulated cock beading

APPENDICES

  Sources of Supply 179

  Glossary 180

  Bibliography 183

AN INTRODUCTION TO FEDERAL FURNITURE

The waning years of the 18th century marked an exhilarating period in American history. With the end of the Revolutionary War in 1781 and the ratification of the U.S. Constitution in 1788, Americans embarked on one of the most radical political experiments in history. The product of their struggle was the Federal Republic—an achievement of which they were acutely proud. At the same time they were also unknowingly laying the groundwork in America for what would begin in England and spread elsewhere as another of history's greatest changes: the Industrial Revolution.

The arts of America bear the influence of this exciting era, and many innovations in style heralded the new republic's birth. In furniture the emerging style in America was known as Federal and was produced roughly from around 1790 to 1820.

A large, well-established middle class dominated the populace of Federal-period America. This population was well educated, and politically, technologically and artistically sophisticated. While Hollywood has thoroughly familiarized us with the pioneers who settled the American frontier, we remain largely unaware that our Colonial and Federal forebears also created wealthy, cosmopolitan centers like Philadelphia, Boston and New York. The social conditions of these Federal-period cities and the new republic's established commercial network made possible a high level of accomplishment in the arts and in manufacturing, arenas that converged in the woodworking trades of architecture and furnituremaking.

During the 17th and early 18th centuries, England had provided the major influence on American architecture, furniture and decorative arts. In the mid-18th century, England, like the rest of Europe, became fascinated with the archaeological discoveries at classical Greek and Roman sites. The decorative objects and the paintings of daily life yielded by sites like Pompeii gave rise to an enthusiastic revival of interest in the classical world. In reaction to the excess of the Gothic and rococo styles from the Chippendale period in the mid-18th century, the neoclassical movement produced a reinterpretation of Greco-Roman antiquity that emphasized simplicity, geometric forms and classical ornament. With the end of the Revolutionary War and the normalization of relations and commerce between England and America, neoclassicism spread to the new republic. For Federal-period Americans, the similarities of their own political experiment and the democratic experiences of the classical world added significance to their embrace of the neoclassical movement that went far beyond the desire to copy the most up-to-date European fashion.

The new Federal furniture was light and delicate in appearance. Favoring simple, geometric lines, it observed rigid symmetry in its overall design and borrowed enthusiastically from classical decorative motifs. Among these motifs were vases, urns, plumes, swags, bows and reeding; patriotic elements like the eagle found their way into many Federal pieces as well. In addition to classical ornament, Federal furniture also made frequent use of string and pictorial inlay and veneering.

The characteristic delicacy of Federal furniture is also the feature that most obviously distinguishes it from the larger, more robust Chippendale furniture that immediately preceded it and the heavier Empire style that followed. Federal furniture's apparent daintiness, however, was largely an illusion, created by removing from the individual elements of a piece all wood unnecessary to the structural integrity of the whole. Sometimes this delicacy was achieved by scaling down the piece, so that while adequately sized for its function, it was generally smaller than a comparable Chippendale or Empire example. Yet despite its appearance, Federal furniture was by no means fragile. On the contrary, the pieces presented in this book—all of which are from the collection of Federal furniture my wife, Carol, and I own—are an average of 175 years old, and all still remain stable and in daily use.

The introduction of neoclassicism in America was hastened by the importation from England of pattern, or drawing, books published in the late 18th century by individual cabinetmakers or others in the furniture trade. Comparable to what today would be a cross between a modern furniture catalog and a home-and-garden magazine, these drawing books illustrated the latest fashion in furniture and interior decorating and provided patterns for cabinetmakers working outside London who needed to accommodate their customers' requests for the most up-to-date designs. The engravings in the drawing books frequently presented both what the latest furniture was to look like and how it was to be accessorized, arranged and used in the home.

Although numerous pattern books were published, the best known are *The Cabinet-Maker and Upholsterer's Guide* (1788) by George Hepplewhite and *The Cabinet-Maker's and Upholsterer's Drawing-Book* (1791-93) by Thomas Sheraton. The engravings in these books, two of which are found on the facing page, contrast markedly with the plans we use today in building furniture. They include very few measurements and usually present only front views of pieces. For the user of one of these books, additional information was unnecessary; a trained cabinetmaker needed only a picture of the desired piece to proportion and construct it.

Hepplewhite and Sheraton usually illustrated furniture that was far more elaborate than the actual pieces inspired by their books. It is unlikely that they intended the furniture to be so intensely developed, but probably overadorned their engravings to give cabinetmakers and their customers a wide selection of ornament from which to choose.

It is often thought that Hepplewhite and Sheraton designed the furniture that bears their names, but instead of promoting their own designs, both men merely illustrated the style then current in England. Ironically, neither Hepplewhite nor Sheraton left any furniture that can be attributed to their hands.

Actually, the traditional distinction between Hepplewhite and Sheraton furniture is misleading, since the pieces illustrated in their pattern books were quite similar. This system of classification arose in the late 19th

Made around 1770, the robust Chippendale side chair shown at left above features square Marlborough legs and a shaped and pierced "ribbon back." The more delicate, Federal-period Sheraton side chair, center, has a serpentine-shaped seat, turned and fluted front legs, and a square back that the maker undoubtedly copied from Sheraton's second design in the lower engraving on the facing page. The Empire side chair, right, made around 1820, is based on the Klismos chair illustrated on ancient Greek vases.

Sofa.

From George Hepplewhite's pattern book, this sofa design features the turned legs that are usually associated with Sheraton furniture. (Both engravings courtesy of Dover Publications.)

CHAIR BACKS.

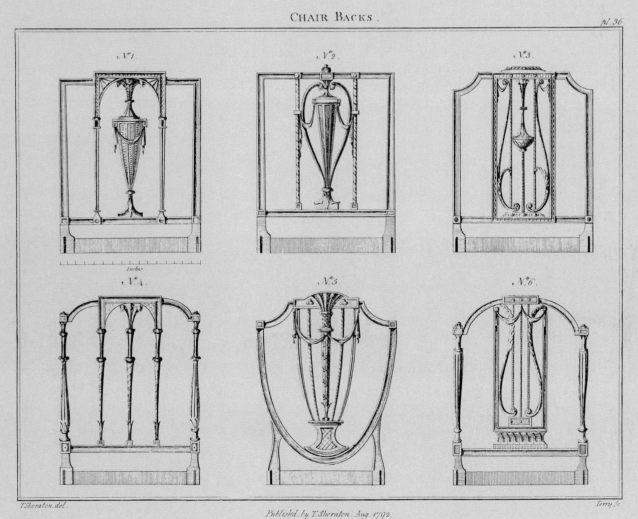

From Thomas Sheraton's pattern book, this engraving displays a variety of chair-back designs and the minimal dimensions needed for their reproduction.

and early 20th centuries when antique collectors and the museum world tried to organize and codify, somewhat arbitrarily, the various styles of furniture being collected. A Sheraton chair, for example, is generally perceived as having a square back, turned legs and feet, and often reeded decoration on both turned and flat surfaces; yet it is possible to find examples of Hepplewhite chairs with one or several of these characteristics. By contrast, the traditional Hepplewhite-style chair is characterized as having a curvilinear back (often in the shape of a shield), tapered legs and spade feet—all features that are occasionally found on Sheraton furniture as well. And sometimes a feature designated as Sheraton or Hepplewhite is actually an amalgam of designs from both pattern books.

Just as Federal-period cabinetmakers found motifs and features intermingled in pattern books, they too borrowed freely from various sources for their own designs. They occasionally incorporated an element that remained popular from an earlier period or style. Such an element, called a survival feature, is more common on informal and country furniture than on formal. One of several examples of survival features found in this book is the thumbnail molding on the desk on frame on p. 138, a feature carried over from the Chippendale period.

Late in the Federal period, cabinetmakers also borrowed from the newly emerging Empire style, called Grecian by the men who made it. This style of furniture was heavily influenced both by Greek classical forms and by archaeological discoveries then being made in Egypt.

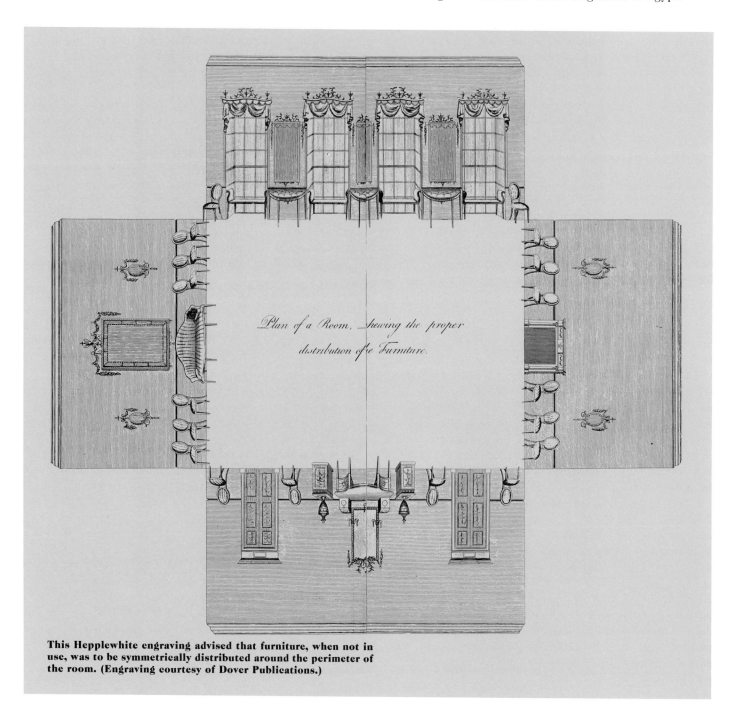

Plan of a Room, shewing the proper distribution of the Furniture.

This Hepplewhite engraving advised that furniture, when not in use, was to be symmetrically distributed around the perimeter of the room. (Engraving courtesy of Dover Publications.)

Cabinetmakers and their clients

In the Federal period, almost every large city had numerous cabinetmaking shops where one could purchase ready-made furniture or place a special order. Most major cities, among them Philadelphia, New York and Boston, also shipped Federal furniture as cargo to ports all along the East Coast, where it was usually purchased by furniture dealers, who were often cabinetmakers themselves. Any good-size town and many rural villages also had at least one cabinetmaker creating furniture for local use.

The great variety of cabinetmakers and the differing needs of their customers produced several categories of Federal furniture: formal, or high-style, furniture; informal furniture; and country furniture. Formal furniture was usually made in cities with an established cabinetmaking industry by craftsmen who had trained in traditional apprenticeships. Their work was fashioned after that in the pattern books and ornamented in varying degrees. Whatever the extent of its decoration, formal furniture was usually made of mahogany, though occasionally cabinetmakers worked with native woods like cherry or used a highly figured variety, like crotch-grain birch, for veneer.

Informal furniture was made both by urban cabinetmakers—sometimes in the same shops that produced more expensive, formal pieces—and by rural artisans. This utilitarian furniture generally carried less ornament than did formal work, and it was frequently painted. The wood used for informal furniture was usually a native species like cherry, birch, maple, pine, tulipwood, poplar or walnut.

Country furniture was made by rural craftsmen. This furniture is often similar in appearance to informal furniture, and frequently it's impossible to distinguish between the two. While generally simple, country furniture could be ambitious in design. Yet even the best country furniture usually indicates the maker's inexperience with high-style interpretations of Federal furniture, perhaps the result of a more informal apprenticeship.

Country furnituremakers occasionally used mahogany in their work but more often employed locally available, native woods. These craftsmen seem to have frequently copied designs from memory and clearly felt free to express their individuality in interpreting a design. Their work varied widely in quality; yet a piece like the candlestand on p. 38 displays how successful country furniture could be.

Whether making formal, informal or country furniture, a Federal-period cabinetmaker knew how his work would be used by the client. As advocated in the pattern books, most furniture, when not in use, would be placed against a wall, essentially ringing the room (see the engraving on the facing page). When needed, it would be moved to the center of the room. Most pieces therefore had to be portable, a requirement made possible by the furniture's delicate design and light weight. The custom of moving furniture about offered cabinetmakers an opportunity to enhance their designs, and they frequently fashioned pieces like the tip-top table on p. 50 that altered position—and thus character—for storage and use.

Often Federal furnituremakers designed pieces that also changed character in the varying light of day and evening. They knew that a piece would be seen in its entirety in the even, natural light of day; and that, by contrast, in the oblique candlelight of evening, the piece would lose detail, and its proportions might become distorted amidst the shadows. To use these lighting conditions to advantage, these craftsmen created such intriguing designs as those for the card table on p. 10 and the bellows on p. 108.

The cleverness and subtlety of Federal cabinetmakers' designs displays considerable sophistication. Our Federal ancestors certainly developed and nurtured a keen visual sense, which we, I suspect, have lost from exposure to such passive forms of entertainment as television. Unlike the diversion we electronically pipe into our houses, visual entertainment was built into the Federal-period home itself. A Federal interior was a complex and well-planned composition, meant to be studied over time and enjoyed. Architecture and furniture together contributed to a harmonious whole that engaged and entertained the eye.

Perhaps because Federal Americans created their own diversion, they lauded cleverness in conversation and in decor. For this reason, cabinetmakers incorporated delightful surprises and subtleties in their work. Such visual cleverness, for example, can be seen in the choice of veneers on the Lord box on p. 44 and the unusual design with which the maker of the secretary on p. 58 circumvented the rigid symmetry of Federal furniture.

Because almost all Federal furniture, formal or informal, was made of wood, Federal cabinetmakers and their customers regarded wood differently than we do today. Though their formal furniture displays an appreciation for bold figure, they understood that furniture's success did not always depend on seeing the wood itself. An opaque, painted finish was seen, on occasion, as a means of enhancing the success of a piece. Certainly the painted finish on a piece like the Windsor chair on p. 118 serves to unify it and elevate it from a study in grain to a sophisticated composition in line.

From my study of Federal furniture, I found that even the most ordinary, functional furniture of this period was better designed and better constructed than modern mass-produced furniture. (Only time will tell whether the work of contemporary custom furnituremakers is as enduring as Federal furniture.) Yet despite excellent workmanship, this furniture has inevitably suffered various degrees of damage during nearly two centuries of use, most of it due to wear and abuse. The cracking, warping and shrinking found in many pieces, however, is the product of wood movement. In the environment for which it was created—homes heated by fireplaces—this furniture remained relatively stable. Yet in the much drier environment produced by modern central heating, the wood has unavoidably undergone change.

Living with Federal furniture

The individual pieces of furniture presented in this book have a great deal in common with one another. Not only were they all made at about the same time, they were also fashioned as middle-class furniture, that is, neither overly elaborate nor exceedingly simple. Yet these pieces have something else in common, too. Carol and I have assembled them along with other Federal pieces to furnish our Federal-period house, which was built around 1800.

When we bought our home in 1976, it had changed so little over its lifetime that we decided to restore it exactly to its original appearance, including duplicating the original colors and wallpapers. As the walls, woodwork and floors were restored, we added to our growing collection of Federal-period furniture.

A document we have found vital in furnishing our home is the inventory of the contents of the house taken in 1805. Since consumer goods were very expensive before the Industrial Revolution and household furnishings generally made up a substantial part of a personal estate, the judge of probate usually ordered a household inventory taken upon someone's death. The 1805 inventory to which I refer is that of the estate of master mariner John Seaward, Jr., who built this house sometime between 1794 (when he bought the lot) and 1803 (when he wrote a will leaving the house to his wife, Hannah). In March 1805, Seaward sailed out of Boston as captain of the ship *Peter* and died while in Savannah, Georgia.

This inventory, whose text is provided on the facing page, gives a fascinating look at the contents of a typical middle-class, Federal-period household. Among other things, the modern reader will doubtless be impressed by the number of chairs listed—five different sets, totaling a surprising 40 chairs in the house's six completed rooms. (Though the inventory lists four sets in the kitchen, it's unlikely to have held 30 chairs. Probably chairs from various sets were in the kitchen and the inventory takers asked Mrs. Seaward how many of each she had.)

We haven't adhered slavishly to this inventory in furnishing this house, though we have bought some pieces because similar items were once part of the house's furnishings. We have arranged this furniture as it would have been in a typical Federal house, often placing pieces in locations suggested by the inventory and, insofar as possible, using these pieces as originally intended.

As a woodworker and Windsor chairmaker since 1971, as well as an inveterate student of Federal-period life, I wanted to address the subject of Federal furniture both from the point of view of the people who lived with this furniture and from the perspective of the craftsmen who made it. Unfortunately, scholars studying historical furniture are seldom concerned with the craftsman's point of view, and few are themselves woodworkers. For these reasons, much valuable information has gone undetected, and our understanding of the subject is incomplete. I am therefore pleased in this book to invite you into my home and to share with you my findings about Federal furniture and Federal-period life.

Using this book

This book consists of 20 chapters, each devoted to one piece of furniture and all arranged in four sections by room. Every chapter contains a general discussion of the design and construction of the piece, as well as a project section on a particular aspect of construction or ornament that is either typically Federal or unusual to modern woodworkers—for example, how to produce the simulated cock beading on a drawer front. The project section contains step-by-step instructions, detailed drawings and process photographs; and each chapter concludes with a complete set of measured drawings for the full piece.

The 20 pieces included in this book were carefully selected from the larger collection of Federal furniture with which we live. First and foremost, I chose these pieces because they are good examples of Federal-period design and workmanship. They are not necessarily what the antique market would deem the most "important" pieces in the collection, but they represent the broad spectrum of Federal style. I hope they will appeal to differing tastes and add to the furnishings of many different homes.

If you, too, are a woodworker, you will be interested in what can be learned from Federal-period cabinetmakers. They used some woodworking techniques that are no longer widely known. They also used hand tools, some of which, though still available, are not well known either. Since I own few machines and usually work with hand tools, I have chosen to show in this book how to do the projects with these traditional tools. Often, however, I suggest alternative electrical tools that can be used for a particular job, and when using an unusual antique tool, I have offered advice on how to adapt another commonly available tool.

Some of the pieces presented in this book could be interpreted differently from the original or could be scaled up or down in size. In both cases, I have mentioned the possible changes, but I urge you to think through each change thoroughly before beginning work on a project, since limited space obviously prevented including all the information needed for such changes.

Also I often mention the finish used on the original piece. In some very humid or very dry climates, the original finish might not work well. For this reason, keep local conditions in mind when choosing a finish.

I hope you find the furniture in this book as interesting as I do and that you will decide to make some of the pieces, either for yourself or for your customers. If you do, please send me a slide of your work.

By the Hon. Nathl Rogers, Rockingham—ss.
Judge of the Probate of Wills &c. for said County.

To Capt. Edward Sargent, M. Daniel Smith and M. Samuel Drowne, all of Portsmouth in said County

Greeting.
You are hereby authorised to take an Inventory of the Estate of John Seaward, late of said Portsmouth, mariner deceased who lately died testate to be shewn unto you by Hannah Seaward Executrix of his last Will & Testament and to make a just and impartial Appraissment thereof according to the best of your Judgment, and to return the same under your, or any two of your Hands, into the Registry of the Court of Probate for said County, upon Oath, to your Fidelity, herein, at or before the Third Wednesday of September next, together with this Warrent.

Dated at Portsmouth the 19th day of June, Anno Domini 1805
By Order of the Judge W. Parker Reg

Inventory of the Estate of John Seaward, late of Portsmouth, Mariner deceased, taken by us the undersigned, and appraised—
Pursuant to the annexed Warrent—

Viz. 1 Mahogany Bureau	$18.
2—ditto—Card Tables	24.
2 Oval Gilt Framed Looking Glasses	12.
1 large easy Chair & Covering	16.
8 mahogany mohair bottom'd chairs and two armed—ditto—	40.
1 high post birch Bedstead, with Bed and furniture	90.
1 pair brass Front Andirons, Shovel, Tongs & hooks, & 1 pair Bellows	15.
2 pictures	1.
2 small pieces wax work, Glass & Framed	.50
1 pair brass Candlesticks, Tray & Snuffers	1.
a Quantity of China, glass, & Earthern ware in a closet	70.
1 hearth brush, Carpenters Hammer, & glass Lantern	2.
1 large Bible	4.50
1 pair Iron dogs, 2 Iron pots, Shovel Tongs & Sad Irons	2.50
1 Tub, 1 pail, 1 birch Square Table, with leaves	4.
2 Small pieces, Home made Carpeting	2.
3 Japaned waiters, 1 Toilet Table	2.
1 Corded Bedstead	1.50
1 Dozn green, & 6 yellow Windsor Chairs	12.
6 Maple carved, back Flag Bottomed Chairs	4.
6 Common Chairs	2.

Amount Inventory, Sum brot forwd, Dollars	**$324.**

1 Large Spinning Wheel, 1 Foot—ditto—	$2.
1 Bread Trough, Bowle, Tray, & 2 measures	2.
1 Tin Roasting Kitchen & Spit	2.50
a Quantity old Tin ware	1.
Iron ware	5.50
1 Case 15 Two Quart Empty bottles	2.50
a Quantity, Old earthern ware	1.
1 Brass warming pan	2.50
Salt mortar, & Sieve	.50
1 mahogany 4 feet, (old), Table	4.
some old Empty Casks	2.
2 large Gilt Framed looking Glasses	40.
1 Mahogany Desk	18.
1 Birch 4 Feet Table & covering	8.
1—ditto—3 feet table, with leaves	2.50
1 Cloathes Horse	1.
1 brass fire set small size	10.
1 Pembroke, Mahogany table	8.

1 large Japan'd Tea Tray $4. Candle Stand 50 cts	4.50
1 small Gilt framed looking Glass	5.50
1 Violen	2.
1 maple 4 feet table with leaves	3.
23 Framed pictures different sizes	15.
1 Japaned Tea Tray	2.
2 Small Trunks	2.
13 Volumes, Books	10.
1 Small Shaving Glass	.30
2 large, Floor carpets	50.
Bed Furniture	46.
1 Birch high post Bedstead, Bed, and Furniture and window Curtains	90.
1 Feather bed, Bolster and pillows	30.

amount carried forward—Dollars	**$697.30**

5 Table Clothes, sundry Towels. napkins & pillow cases	$25.
2 Chests & 3 Trunks	15.
1 looking Glass & small Oval table	2.
Copper ladle & Skimmer	1.50
some Kitchen Utensils & sundry pieces. old carpets	8.
1 Portmanteau	3.50
1 small plated Tea Pot, Six large Silver spoons, 12—ditto—Tea spoons, & a pair of Sugar Tongs	45.
Sundrie Earthern pickle pots	2.
2 Fire Buckets	6.
1 Hadleys Quadrant, & Spy Glass	10.
1 Chaise & Harness complete	150.
1 Gold Watch $45, 1 Silver Watch $15	60.
1 Dutch, Liquor Case, & Bottles	5.
Brass, Top Shovel & Tongs	1.
Wearing Apparel of said deceased	30.

whole amount Personal Estate	**Dollars $1061.30**

Real Estate
a Lot of land in Portsmouth, situate by the northwardly, side of Maudlin Lane with the dwelling House, out houses & and all buildings thereon, and all appurtenances, thereto, belonging
$2800.

whole Amount of Inventory dollars	**$3861.30**

Portsmouth
July 2, 1805

Edward Sargent
Danl Smith
Saml Drowne

State of New Hampshire Rockingham ss
Portsmouth August 6th, 1805, then Messrs. Edward Sargent, Daniel Smith & Samuel Drowne above named personally appeared and made Solem Oath that they have faithfully and impartially appraised all the Estate of the said John Seaward deceas'd that was shewn them by the Executrix of his last Will agreeable to the foregoing Inventory, by them severally signed according to their best skills and Judgment.
sworn before Issac Rindge, Just: Peace

Rockingham ss. Greenland, August 31st 1805, Then Mrs. Hannah Seaward, Executrix of the last Will of the within named John Seaward deceased, made solemn Oath that she had shewn all the Estate of her late husband, the said John Seaward, that has come to her hands agreeable to the foregoing Inventory, & that if any other Estate of said deceased should hereafter come to her hands she would exhibit the same to the Judge of Probate for said County of Rockingham in the Additional Inventory.
sworn to before Enoch Clark, Just: Peace

THE PARLOR

In a Federal-period home, the parlor was usually the best and most formal room, but it was also one of the most comfortable rooms in the house. It was the heart of social and family life, and most entertaining was done here. This was an inviting place to take tea, or to dine alone or in groups too small to warrant setting up the dining room. It was also the usual spot to receive guests, as the many calling cards found behind our parlor mantle indicate. The early 19th-century playing cards also found there suggest that in our parlor the previous owners of the house and their guests partook of this most popular of pastimes, probably on the pair of mahogany card tables listed in the 1805 inventory of the house.

Our parlor reflects its formal purpose. The woodwork is both more abundant and more completely developed than that in any other room in the house. The mantle and the abutting china-closet door make the fireplace wall the focus of the room. The mantle, which is 5 ft. 7 in. high and has a shelf 6 ft. 4 in. long, contains an elaborate cornice made up of a crown molding and a denticulated bed molding. The mantle's frieze is 13½ in. high and ends on either side with a pronounced *S*-shaped cyma curve. Called a lyre-shaped frieze, this was a common detail on mantles in the Portsmouth area during the early Federal period. The fireplace jambs are surrounded by a two-step architrave, identical to those found around the doorways.

The 1805 inventory shows that when Capt. and Mrs. Seaward, the builders of the house, furnished it, they placed most of the formal and expensive objects in their parlor. Continuing the tradition, we also keep our finest furniture in this room. Since most formal Federal furniture was made of mahogany, many of the mahogany pieces included in this book will appear in this section.

The expense in the Federal period of the mahogany furnishings and the fabrics in the parlor resulted in another custom of the day that, to us, seems unusual. Since the ultraviolet rays in direct sunlight can bleach dark woods, damage shellac finishes and deteriorate fabrics, families sequestered themselves during the day behind drawn shutters or venetian blinds in the dimly lit parlor. At night the shutters afforded privacy. In the summer eliminating direct sunlight from the room also helped keep it cool, and in the winter the drawn shutters reduced drafts. Each of our parlor windows therefore has an interior shutter, which slides into a special casing built into the wall. Like the house's previous owners, we too keep these shutters drawn during the day. If we want to use the room, we open the shutters partway, and close them again when we leave.

A card table was a standard fixture in the Federal-period household and was often the most elaborate piece of furniture a family
owned. (Project: String inlay, p. 14.)

Card Table

Chapter 1

A t no other time in our history were Americans more fascinated with card playing than during the Federal period. Without television or movies, people amused themselves by socializing with friends. Card playing was an ideal pastime in that it gave the participants a reason to gather and engage in conversation while also offering them amusement and diversion.

So much time was devoted to card playing that a special piece of furniture was created for just this purpose. The wooden card table, with one hinged leaf that closed book-fashion, was developed in the early 18th century. Although these tables were made until the mid-19th century, the form was never before or after as popular as it was during the Federal period. A household that did not own at least one card table was as unusual as a modern household without a television. Of all the furniture that has survived from the Federal period, only chairs are more abundant than card tables.

Our technology and new materials have given us a homely card table with a cardboard top and folding legs, which we store in a closet when we're not using it. During the Federal period, card tables were not hidden because they were not ugly. Cabinetmakers lavished their skills on card tables, producing what were often the most elaborate pieces of furniture a family owned. When not in use, these tables were prominently displayed in the front hallway or the formal parlor, often against a pier (the wall area between two windows or doorways). The closed table made a good surface on which to display a flower arrangement or a treasured object.

The care and effort required to make this table is evidence of the status given card tables by Federal-period cabinetmakers and their customers. The table has a visual intensity unusual for such a compact piece of furniture, which is created by the string inlay on every visible surface except the top and the insides of the legs.

String inlay, also called stringing, is a very thin strip of wood, usually of a contrasting color to the surrounding wood, that is set into a narrow groove, or inlet. Stringing was commonly used in formal Federal furniture, perhaps because cabinetmakers appreciated its ability to draw the viewer's eye. On this table, which is primarily mahogany, the light-colored inlay acts as a visual fence, bounding each area and preventing the eye from moving easily from one to the other. For a brief moment, the viewer's attention is trapped inside each area, but it is not held immobile. The eye scans the perimeter several times, then moves on to the next surface and is again briefly seized and spun around the outline of the stringing.

Each time I view this table, my eye is drawn first to the skirt. There it moves quickly around the long rectangle, like a marble spinning inside a tin can. The concave corners enable my eye to jump from a horizontal line to a vertical to the other horizontal. (On less well-thought-out tables, where the corners of the stringing are square, the eye will follow the horizontal lines into the corners, and the quick scanning motion is subverted. The effect is like trying to spin a marble in a box instead of a can.)

From the skirt, my eye usually falls to a leg, where the stringing pulls it quickly down the long taper to the ankle, across the ankle banding and back up the other side. After scanning the leg several times, I am always drawn back to the four parallel lines around the edge of the folded top. It is as if each pair of lines runs in the opposite direction from the other pair: whichever way the eye begins to travel, the other pair of lines automatically pulls it back the other way. I haven't yet figured out why this happens, and, as a result, I spend more time looking at the edges of the leaves than at the skirt or legs. I enjoy this mystery and hope that when I do finally understand it, the card table will not lose any of its interest.

The family that originally owned this table would have worked all day, so most of the time spent with this piece would have been in the evenings, when the room was illuminated by candlelight. Under the soft, dim light of candles, the table's mahogany loses most of the subtle shading that makes up its figure, and the wood becomes a uniform red-brown. This fact obviously affected the maker's decision to use string inlay to outline each of the table's parts. Without the stringing, the table would read as a mildly interesting geometric form lurking in the shadows of the room.

Near the bottom of the tapered legs, two horizontal lines of light stringing flank a dark, thicker core of ebony veneer to define the ankles. If the stringing simply ran vertically to the foot, the eye would travel down to the floor and not easily jump from one edge of the leg to the other. The same triple banding is used as a border to delineate the lower edge of the skirt. The effect is strongest under candlelight. The banding creates a sharply defined line that prevents the edge of the mahogany skirt from fading into the shadows under the table.

The skirt banding serves a functional purpose as well. Its lower, light-colored edge has been well worn by the countless legs that have rubbed against it over the years. If the mahogany veneer had been run out to the edge of the skirt, it would have been subjected to this wear and would certainly have chipped, pulled loose or worn away to expose the pine secondary wood underneath.

From whatever direction you view the folded table, you see exactly the same thing. Looking at it head-on or from either side, you see an arc of skirt framed by two legs. The veneer used on the skirt is made from three adjacent, or sister, cuts taken from the same flitch, so that each surface is as nearly identical to the other two as wood can be. From a front view of the table, you glimpse two blank surfaces on the rear legs. It may seem odd that they have no stringing, but this would have scuttled the maker's noteworthy design. With inlay only on the extreme left face of the left leg and right face of the right leg, the table breaks into a symmetrical triptych—three identical sections made up of two legs and a panel, each one sharing a leg with its neighbor.

When the table is open, this careful arrangement no longer exists. The maker knew that participants in a card game commonly draped a green, floor-length wool cloth over the table, almost completely hiding it from view. Even if this were not the custom, one is more likely to interact visually with the piece when it is folded and against the wall than while playing cards on it.

This card table is a well-conceived design, but it is not a particularly complex woodworking project. Beneath its mahogany veneer, the curved skirt is two layers deep and is bricklaid as a single long curve rather than as three distinct sections. The maker laid out three curved segments of pine as the top layer of the skirt and glued onto these another layer consisting of two longer curved segments, probably rough-cut to shape. Once the glue hardened, the inner and outer surfaces of the segmented skirt were planed smooth.

There are about a dozen nail holes in the lower edge of these pine sections, indicating that the mating surfaces were glued and the pieces nailed together. The nails may have prevented the sections from slipping when being clamped, or eliminated the need for clamps altogether. Either way, the nail heads were never set, and the nails were extracted after they had served their purpose.

Bricklaid construction makes a stronger skirt than would three single pieces cut from a plank. The short lengths of edge grain that occur in a curve are strengthened by the other layer. A skirt comprised of one long, curved, bricklaid piece allows for some joinery techniques that differ from the standard mortise-and-tenon normally used to join a table's legs to the skirt. The two center legs are joined to the skirt with a modified bridle joint. The rear tenon of the bridle is short and is housed entirely within the skirt. While the mortises are cut into the skirt, it remains a single, continuous part. Since the structural integrity of the bricklaid skirt is retained, this again makes for a stronger construction than would three separate, curved sections of skirt, with a tenon on each end, inserted into mortises cut into the legs.

The rear legs are treated differently. The right rear leg (as viewed from the table's front) is fixed and is joined to the corner formed by the end of the curved skirt and the back rail. Standard mortise-and-tenon construction is used, the tenons being cut onto the end of the skirt and the end of the rail.

The card table opens and closes differently than do most other tables. Its movement requires two leaves hinged together and a swinging leg, called a gateleg, that is hinged to the middle of the back rail. The bottom leaf is fixed to the skirt, with the movable top leaf hinged to it. When the table is closed, the two half-round leaves lay together like a closed book. When the table is used, the hinged top leaf is opened to form a round playing surface and the gateleg is swung on its hinge to support the leaf. The gateleg swings on a movable section of the back rail and is attached to it with a mortise-and-tenon.

Some more interesting joinery is required to enable this leg to swing. The back rail itself is two layers thick. The outer layer is made of two separate pieces, the movable rail and the fixed rail, and these are connected in the middle by a series of interlocking knuckles that form a wooden hinge. The method of making this hinge is explained in the project section of the gateleg-table chapter on pp. 94-96. The two rear legs, one fixed and one movable, are joined to the ends of this outer layer. The inner layer of the back rail is joined to the right-hand end of the curved skirt with a series of half-blind dovetails. The left end of the back rail is laminated to the fixed section of the outer layer with glue and screws, and is cut off flush with the inside of the skirt.

Some tables, like the gateleg table on p. 90 and the Pembroke table on p. 156, have rule joints, where the inside edges of the movable leaves meet the fixed top. One function of this rule joint is to prevent the edges of the leaves from shifting vertically. On this card table, however, the two edges of the top leaves merely butt together when the table is open. A short tongue is set into the center of the rear edge of the fixed leaf, and a mortise is made in the rear edge of the hinged leaf. When the top is open, the locator tongue fits into this mortise and keeps the movable leaf from shifting. Otherwise, all that strengthens this butt joint between the leaves when the top is open are the two card-table hinges.

Card-table hinges are unique to card tables. A card-table hinge has two long legs that open like a pair of scissors rather than opening and closing in book-fashion like table-leaf and butt hinges do. Both the table-leaf and butt hinges would have to be set into the playing surfaces of the leaves, which Federal-period cabinetmakers seemed reluctant to do. Instead, card-table hinges are set into the outside edges of the leaves. Made of brass, and therefore decorative, these hinges are available from the reproduction-hardware suppliers listed in the appendices at the back of this book.

During the Federal period, hinged, round card tables, often called demi-lunes, were made in every cabinetmaking center in America. The interpretations that exist are nearly limitless, and you can find examples in the books listed in the bibliography. The use of stringing on this table is masterful, but you could substitute pictorial inlay, which was also commonly used during the period. There are Federal-period card tables made entirely of maple or birch, with the skirt covered with either a curly or flame-figure veneer, so you can reproduce the table in native woods, too. Use the dimensions and construction details from this table to make any other interpretation of this shape that you like.

When a card table is not in use, the movable top leaf is usually closed, but it can be opened halfway and rested vertically against the wall. The semicircular shape makes the table look larger, and if you have a light-colored object (such as a piece of porcelain) that you want to display, the leaf creates a good background. Of course, the table does not have to be merely a surface used to show off other objects. It is still well suited to its original purpose. Often on cold winter evenings my wife and I have friends over, set up the card table near the fireplace and enjoy a leisurely game of Scrabble.

When the card table is not in use, the movable top leaf can be either folded shut book-fashion, or opened halfway and rested vertically against the wall.

SCRATCH TOOL

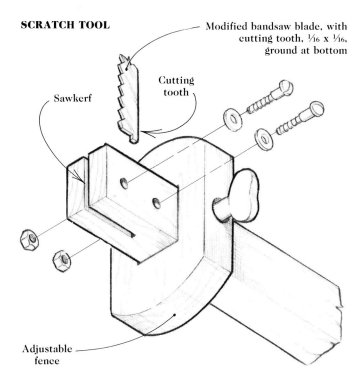

Modified bandsaw blade, with cutting tooth, 1/16 x 1/16, ground at bottom

Cutting tooth

Sawkerf

Adjustable fence

A marking gauge can be adapted for cutting inlets for string inlay. File or grind an old bandsaw blade to the thickness of the stringing to use as a cutter. Slide two 1/8-in. bolts through holes in the shaft to secure the cutter.

String inlay

To make the inlets for string inlay, there is an adjustable tool called an inlay cutter, available through specialty tool catalogs, that will cut straight lines, circles and ovals. This tool is more complex than necessary to do the string inlay on this card table, though. I prefer to use a couple of tools that I can quickly make myself.

I adapted an old marking gauge to use as a scratch tool for making straight inlets. The fence on the marking gauge allows me to cut an inlet parallel to an edge at any distance up to 5 in. from that edge. It is intended for making straight lines but will also work on a long radius, such as the edges of the leaves. I make the cutters for this tool from old bandsaw blades by filing away the teeth and any additional metal until I have a tooth 1/16 in. wide. This cutter will just scratch, rather than cut, a flat-bottomed inlet with square sides the same width as the stringing (1/16 in.). The marking-gauge shaft has a scribe in one end and the tooth mounted in the opposite end. Use a dovetail saw to cut the thin slot for the tooth. Drill two 1/8-in. holes across the sawkerf, about 3/4 in. apart so that the tooth will fit between them. Slide two 1/8-in. bolts through the holes, and place washers under the heads to protect the wood. Insert the cutter into the sawkerf and adjust the setting—the cutter should protrude about 1/16 in. from the bottom of the marking-gauge shaft. Tighten the bolts to prevent the cutter from moving and set the fence to the desired distance.

In discussing the procedure for inlaying the legs, I'll limit my explanation to how to do the stringing on the lower leg. The process is similar for the other stringing.

While the leg stock is still square, cut the inlet for the ankle banding only on the front of the leg. (If you proceed to cut inlets for the ankle banding on the sides and back of the untapered leg, they will only be lost during the tapering process.) With a mat knife scribe two lines for a 1/4-in.-wide inlet, using the technique for cutting stop dadoes shown in the shelf project on p. 128, and remove the wood with a 1/4-in. chisel. After tapering the sides and back of the leg with a hand plane to the dimensions given on p. 18, you can continue the front ankle inlet around to the sides, and from the sides around to the back.

Next measure 4 3/4 in. from the top of the leg and draw a light pencil line across the front surface of the leg. This is the point where the two vertical lengths of stringing stop and turn inward. When you cut the vertical inlets, this line will tell you where to stop.

Hold the leg between benchdogs on the workbench and set the fence of the marking gauge against the edge. Start the cutter in the ankle inlet and draw the marking gauge up one edge of the leg. The tooth should scratch a clean, square-bottomed groove (it may be necessary to make more than one pass). After scratching every 6 in. to 8 in., lift the tool and remove the chip that will have clogged the tooth. You can make a clean stop cut at the upper end of the inlet by pushing the cutter down on the pencil line that marks the top of the inlet and pulling the tool back toward the ankle. Repeat this process to cut the inlet on the other edge of the leg.

String inlay, a common ornament on Federal furniture, both guided the viewer's eye about the piece and, in the evening by candlelight, kept the table's lines from being lost in the shadows.

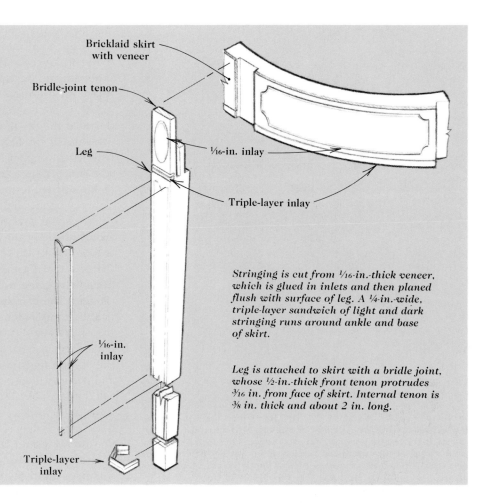

Bricklaid skirt with veneer

Bridle-joint tenon

Leg

$\frac{1}{16}$-in. inlay

Triple-layer inlay

$\frac{1}{16}$-in. inlay

Triple-layer inlay

Stringing is cut from $\frac{1}{16}$-in.-thick veneer, which is glued in inlets and then planed flush with surface of leg. A $\frac{1}{4}$-in.-wide, triple-layer sandwich of light and dark stringing runs around ankle and base of skirt.

Leg is attached to skirt with a bridle joint, whose $\frac{1}{2}$-in.-thick front tenon protrudes $\frac{3}{16}$ in. from face of skirt. Internal tenon is $\frac{3}{8}$ in. thick and about 2 in. long.

Draw the marking gauge from the ankle inlet to the top of the leg to make a clean, square-bottomed groove (above). After scoring every 6 in. to 8 in., clean away the chip that gathers around the tool's tooth (left).

With a square, lay out the inlet for the ankle banding on the leg's front (top). Score the edges with a mat knife and remove the wood with a chisel (bottom). After tapering the leg, complete the inlet around the leg.

To lay out curved stringing, use dividers with a pair of scribes, 1⁄16 in. apart, filed into the end of one leg. By trial and error, set the dividers to the correct radius and find the location for the pointed leg in the top of the vertical inlet. Scribe the radius for one side, which will produce a pair of parallel lines. Repeat this on the other side to form the *V* in the middle of the leg.

After using the dividers to scribe the parallel lines for the curved inlet, score along those lines with a mat knife. Lift out the chip with a chisel (this one was ground to 1⁄16 in.). Use the chisel to clean up the intersection of the two curved inlets and the points at which they meet the vertical inlets.

Now cut the two radii that turn inward at the top of the leg. I use a pair of modified dividers to lay out and cut this curved groove for the stringing. One leg of the dividers is pointed, and the other leg has a notch filed into its end that forms scribes, 1⁄16 in. apart—the same distance as the width of the tooth in the marking gauge. Place the pointed leg near the top of one of the vertical inlets and set the dividers to one-half the distance between the inlets. You will have to play with the opening of the dividers to find the exact radius—it should be somewhere near 5⁄8 in. You will also have to find by trial and error where to place the pointed divider leg in the straight inlet.

When you have found the correct setting, swing the notched end of the dividers so that it scribes two parallel curved lines, or concentric arcs. Do the same with the pointed leg of the dividers positioned in the other straight inlet so that the two pairs of curved lines intersect in the middle. This method only scribes the edges of the curved inlets. Now deepen the scored sides of these inlets with a mat knife, and lift the chip out with a 1⁄16-in. chisel. The chisel will also clean up the intersection of the curved inlets with the straight vertical inlets.

Because I think white birch was used for the stringing on the original table (it would be impossible to positively identify the wood without extracting it for testing), I chose this wood for my stringing too. Any light-colored hardwood will do, however. Essentially I make a sheet of white-birch veneer by resawing thin slabs from a board on the bandsaw. I then thickness-plane them as thin as possible and finish them down to 1⁄16 in. with a smoothing plane. I cut the stringing from this birch veneer with a mat knife and straightedge. As long as the veneer is 1⁄16 in. thick, it does not matter if you cut the stringing slightly wider than 1⁄16 in. If need be, the 1⁄16-in.-thick stringing can be turned on its side to fit into the inlet, and any extra depth that projects above the leg's surface can be planed flush with a smoothing plane.

After test-fitting the stringing in the inlet, run a bead of glue in one vertical inlet with a glue syringe. Use a chisel to slice a square end on the stringing, and butt the square end tightly against the top end of the straight inlet. Push the first inch or so into the inlet; you should have no trouble making the rest of the stringing fit once this end is in place. It almost seats itself if you press it in with the face of a hammer. Don't worry about length; any excess can be sliced off flush in the ankle inlet with either a chisel or a mat knife.

Fitting the curved pieces is more difficult. Roll one end of the stringing around a cylinder of about the same radius as the inlet. A chisel handle will work just fine here. Do not try to cut the stringing to length right now. This can be done more easily and more accurately after most of the stringing is in the curved inlet. Again, test-fit the stringing, then run a bead of glue in the curved inlet. Butt the end of the curved stringing tightly against the stringing in the straight inlet, and work the curved piece into the groove, using the hammer if necessary. As you near the bottom of the *V*, you will be able to see exactly where to trim off the excess stringing. Do the same for the other curved side.

The ankle stringing is a ¼-in.-wide sandwich of the same light-colored wood used for the other inlay, with a thicker, dark ebony core. The original, three-tiered veneer was undoubtedly cut in a single slice from three slabs of wood planed to the desired thickness and glued together. Make a similar sandwich of veneer for your ankle banding and fit it into the inlet as you did for the vertical inlay.

Plane all the stringing flush with the face of the leg. Now sand with 220-grit paper—the fine sawdust will mix with the glue and fill in any slight gaps. String inlay is meant to be enjoyed from a distance, and small imperfections are not noticeable. The finish will usually fill any gaps left after sanding.

After laying a bead of glue into the straight inlet, cut a square end on the stringing and push it into the top end of the groove (above). Use the face of a hammer to seat the rest of the stringing (left). You can trim off any excess stringing in the ankle inlet with a chisel or a mat knife.

Before filling in the curved stringing, "prebend" one end by rolling the stringing around a cylinder of about the same radius as the inlet.

Once the stringing is in place, plane it flush with the face of the leg. Sanding with 220-grit paper will fill in any slight gaps in the grooves, but slight imperfections will not be noticeable.

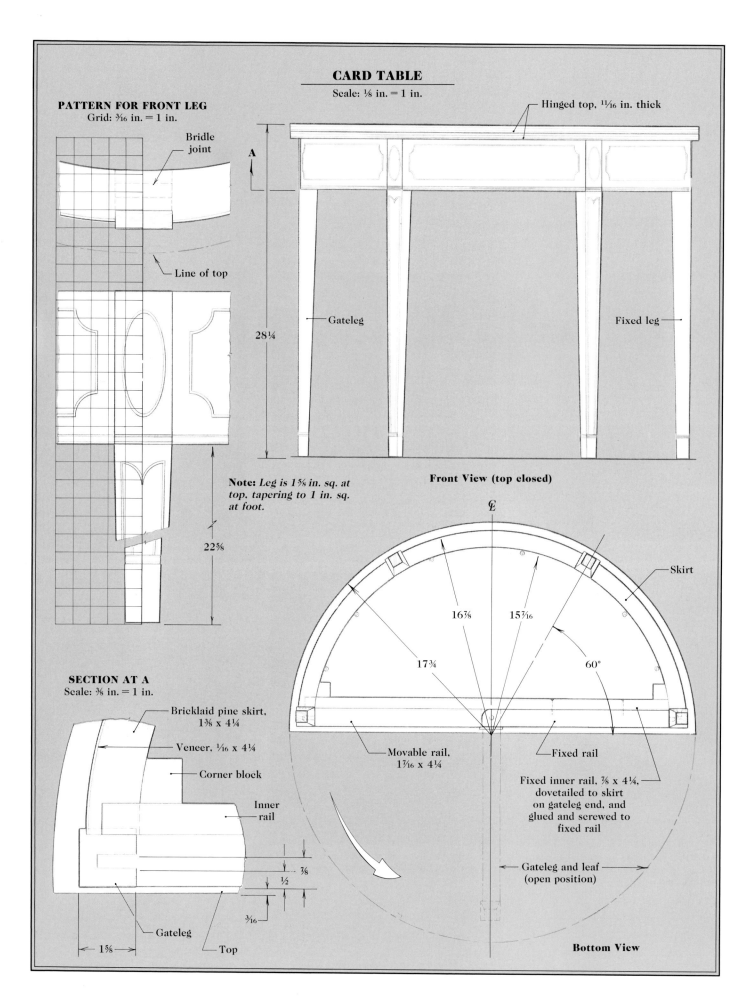

CARD TABLE
Scale: ⅛ in. = 1 in.

PATTERN FOR FRONT LEG
Grid: ³⁄₁₆ in. = 1 in.

Bridle joint

Line of top

A

28¼

Note: *Leg is 1⅝ in. sq. at top, tapering to 1 in. sq. at foot.*

22⅝

Hinged top, ¹¹⁄₁₆ in. thick

Gateleg

Fixed leg

Front View (top closed)

₵

16⅞   15⁷⁄₁₆

17¾   60°

Skirt

Movable rail, 1⁷⁄₁₆ x 4¼

Fixed rail

Fixed inner rail, ⅞ x 4¼, dovetailed to skirt on gateleg end, and glued and screwed to fixed rail

Gateleg and leaf (open position)

Bottom View

SECTION AT A
Scale: ⅜ in. = 1 in.

Bricklaid pine skirt, 1⅜ x 4¼

Veneer, ¹⁄₁₆ x 4¼

Corner block

Inner rail

⅞

½

³⁄₁₆

Gateleg

Top

1⅝

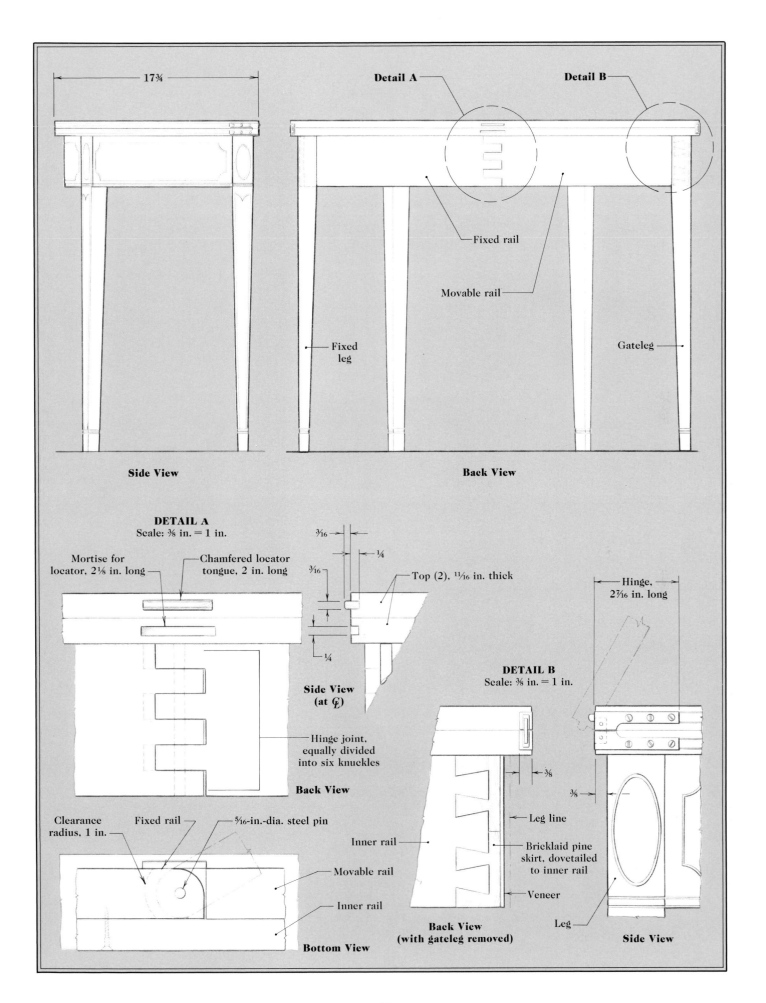

17¾

Detail A

Detail B

Fixed rail

Movable rail

Fixed
leg

Gateleg

Side View

Back View

DETAIL A
Scale: ⅜ in. = 1 in.

Mortise for
locator, 2⅛ in. long

Chamfered locator
tongue, 2 in. long

3/16

¼

3/16

Top (2), 11/16 in. thick

¼

**Side View
(at C̸)**

Hinge joint,
equally divided
into six knuckles

Back View

Clearance
radius, 1 in.

Fixed rail

5/16-in.-dia. steel pin

Movable rail

Inner rail

Bottom View

Hinge,
2 7/16 in. long

DETAIL B
Scale: ⅜ in. = 1 in.

⅜

Leg line

Inner rail

Brieklaid pine
skirt, dovetailed
to inner rail

⅜

Veneer

Leg

**Back View
(with gateleg removed)**

Side View

An expensive and prized possession in the Federal period, a large mirror was valued because it could make a room appear bigger and, at night, increase light in the room by reflecting candlelight. Since large mirrors were costly, their frames were often elaborately worked. (Project: Rope turning, p. 23.)

Mirror

Ever since it was discovered that a piece of polished metal reflects a viewer's image, mirrors have been integral to grooming. In use since ancient times, polished metal mirrors underwent great improvement in the early Renaissance when it was found that glass with a silvered back reflected a much clearer, less distorted image. For centuries, however, sheet glass without imperfection proved difficult to make, and mirrors remained small.

During the late 17th century the technology was developed for making large, unblemished sheets of glass, and mirrors increased in size. These larger mirrors were highly regarded for their ability to increase illumination in a room by reflecting candlelight. They were also valued because they could make a room appear bigger than it really was. These features made mirrors very popular, even though they remained quite expensive. (According to the 1805 inventory of our house, the secondhand value of the two "large oval gilt looking glasses" that then hung in our bedroom was $45, about one-seventh the annual income of a skilled Federal-period craftsman.)

Because large mirrors were so valuable, it is not surprising that tremendous care and effort went into making their frames. During the Federal period, most frames were gilded. The foundation of the frame was a softwood that could be easily molded and carved, but most of the ornament was cast composition, a mixture of plaster and glue. The wood was covered with a thin skin of gesso to give it the same smooth surface as the composition, and then gilding was applied to the entire surface of the frame. As a result, a woodworker made only part of the frame, and other artisans completed the rest.

I chose to include the piece shown here rather than one of our gilded mirrors because the frame is made mostly of wood and it is the most successful example of its type I have seen. The mirror has an honored place in our house, hanging in the pier between the front-parlor windows.

This mirror was made late in the Federal period around 1820 and displays the influence of the emerging Empire style. This type of mirror, with two vertical columns and two sections of glass divided by a horizontal muntin, had been popular for as long as 20 years before this example was made. The two split columns are its most up-to-date feature. They are heavier in appearance than those on earlier mirrors and have rope turnings, also known as spiral or twist turnings, which were a popular Empire-period motif often used on the legs of tables, the crest rails of chairs, and the engaged columns of bureaus and sideboards. (Had the mirror been made a few years earlier in the height of the Federal period, these columns would probably have been a carved cluster of reeds.) The decorative carving on the top and bottom thirds of the columns is typical of the late Federal period and presents a stylized version of the classical acanthus leaf.

This type of mirror is known as an architectural mirror because the frame is made up of elements found in classical Greek architecture. It has, for instance, an entablature, which is the combination of elements on a Greek temple above the columns and below the triangular pediment that shapes the slope of the roof. The cornice, or uppermost molding of the entablature, is stepped, or broken forward. Under the cornice is a veneered frieze panel, which includes stepped areas on either side and sits atop two raised and reeded architraves, the lowest element of the entablature. The two split columns with rope turnings are mounted on plinths, the square blocks that serve as the bases of the columns.

The frame, however, is not merely miniaturized architecture. It is a well-thought-out piece of furniture that relied on the Federal-period furniture idiom in its use, for example, of veneer and moldings. Yet the introduction of architectural elements into the piece allowed the mirror to relate to the room in which it hung, as well as to the other furniture around it.

The wide frieze panel below the cornice is covered with bookmatched, crotch-grain, San Domingo mahogany veneers. Bookmatched veneers were commonly used by Federal-period cabinetmakers, and the maker of this frame could have expected them to appear on other surfaces in the room. The frame's horizontal bottom rail and the two vertical stiles are covered with veneer of the same color. They also share the same plane, a fact that the veneer reinforces.

The same dark, heavily figured veneer is also found on the two plinths and on the two stepped areas of the frieze. These are the only other flat surfaces on the mirror, and the eye is informed of this by the recurrence of the veneer. The brass medallions mounted on the plinths and stepped areas of the frieze emphasize the fact that, although related to the rail, stiles and frieze, these areas are set in another plane.

All the other elements of the mirror are made of Honduras mahogany, which is light gold in color and contrasts nicely with the rich red-brown of the San Domingo mahogany veneer. The use of two tones of mahogany is a sophisticated design element and is also found on the secretary (p. 58), which is located across the room. In the same way that color defines the flat surfaces on this piece, it also unites the frame's three-dimensional elements.

The various effects created by these turned, carved or molded elements combine to produce the mirror's overall statement. The deep, projecting cornice makes the piece top-heavy so that it looms over the viewer and seems larger than it is. Its dominant presence is magnified by the fact that it steps out above the frieze and architraves, making the entire cornice appear to project even farther into the room. The same stepped design was commonly used on Federal-period mantel cornices.

The smaller moldings around the inside and outside of the frame draw pronounced lines around the frame's inner and outer edges, and create a boundary for the darker, flat, veneered surfaces. The moldings are raised slightly above the veneer so that they also border the frame in three dimensions. The outermost molding strip has a rounded upper edge, which relates it to the reeding on the architraves by turning it into a single reed. The molding on the inside of the frame is typical of Federal-period moldings used as backbands on door and window architraves in that it steps very quickly downward and leads the eye into the "other room" of the reflection in the same way that stepped backbands and architraves lead the eye through doorways. Since the thickness of this molding is less than half that of the veneered frame, its rear surface creates the bottom of the rabbet into which the mirror glass is set.

The same molding, with an extra step added to it, is set on the bottom edge of the bottom rail and separates the two plinths. The extra step makes the molding larger than that around the glass and also projects toward the viewer, creating a raised lip. This molding prevents the eye from falling away from the mirror, while maintaining a consistent molding shape throughout the piece.

On each of the frame's two split columns, the rope twist leads the viewer's eye outward. Its purpose is to suggest that the mirror is wider than it really is. This complements the projecting cornice by keeping its grandeur in proportion.

The reeding on the architraves and muntin is a detail closely associated with the Sheraton furniture style from which this mirror evolved. Its use here not only relates the mirror to the room and to other furniture nearby, but also expands the textural smorgasbord created by the carving, molding and turning.

Although the architectural elements of the mirror appear complicated, they are not. Nor does their use in the piece require any complicated joinery. The mirror is little more than a flat frame mortise-and-tenoned together, with the various elements applied to it. The stepped effect of the entablature is produced by the two mahogany blocks, each veneered with crotch-grain on the face, which extend up beneath the cornice. The cornice is in turn stepped out above them. The various sections of the cornice are cut from a single length of molding, and each of the joints is a simple miter. The plinths are also mahogany blocks with crotch-grain veneer on the face. They are capped top and bottom, as are the reeded architraves, with ¼-in.-thick slices of mahogany.

The split columns are each half of a turning and are glued and nailed to the veneered frame. The direction of the spiral twists poses a potential construction problem. The maker obviously intended the twists to spiral up and diverge outward. To do this he could not use two halves of the same turning—the spirals would both slope in the same direction and would pull the viewer's eye to one side or the other. Inverting the column would not change the direction of the spirals, and, as well, the turnings have a distinct top and bottom. The maker of this mirror therefore produced two turnings with opposite twists, one left-handed, the other right-handed.

After having spent so much time producing these turnings, the maker certainly would not have discarded the unused halves. It is therefore likely that he made at least a pair of these mirrors. The piece exhibits enough virtuosity to make me suspect that frames were his specialty and that this was a production item. If you choose to make this mirror, you might as well make a pair, too.

Since it is no longer possible to obtain San Domingo mahogany, the color of the wood you use for the turned, molded and carved parts might not differ noticeably from the veneer. This poses a problem because, although the effect of the two-toned mahoganies is very subtle, their use is essential to the mirror's design. I would therefore suggest that you veneer the pine frame and then wipe the veneer with a dark stain or a saturated solution of potassium permanganate, which will darken the wood. If you use the potassium permanganate solution, don't get carried away with applying it. You don't want to soak the veneer so thoroughly that it cracks when dry.

My mirror was finished with shellac, which has darkened with time. As a result, some of the two-tone effect is lost, but I would not strip the finish since it is original.

Finding the original glass in a mirror this old is rare. With time, a mirror's silvered surface would have lost its reflective ability, and was usually replaced by those not content to consider themselves in a glass darkly. This is probably what happened with this mirror.

The upper section of the mirror was probably reverse-painted since it was common in the period to combine a painted section and mirror glass, but this painting has also been lost with time. In reverse painting, the painter works on the back of a glass panel, and under candlelight the resulting portrait or scene takes on a very lifelike depth and color. For those who want to include a reverse painting on their mirror, I have included a supplier who does custom work in the list at the back of the book. My wife, Carol, has often suggested that a view of our house would look nice in the upper panel of our mirror.

When installing mirror glass or a reverse painting, avoid using either nails or glazing points, which can scratch the silvering or painting. In Federal-period mirrors, glass was instead held in place with glue blocks that were usually a right triangle in cross section, as shown in the plan on p. 29. A ¼-in.-thick backboard should be tacked to the rear of the frame to keep out dust.

The original mirror weighs just over 20 lb. and must therefore be hung in a foolproof manner. I suspended ours with picture-frame wire, strung between two eyehooks screwed into the frame. It is hung from an 8d finish nail driven into the frieze under the parlor cornice at about a 45° angle. I slipped a hollow copper rivet over the end of the nail because the flange looks like the mushroom knobs commonly used as hangers in the Federal period.

Rope turning

The various names given to the detail on the center of the mirror's split columns—rope, twist or spiral turnings—are misleading in that this detail is carved, not turned. Visualizing and understanding the makeup of these spirals is much more difficult than actually creating them. To help grasp the idea of their design, think about the threads of a screw and, by contrast, the strands of a rope.

Screw threads have what is called pitch and lead. Pitch refers to the number of threads per inch; in other words, a count of the number of times a ridge and adjacent groove occur on a single inch of the shank. Lead is the distance the thread travels along the shank in a single spiral. These terms roughly describe the relationship of the spirals on these rope turnings. But a screw has only a single worm that spirals up its shank. The turnings on this mirror are more akin to a rope, in that they are composed of several strands that spiral perfectly parallel to each other. Lead can be varied to alter the visual impact, but what most interests the woodworker making rope turnings is pitch, which is determined by the number of strands in the spiral and their individual thickness.

To begin this project, turn a mahogany blank, or whatever primary wood you have selected, to the outside dimensions of the column shape shown on p. 27. Use a pair of dividers to divide the area to be carved into 11 equal sections along its length. This distance is ¹⁵⁄₁₆ in. Turn the lathe on and lightly touch a soft lead pencil to each of the marks. This will result in 10 perfect rings around the diameter of the turning. Do not scribe these lines, as the scratches would remain in the finished spirals.

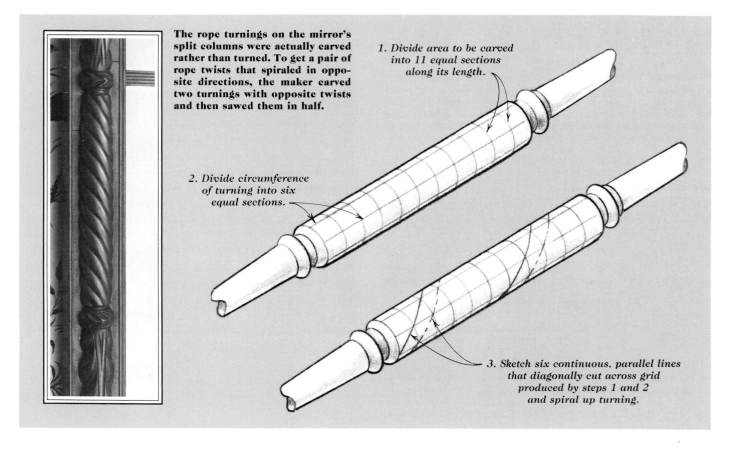

The rope turnings on the mirror's split columns were actually carved rather than turned. To get a pair of rope twists that spiraled in opposite directions, the maker carved two turnings with opposite twists and then sawed them in half.

1. Divide area to be carved into 11 equal sections along its length.

2. Divide circumference of turning into six equal sections.

3. Sketch six continuous, parallel lines that diagonally cut across grid produced by steps 1 and 2 and spiral up turning.

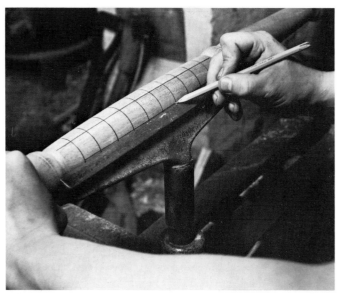

With the tool rest positioned at center height, draw a uniform grid on the turning. Begin by placing the rest against the work and rotating the turning to one of the sets of horizontal markings already made. Then pencil a line through the vertical markings. Repeat the process for the remaining markings.

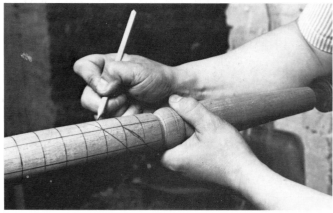

To begin tracing out the strands of the spiral, start at the lower right corner of one of the end squares and draw a diagonal line to the upper left corner of the square. Continue the diagonal line into the next square on the row above and proceed in this fashion until you have drawn one continuous spiral up the turning. Repeat this process to make six lines that spiral from one end of the turning to the other.

Use a parting tool to cut a groove along the lengths of the six spiraling lines. Work all six grooves as far as you comfortably can, then rotate the turning to complete them on all the spirals.

The next step is to divide the area lengthwise around the circumference, but before beginning, pull the plug of the lathe motor to avoid the chance of an accidental start-up. There are six separate strands that make up the design, so the circumference will need to be divided into six equal sections. On the turning in the photographs, the circumference is 6 in. at its widest part, so the dividers are set to 1 in. Use a pair of dividers to walk off this distance on one of the two centermost lines.

Remove the turning from the lathe and adjust the height of the top edge of the tool rest to align exactly with the drive and tail centers of the lathe—you'll have to move the tailstock in to do this accurately. Then swing the rest out of the way, keeping it at the same height, and position the tailstock to remount the turning. Push the adjusted tool rest against the turning, and rotate the piece until one of the six points comes into line with the top of the tool rest. With a soft lead pencil, lightly trace a horizontal line that intersects the ten vertical lines. Rotate the turning to the next penciled point and trace the next horizontal line. Repeat this process for all six points.

The result should be a uniform grid. Begin at one of the end squares and sketch a line from the bottom right corner to upper left corner. Continue the line from the adjacent lower corner of the next square to the opposite upper corner. Keep repeating this process, slowly revolving the turning as you sketch, until you have a single spiraling line up the turning. While there is still only one line, you can best see the lead of the spiral. In a single twist it travels just under 5¾ in.

When this line reaches the other end, return to the beginning of the grid and start the sketching process anew, beginning in the lower corner of the next square above or below the one where the previous spiral was started. Repeat the process until there are six lines that spiral from one end of the turning to the other.

You are now ready to begin the carving. I find it easiest to do this with the turning still mounted on the lathe. You might want to reposition the lathe to give you access to it from both the front and the back. If you have a lock on an indexing head, you should engage it to keep the turning from rotating while being carved.

Start at the beginning of one of the squares and, using a ¼-in. parting tool, cut a ⅛-in.-deep V-groove along the spiral line. Follow the spiral from corner to corner on each of the squares as far as you can comfortably reach around the work without having to rotate the turning. Try to keep the cut at a constant depth. Return to the beginning and cut the same V-groove on the adjacent spiral. When all six spirals have been worked in this manner, rotate the turning to complete the V-grooves on all the spirals.

The next step is to round the individual strands with a chisel. You will have to cut in only one direction, working with the grain. You can shape the left half of each spiral (as you face the work) by moving right to left, tailstock to headstock, in the same direction as you sketched the line and cut the *V*-groove. To round the other half of the spirals, you will need to stand behind the lathe, or flip the work around if you cannot get behind the lathe. You will still be working right to left, and always with the grain to avoid chipping.

After rounding the spiral with the chisel, smooth away the faceted tool marks with a half-round file. The rounded and flat surfaces of the file meet at a sharp edge. This edge is important for cleaning up between adjacent spirals and creating a smooth, flowing line. Avoid using a square-edged file, which would cut into the sides of the adjacent spiral. Again, you should work from both sides of the lathe to keep from filing against the grain. The surface left by the file will be uniformly round but needs to be smoothed further with 80-grit sandpaper.

With the turning still on the lathe, carve the details on the rings above and below the spiral. (I did not do this on the turning I made in the photographs.) This should be done with a parting tool. The rest of the carving is done after the turning is sawed apart.

To help ensure accuracy when sawing the turning in two, draw a line along one axis, using the tool rest or a yardstick as a guide. Make another line on the opposite side of the piece. The pattern in the end grain, made by the spur drive center, can also be used to help locate these two lines. To saw along the lines, I used a 10-point rip panel saw.

The back edges of the two halves can be planed smooth in either of two ways: You can clamp a jointer plane in the front vise of your workbench and run the back side of the sawn turning over it. Or you can clamp the turning, sawn surface upward, between benchdogs and plane it.

The turning I made in the photographs had a right-hand spiral. To complete the mirror, you need to make a second turning that is identical but which has a left-hand spiral. Do this by laying out the grid with the same divisions, but instead of sketching a line from the lower right corner of the first end square to the upper left corner, sketch from the upper right corner to the lower left corner and continue the spiral in that direction.

If you wish to use spiral turnings in other work, you may need to adapt them. Lead can be increased by placing the vertical lines farther apart, or decreased by placing them closer together. Width of the spirals can be increased by using fewer of them. You might divide the turning horizontally into quarters rather than sixths. Spiral width can be decreased by adding more spirals, dividing the turning into eighths, for example.

Use a chisel to round the strands of the spirals (top). You can work one side of the strands from the front of the lathe, but you'll have to round the other side from the back of the lathe to keep working with the grain (above).

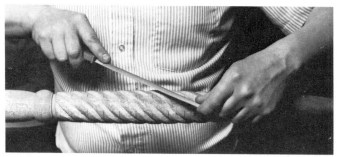

Smooth away the tool marks, using a half-round file and always working with the grain.

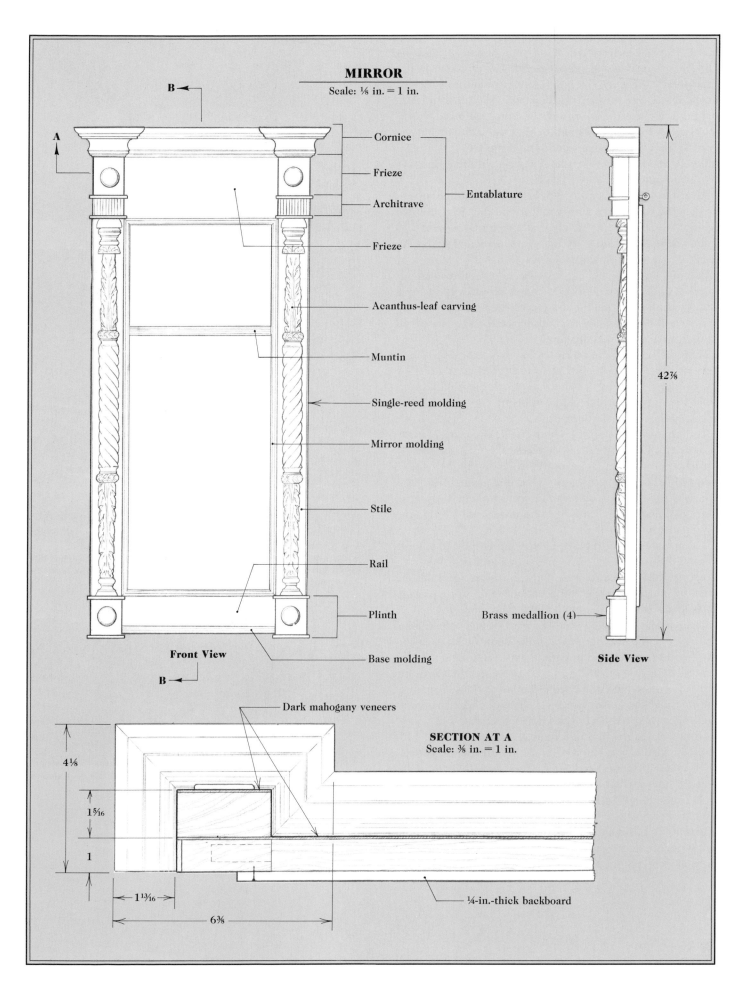

MIRROR

Scale: ⅛ in. = 1 in.

B

A

Cornice

Frieze

Architrave — Entablature

Frieze

Acanthus-leaf carving

Muntin

Single-reed molding

Mirror molding

Stile

Rail

Plinth

42⅞

Brass medallion (4)

Side View

Front View

Base molding

B

Dark mahogany veneers

SECTION AT A
Scale: ⅜ in. = 1 in.

4⅛

1⁵⁄₁₆

1

1¹³⁄₁₆

6⅜

¼-in.-thick backboard

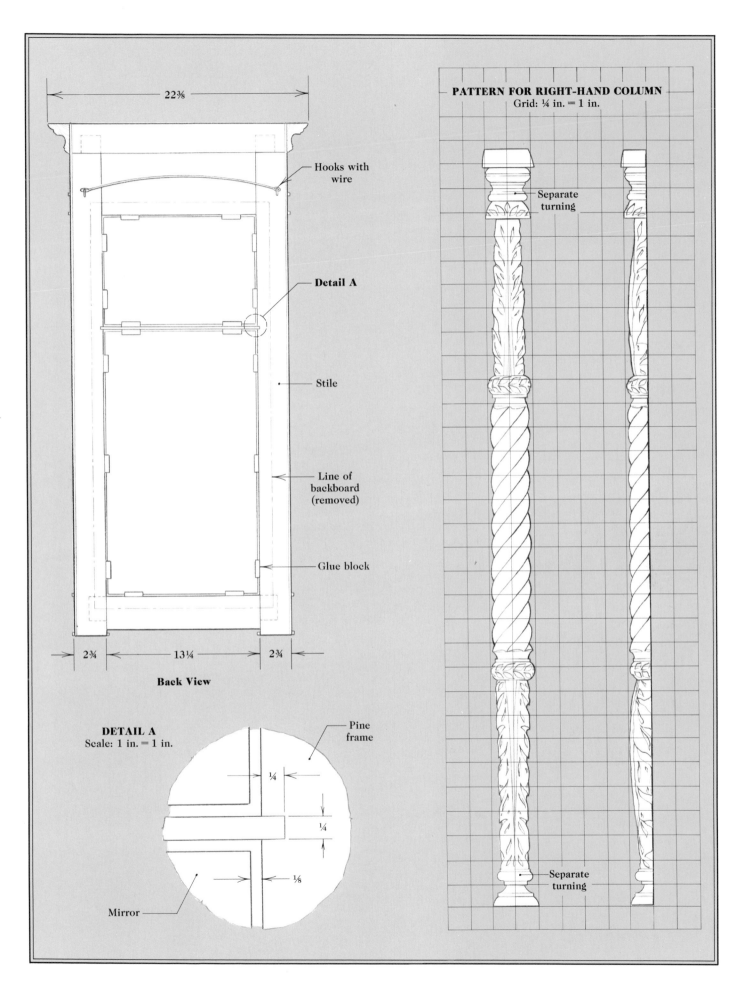

22⅜

Hooks with wire

Detail A

Stile

Line of backboard (removed)

Glue block

2¾   13¼   2¾

Back View

DETAIL A
Scale: 1 in. = 1 in.

Pine frame

¼

¼

⅛

Mirror

PATTERN FOR RIGHT-HAND COLUMN
Grid: ¼ in. = 1 in.

Separate turning

Separate turning

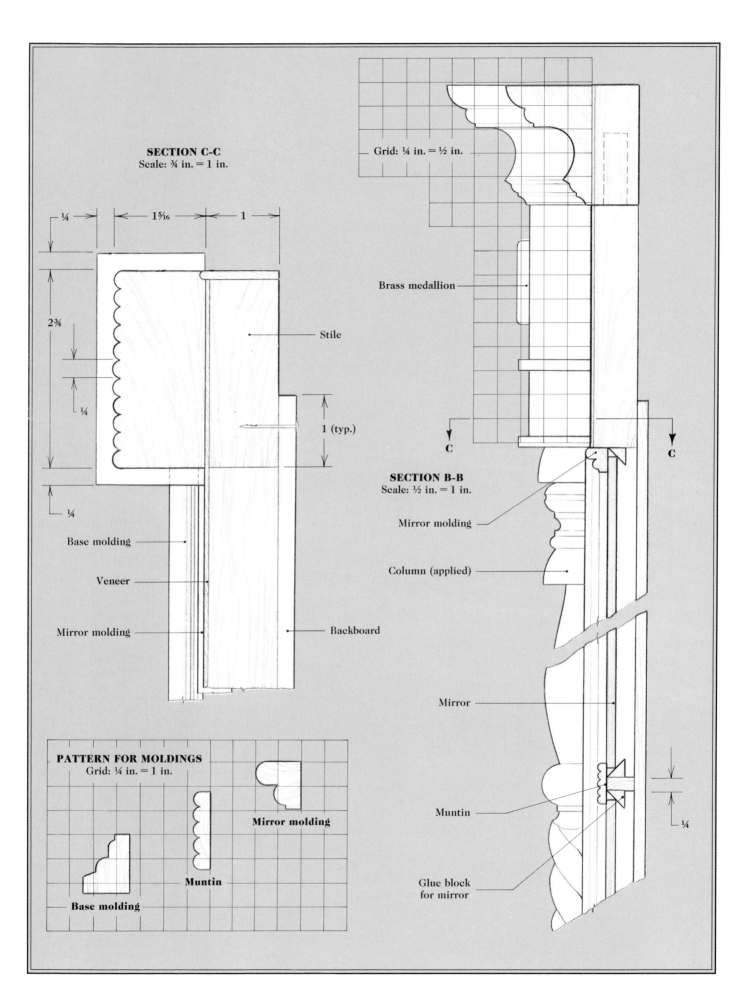

SECTION C-C
Scale: ¾ in. = 1 in.

¼ 1⁵⁄₁₆ 1

2¾

¼

Stile

1 (typ.)

¼

Base molding

Veneer

Mirror molding

Backboard

PATTERN FOR MOLDINGS
Grid: ¼ in. = 1 in.

Mirror molding

Muntin

Base molding

Grid: ¼ in. = ½ in.

Brass medallion

C

C

SECTION B-B
Scale: ½ in. = 1 in.

Mirror molding

Column (applied)

Mirror

Muntin

¼

Glue block
for mirror

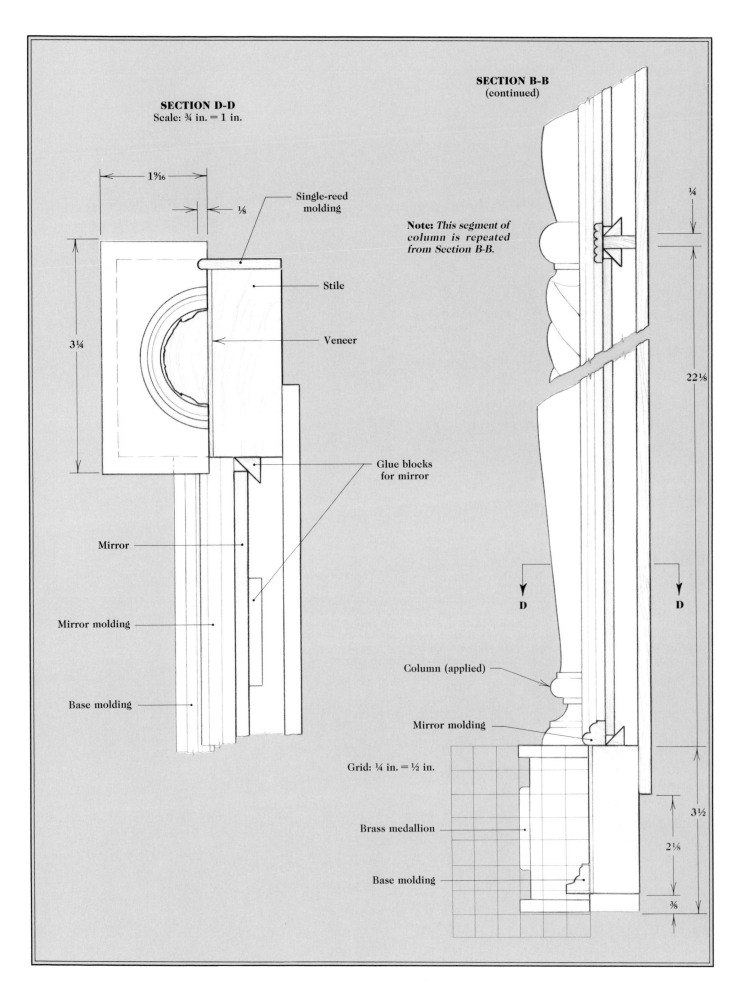

SECTION D-D
Scale: ¾ in. = 1 in.

1⁹⁄₁₆

⅛

Single-reed
molding

Stile

3¼

Veneer

Glue blocks
for mirror

Mirror

Mirror molding

Base molding

SECTION B-B
(continued)

¼

Note: *This segment of
column is repeated
from Section B-B.*

22⅛

D   D

Column (applied)

Mirror molding

Grid: ¼ in. = ½ in.

3½

Brass medallion

2⅛

Base molding

⅜

Unlike most pieces of furniture in this age of wood, this formal sofa is visually dominated by an expanse of fabric, not wood. During the Federal period, all fabric was handwoven and therefore costly, making a piece like this out of reach for most households. (Project: Reeding by hand, p. 33.)

Sofa

Chapter 3

This sofa represents a departure from the approach to designing and building furniture seen in the other pieces in this book. Those pieces use wood not only for their frames and other unseen parts but also for most of their visible surfaces. In this sofa, wood serves as a frame for the upholstery but plays a relatively minor visual role.

The sofa's legs, arm posts and the faces behind these posts are its only visible wooden elements. The piece confronts the viewer with such a vast expanse of fabric that these wooden areas help establish the sofa's identity as a piece of seating furniture, and this wood is intensely worked with ornament of the period. The reeded arm posts and the turned legs are characteristic of the Sheraton style of Federal furniture, though it is unusual to find a sofa where the arm posts are reeded and the legs are not. This leg is a typical Sheraton turning, with a major vase, rings, a cove and an urn-shaped foot, compressed into only 10 in. The result is one of the most appealing turnings I have ever encountered, and perhaps the cabinetmaker used this design instead of a reeded leg because he admired it too.

Since this is an elegant piece, designed for a parlor or other formal room, the arms and legs are made of mahogany. The flat sides and fronts of the square blocks separating the legs and the arm posts are veneered with crotch-grain birch panels surrounded by birch and ebony stringing and strips of mahogany veneer. This motif, without the contrasting stringing, is repeated in elongated form on the exposed faces behind the arm posts.

While the sofa's exposed wooden elements are visually arresting, the woodwork that is unseen is equally important. The birch frame is the foundation for the upholstery. It serves the same purpose as a skeleton, supporting and giving definition to a flesh of fabric and stuffing. And just as a skeleton determines the general dimensions of a body, the frame creates the shape of the sofa. It is responsible for the slightly arched back and for the echoing curve of the front rail's long, gentle bow. The concave upper edge of the arm, sloping forward to the exposed posts, is also a function of the frame.

The shape of the sofa associates it geographically with Boston and the North Shore, the latter a string of port cities and urban cabinetmaking centers stretching northward along the New England coast. Portsmouth, New Hampshire, where we found this sofa, is included in this area.

Although the frame determines the sofa's size and general shape, the personality of this piece is largely a function of its visible exterior. The skin over the wooden skeleton and padded flesh is the cloth covering, which becomes the sofa's most pronounced feature. This outer fabric does not override the importance of size and shape in the sofa's overall look (the piece would still appear odd in a small room), but it dominates the piece and enables it to harmonize with the room's other fabrics, wallpaper and paint. In this respect, the sofa is similar to the architectural pieces shown in this book—the mirror (p. 20) and the secretary (p. 58). Their architectural elements relate them to the woodwork of the room and to the surrounding furniture. The same is true of the color and pattern of the fabric covering this piece. The sofa is not merely in the room, but of the room.

A sofa is a rather inflexible piece of furniture. Its covering closely links it to its surroundings and its great size limits its portability. Its placement in a room and the selection of its covering are not generally isolated decisions but rather part of a complex decorating scheme. The limitations created by these factors, however, are also a sofa's strengths. More than most other pieces of furniture, a sofa helps create a decor.

Federal-period Americans appreciated the complex contribution a sofa made to a room, but they admired this piece of furniture for other reasons as well. Theirs was an age of wood, and upholstery was welcomed since it produced sofas and chairs that were both softer and, on a cold winter night, warmer than wooden ones. Before the Industrial Revolution and the development of textile-making machinery, however, all cloth was spun and woven by hand. This made upholstered furniture very costly, and ownership of such a piece therefore indicated status.

Curiously, the woodworking on a Federal-period sofa was its least expensive element. But this did not mean that the worksmanship on these pieces was of poor quality. On the contrary, it was well conceived and executed. Given the great expense of the fabric, it would have been foolish to skimp on the frame or other wooden parts.

Many period cabinetmakers offered upholstering as a service to their customers, and independent upholsterers often set up business near cabinetmaking shops. Whether or not the maker of a frame actually did the upholstery, there was a collaboration between the two crafts. As a result, the upholsterer understood furnituremaking and design, and the cabinetmaker knew how to build a frame that, when upholstered, would result in the desired shape.

This close association between maker and upholsterer is uncommon today. Thus a modern upholsterer may neither share nor understand an earlier cabinetmaker's intent, and may be unfamiliar with the techniques needed to correctly interpret a Federal-period sofa.

When we bought this piece, it had been freshly reupholstered, but with results that differed greatly from the way it looks now. The upholsterer had relied on modern materials and techniques. He used coiled springs, for example, unaware that their patent was not granted until 1828, two decades after this sofa was made. As a result, his reupholstered seat had a dome to it rather than the nice tight, flat surface produced by our subsequent reupholstering, which more accurately reflects the period. He also overstuffed the sofa with foam rubber, so that it looked bloated and the exposed wooden parts seemed spindly. Our reupholstering produced instead the lean, trim lines the cabinetmaker intended and also a comfortable firmness, which is extremely different from the mushiness of springs and foam rubber.

Having witnessed the transformation of the sofa when correctly upholstered, I suggest that, if you are unable to do the upholstery yourself, you resolve to find an upholsterer who can accomplish the proper effect. To help you select a skilled upholsterer and know generally what needs to be done, I will outline the steps involved in Federal-period upholstery. For those interested in a more detailed description of these upholstery methods, I have included an 1834 source in the bibliography.

Our frame was upholstered by Patrick Edwards, of San Diego, California, a well-known expert on American Empire furniture who also specializes in early upholstery techniques. He prefers to work with tacks and a hammer, and refuses to use staples. He first builds up a layer of woven jute webbing and pulls it taut. This creates a firm foundation for the upholstery and strengthens the wooden frame. Next he stretches a layer of burlap and then lays on the stuffing. Instead of foam rubber, he used specially treated horsehair that curls. This makes the upholstery springy, so that it bounces back when sat on. Until World War II, horsehair was a common stuffing for mattresses, which is where we found the quantity we needed for the sofa. Nowadays upholstery supply houses stock rubberized horsehair, a natural bristle coated with rubber.

Another layer of burlap is laid over the horsehair, and a sharp, straight line is obtained by stitching the two layers of burlap with a rolled edge. Then the burlap-and-horsehair sandwich is sewn together with twine to the webbing, in quilting fashion, to prevent the stuffing from gathering and the cloth from shifting. Edwards then spreads cotton batting over the top layer of burlap and covers it with muslin. This helps produce a smooth, tight surface and also prevents the stiff ends of the horsehair from sticking the sitter. The cover is put on last, and the methods used for fitting it are similar to modern practices.

The final touch in the upholstering is the addition of a cloth tape to finish off the work and produce a smooth line around the visible wood surfaces. On Federal pieces, this tape was sometimes secured with brass tacks.

Knowing that the outer fabric we chose for our sofa would relate the piece to the room and surrounding objects, we proceeded slowly with the selection. In fact, we left the sofa in its muslin covering for a year while we restored the parlor and planned our decorating scheme. In the end, we decided to return the woodwork and wainscot in the room to their original painted colors, a light beige with a deep brown mopboard. We did not know what the original wallpaper had looked like, but followed the example of the original samples in the front hall and the bedchamber. Both of these papers had as a background color a paler shade of the color used for the walls and woodwork of the room in which they were hung. This precedent helped us finally select a reproduction of a late 18th-century French wallpaper. The result of our work is a two-tone beige room with a strong brown line around the floor and, on the wall above the wainscot, a black, single-screen pattern of tendrils and birds. This is a very calm environment, which we felt could carry a large, lively counterpoint. We therefore chose a cranberry-red reproduction fabric for the sofa, which would pick up the red of the plastered cheeks and jamb of the fireplace, as well as that in several of the watercolor prints on the walls and in the cockscomb that Carol uses in dried flower arrangements on the mantel.

We tried placing the sofa in other spots in the room before concluding that it works best under the two symmetrical windows, between which the architectural mirror hangs. Like the secretary facing it on the opposite wall, the sofa is a domineering piece. It is long and low, and takes up most of its wall. I have always thought that it would be nice to place the sofa in the center of the room facing the fireplace, a practice that became popular during the Empire period. In our parlor, however, the fireplace is offset and the floor space in front of it is a traffic area.

Reeding by hand

Among the neoclassical ornament inspired by Greek and Roman architecture was fluting, which mimicked the multiple, parallel concave grooves found on classical columns. During the Federal period, reeding, or parallel convex moldings, was increasingly used instead. Reeding commonly decorated Sheraton-style turned legs, bed posts, engaged columns, applied paterae (small round or oval carved ornaments) and, as on this sofa, arm posts. Period cabinetmakers working in different regions developed various, identifiable styles of reeding.

There are two methods for making reeds on turnings. The simplest, done with a reeding plane called a center bead plane, can be worked only on cylinders or very gradual tapers. That technique is explained in the chapter on the Fancy chair (p. 100). The second method is used on vase-shaped turnings, such as the arm posts on this sofa. Because the turning profile curves as it changes diameter, it would be impossible for a plane to track along both the convex and concave surfaces. Also, a plane can cut only a reed of uniform width, and on this turning the reeds narrow after they pass over the swelling of the vase shape to fit the decreased diameter of the neck. Therefore this type of reeding must be done by hand.

Before beginning the reeding, turn the sofa leg and arm post to the profile shown in the drawing at right. Then, with the work spinning in the lathe, scribe a line around the fullest point of the vase on the post. This marks the beginning of the reeds. Do nothing more until you have pulled the plug on the lathe motor to eliminate the possibility of an accidental start-up.

There are 14 individual reeds on this arm post, each about ⅜ in. wide at their maximum. Walk them off on the scribed line with a pair of dividers. The diameter is small enough that it is unlikely that the 14 segments will be perfectly even—the last reed will probably be slightly smaller or larger than the others. When doing the carving, you will be able to space out this discrepancy over several reeds so that it will not be noticeable.

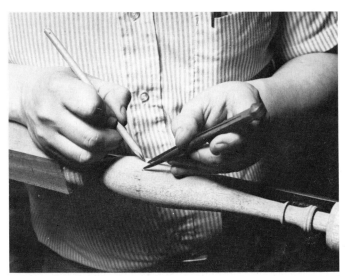

After scribing a line around the widest part of the vase, walk off and mark 14 equal segments for the reeding.

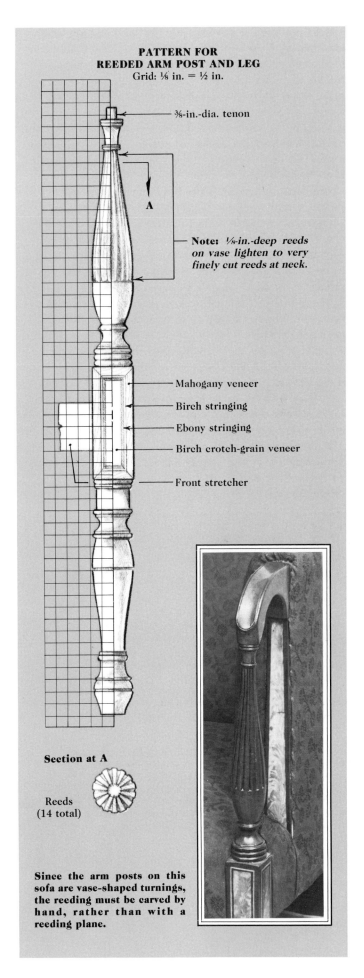

**PATTERN FOR
REEDED ARM POST AND LEG**
Grid: ⅛ in. = ½ in.

⅜-in.-dia. tenon

Note: ⅛-in.-deep reeds on vase lighten to very finely cut reeds at neck.

Mahogany veneer

Birch stringing

Ebony stringing

Birch crotch-grain veneer

Front stretcher

Section at A

Reeds
(14 total)

Since the arm posts on this sofa are vase-shaped turnings, the reeding must be carved by hand, rather than with a reeding plane.

Next remove the turning from the lathe and adjust the top edge of the tool rest to the exact centerline between the drive and tail centers, as explained in the chapter on the architectural mirror (p. 20). Remount the turning and place the rest roughly parallel to it and about an inch away. Now sharpen a soft lead pencil and set it on the rest with its point on the scribed line. Rotate the turning until one of the 14 marks comes into contact with the pencil lead. Holding the pencil on the rest and perfectly parallel to the lathe bed, draw a line from the mark down the neck of the vase to the ring at the bottom. (In the photo below, I'm darkening the line I've already drawn.) This line should be straight, even though it follows the curve of the arm post. You can check it with a short, straight edge, such as the blade of a try square. Then rotate the turning to the next mark and trace the second line. Repeat this process until all 14 lines have been marked.

Now you are ready to carve the reeds. Lock the drive shaft of the lathe to keep it from turning. With a small parting tool, start at one of the lines and take a heavy cut, about ⅛ in. deep, as you move over the vase. As you move down the neck, lighten the cut; for the bottom 1½ in., it should be quite fine. Rotate the turning so that the next line is comfortably positioned for you and carve it in the same manner. Repeat this process for the remaining reeds, but begin planning ahead as you approach the final reed if it is larger or smaller than the rest. To distribute any discrepancy over the last several reeds, slightly adjust the position of the parting tool on the pencil line.

Cutting the V-grooves distinguishes the individual reeds, but they still need to be uniformly rounded. Start this process using the same small parting tool. Roll the tool slightly, so that one side of the V-shaped cutting edge will trim the sharp arris of the adjoining reed. Be careful not to take too heavy a cut. After following the reed all the way down the neck to the ring, return to the scribed line and place the parting tool in the same groove. This time, roll it in the opposite direction to remove the arris of the other reed. Repeat these two cuts in each groove to rough out all the reeds.

I suggest making rough-shaping cuts all the way around the post rather than trying to complete each individual reed, one at at time. Working one step at a time on all the reeds will ensure that they will all be uniform.

Once you have worked your way back to the groove in which you began, you can start finishing the individual reeds. I use a flat carving chisel, beveled on both sides of the cutting edge, to complete the rounding of the reeds.

After finishing a series of three or four reeds, you can go back and clean up the corner formed by the beginning of the V-groove and the scribed line. This cleanup can be done with a mat knife.

When all the reeds have been rounded and the corners cleaned, smooth the surface of each reed with a cabinet scraper. Hold the scraper blade so that one corner is in the groove, and roll the edge as necessary over the reed. You can use small pieces of sandpaper to clean up any irregularities not smoothed by the scraper.

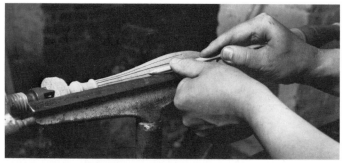

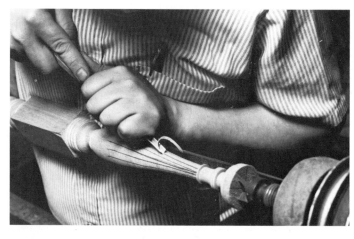

With the tool rest at the centerline of the lathe and roughly parallel to the turning, draw a line from each of the 14 marks down the neck of the vase to the ring scribed at the bottom (above). Once all the lines have been drawn, begin carving out the reeds with a V-shaped parting tool (right).

After the initial cuts have been made, shape the sides of the reeds with the parting tool (right). This time as you cut, roll the tool slightly toward the center of the reed being shaped. Then use a scraper blade to smooth and clean up the rounded curve of the reeds (far right).

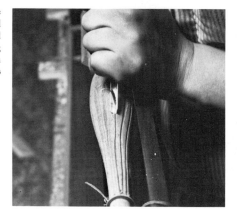

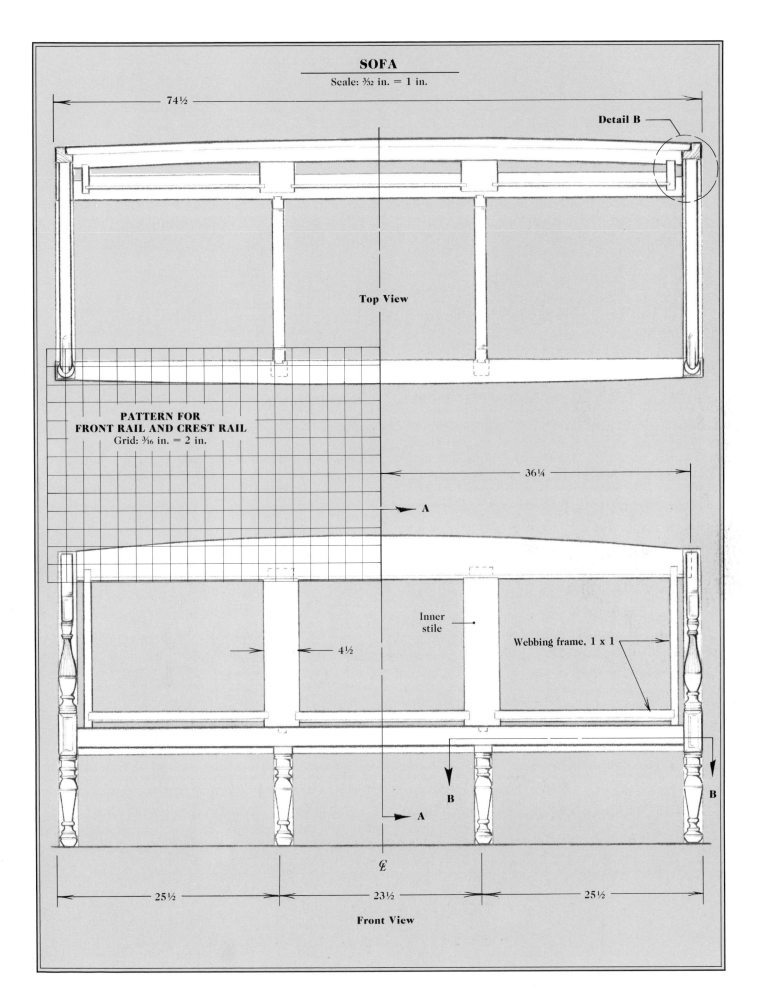

SOFA

Scale: ³⁄₃₂ in. = 1 in.

74½

Detail B

Top View

**PATTERN FOR
FRONT RAIL AND CREST RAIL**
Grid: ³⁄₁₆ in. = 2 in.

36¼

A

Inner
stile

4½

Webbing frame, 1 x 1

B

B

A

℄

25½

23½

25½

Front View

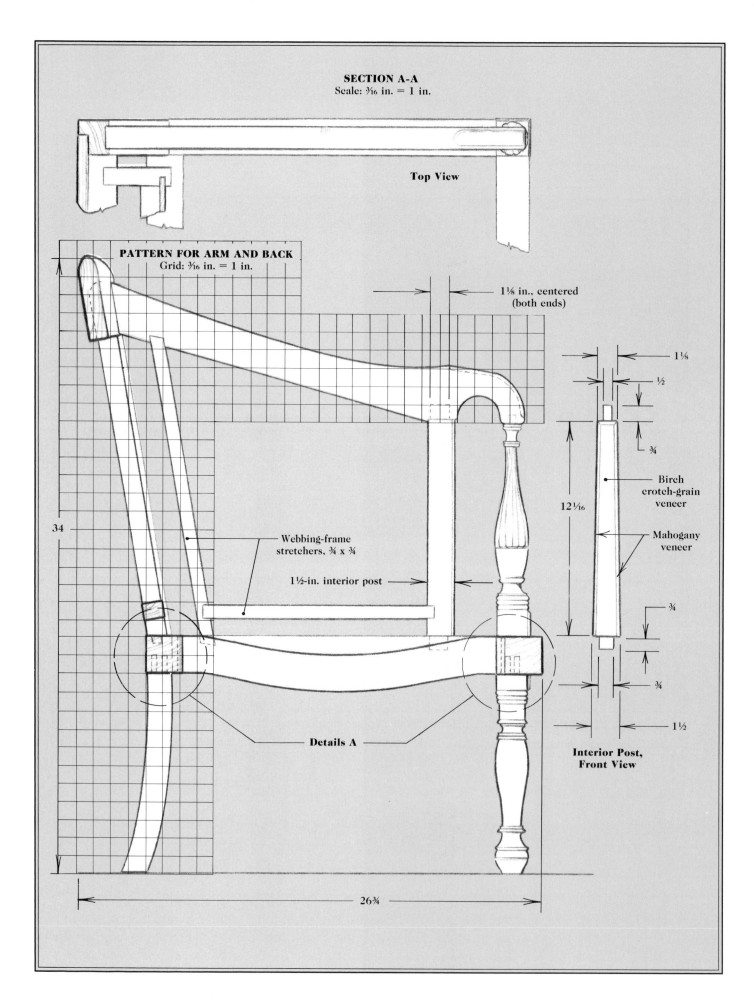

SECTION A-A
Scale: ³⁄₁₆ in. = 1 in.

Top View

PATTERN FOR ARM AND BACK
Grid: ³⁄₁₆ in. = 1 in.

1¹⁄₈ in., centered
(both ends)

1¹⁄₈

½

¾

Birch
crotch-grain
veneer

12¹⁄₁₆

Mahogany
veneer

34

Webbing-frame
stretchers, ¾ x ¾

1½-in. interior post

¾

¾

Details A

1½

**Interior Post,
Front View**

26¾

SECTION B-B
Scale: ¼ in. = 1 in.

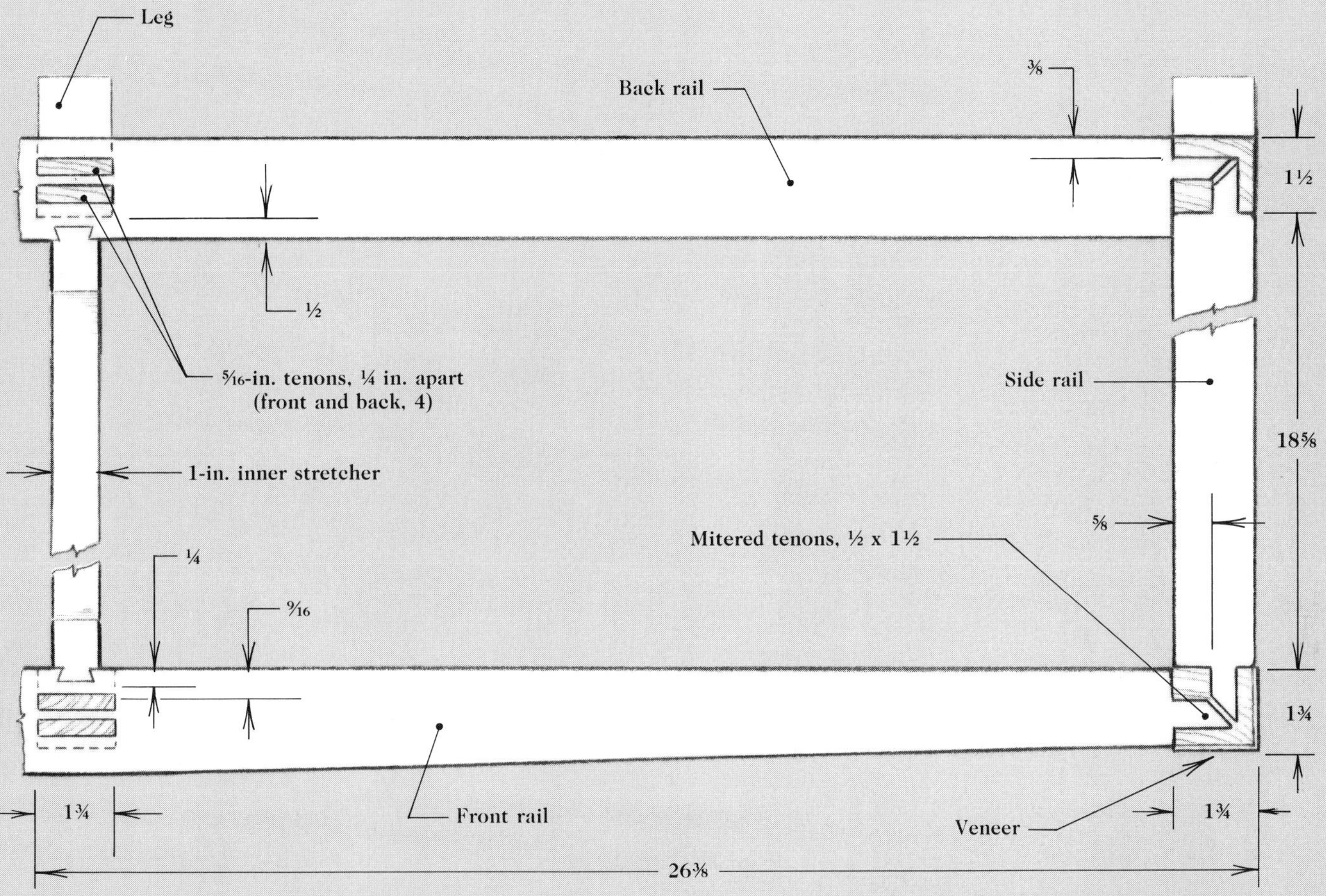
Leg
Back rail
⅜
1½
½
Side rail
⁵⁄₁₆-in. tenons, ¼ in. apart
(front and back, 4)
18⅝
1-in. inner stretcher
⅝
Mitered tenons, ½ x 1½
¼
⁹⁄₁₆
1¾
1¾
Front rail
Veneer
1¾
26⅜

DETAILS A
(taken at inner leg)
Scale: ½ in. = 1 in.

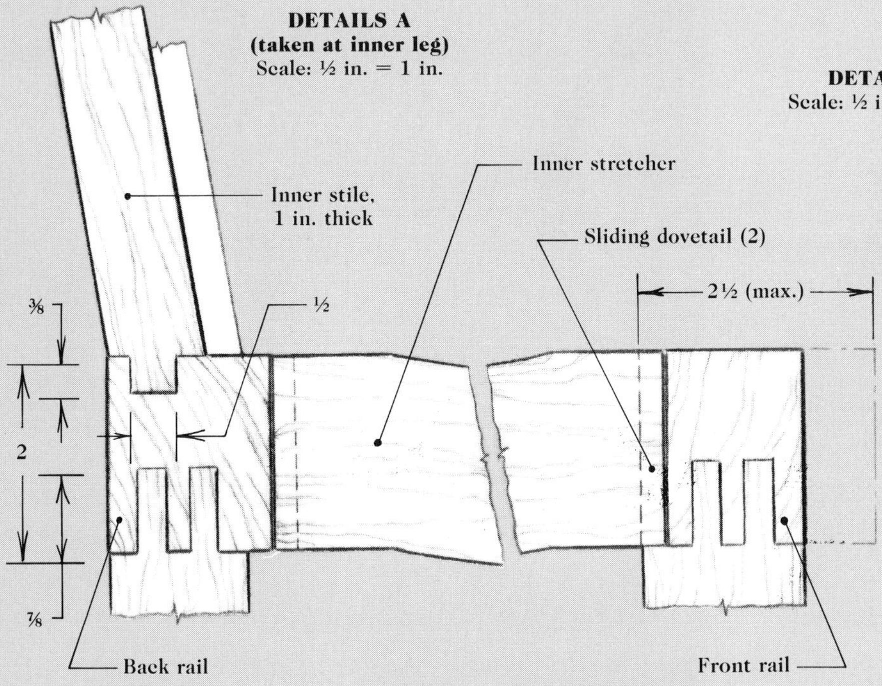
Inner stile,
1 in. thick
Inner stretcher
Sliding dovetail (2)
2½ (max.)
⅜
½
2
⅞
Back rail
Front rail

DETAIL B
Scale: ½ in. = 1 in.

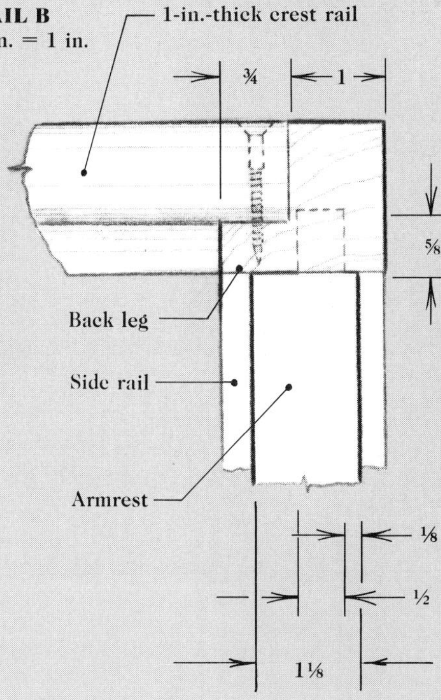
1-in.-thick crest rail
¾
1
⅝
Back leg
Side rail
Armrest
⅛
½
1⅛

Tip-top stands were immensely popular during the Federal period and were produced both in formal styles by urban workshops and in more spontaneous forms, like this piece, by rural craftsmen. (Project: Sliding dovetails, p. 40.)

Candlestand

Chapter 4

T ip-top stands have a dual personality, changing character when their tops are raised or lowered. This characteristic is shared by two other tables in this book, the card table (p. 10) and the Pembroke table (p. 156). But those two tables remain useful pieces of furniture even with their movable leaves down: a chair can still be pulled up to them, and objects can be set on their fixed leaves. When the top of a tip-top stand is lowered, however, the piece serves no other function than to please the eye. It becomes a piece of sculpture.

Federal-period Americans obviously appreciated furniture for its visual accomplishment, but they were nonetheless a very practical people. It seems odd therefore that they would greatly enjoy a piece of furniture that, much of the time, contributed nothing more than its own presence. But whether this was out of character or not, their fondness for tip-top stands created a real demand for these pieces, and cabinetmakers often invested considerable effort in making them.

I suspect that this particular tip-top table and its larger counterpart (p. 50) were used in a Federal-period home in much the same way that Carol and I use them now. We make a point of dining at them by candlelight several nights a week. When we are alone, we usually eat in the parlor rather than in the dining room, and the large tip-top table is therefore kept in the center of this room. Although the large table will seat four people, there is not enough space left for serving dishes and candles. We make up for this by strategically placing several smaller stands nearby to keep platters and bowls within easy reach. I usually move this small tip-top candlestand to one side of the larger table and place a candelabrum on it. In the summer Carol often uses the stand to hold a vase of freshly cut garden flowers. When the stand is not in use, its top is tipped vertically and the piece is placed against the wall between the secretary and the door to the kitchen.

Because of its small size (the table is only a fraction over 38 in. high with its top tipped vertically), this piece is extremely versatile and fits in nicely almost anywhere in the house. It works well alongside most pieces of furniture, whether formal or informal, smaller or larger.

Unlike most other furniture in this book, this tip-top table is a country piece. This isn't a disparaging observation. In fact, like all other rural art, country furniture often displays an originality absent from more studied urban work. I chose to include this stand rather than a more formal example of a small tip-top to illustrate just this point. It is such a successful piece that it never fails to draw notice from visitors.

Although the maker of this piece was a rural craftsman, this candlestand proves that he was both familiar with more formal cabinet work and skillful enough to produce it, but preferred instead his own highly individual design. His work displays a spontaneity unseen in most other pieces in this book and is most obvious in this piece in the pedestal. Its turnings are well executed, with each element crisp and clearly defined. The presence on the pedestal of a boss (or base), cove and urn is consistent with urban work. More formal Federal-period tables, however, usually break into a tapered column above the urn. On this table the maker chose instead to use a vase shape above the urn and added to it four bands of decorative rings, spaced to be completely visible only when the top is raised. On more formal work these rings were generally turned on the urn itself and spaced much closer together.

Despite the fact that it is country work, this stand embodies the Federal-period idiom as completely as any other piece in this book. It is airy and delicate, even fragile in appearance, an effect strengthened by its small size. With the top tipped vertically, the piece reflects the Federal-period appreciation of geometric shapes. In this position, the oval top seems to hang in space and becomes the stand's dominant feature.

This vertical oval is an excellent place to show off a piece of highly figured wood. Our stand is made of cherry, which has darkened to a rich tobacco brown. Its color is enhanced by two coats of orange shellac. If made in a lighter wood such as birch or maple, the stand could brighten a dark corner. If a darker, plainer wood were used, the piece could be inlaid with a Federal motif, perhaps combined with several concentric ovals of stringing at the tabletop's edge.

While this table must be small to be portable, it must also be stable. The piece is given stability by its three legs, since their feet always rest in a plane, whether or not the floor itself is flat. The maker further braced the table by setting the three feet 15 in. apart and making each foot extend 9 in. from the center of the boss. He designed the oval top so that its major radius is likewise 9 in., and he kept the stand's height low (with its top in the horizontal position, the table is only 28¾ in. high).

While the legs function to stabilize the stand, they are also largely responsible for its sprightly appearance. They are more sophisticated than you might expect to find on country work and illustrate how native ability can make up for a lack of formal training. On urban stands, for example, the legs often end with tapered spade feet or sometimes with bands of veneer inlaid at the ankles. The

maker of this stand, however, used a subtler device. From the boss to the feet, the legs steadily taper in both thickness and width. This results in feet that are only ½ in. thick by ⅝ in. wide, which makes the piece appear to stand on tiptoe, like a water spider on a lily pad.

Whether the eye moves up or down the legs, this double taper makes visual sense. If the eye starts at the feet, which seem little more than points, it is drawn up the legs by the graceful flow of S-shaped cyma curves and the increasing thickness of the legs. If the eye moves downward from the heavy boss, the tapered legs narrow, announcing that they will soon terminate.

When the top is raised into horizontal position, its ⅜-in.-thickness echoes the feeling of delicateness created by the dainty feet. The vase shape on the upper pedestal predicts this thinness by narrowing to a neck that disappears under the overhanging top. The eye follows the curve of the vase until it passes out of sight, and the viewer draws the illusory conclusion that the vase is very narrow at the top. In reality, the pedestal increases in thickness just before it meets the hinge block to ensure ample strength for the tenon joining these parts. (A full discussion of the hinge-block mechanism that allows the tabletop to pivot is found in the chapter on the tip-top table on p. 52.)

Sliding dovetails

The legs of this candlestand and those of the larger tip-top table are secured to the boss with sliding dovetails. The first step in constructing these dovetails is to locate the position of the three mortises on the bottom of the boss. If you remember your high-school geometry, you know that a circle can be walked off in six even segments equal to its radius. Set a pair of dividers to the radius of the boss and locate these six points on the circumference of the boss. Next draw a line from the center to every other point. These lines will bisect the mortises.

A template for the dovetails can be made from a clear-plastic coffee-can cover. Place one leg of the dividers, still set to the radius of the boss, on the center dimple of the cover and score a circle on the plastic. Walk off the same six equal points on the diameter of this circle and score a line from the center to every other point. Then scribe the outline of a mortise that is perfectly bisected by one of the three lines. After the template is cut out, it should fit on the boss so that its scratched lines are directly above the boss' penciled lines. The plastic cover's center dimple will conveniently sit in the hole made in the boss by the lathe center and will help prevent the plastic from slipping.

Trace all three mortises on the boss using the template. Then, using a square, continue the layout for the mortises down the sides of the boss. With the pedestal held in a vise, cut along the lines with a dovetail saw as you would if making half-blind dovetails in a very thick drawer front. Remove the waste with a chisel.

Cut three legs to the pattern in the drawing on p. 43. I waited to taper the legs until after I had cut the tenons. This made it easier to hold each leg in the vise without damaging its tapered cross section. Trace the dovetail

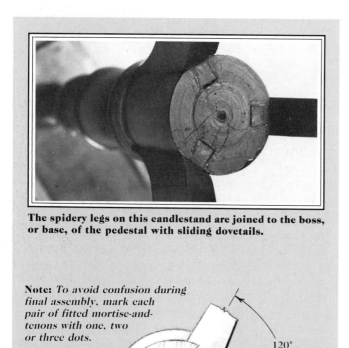

The spidery legs on this candlestand are joined to the boss, or base, of the pedestal with sliding dovetails.

Note: *To avoid confusion during final assembly, mark each pair of fitted mortise-and-tenons with one, two or three dots.*

Leg

1¼r

1⁷⁄₁₆r

120°

Bottom View

shape from the template onto the top end of the leg, being sure to trace the shoulders so they follow the curve of the boss. Then use a square to complete the tenon's layout on the side of the leg. Cut the tenons with a dovetail saw. Be sure to cut outside the pencil marks in this step, which will produce a slightly oversized tenon that will later be fitted to the mortise. The saw will not follow the curve of the shoulders, and the cut will necessarily be straight. However, the bevel of the shoulders will ultimately result in a tight fit between the shoulders and the round boss.

Fitting the sliding dovetails is a matter of trial and error. Find the high spots in either the mortise or tenon and shave the problem areas with a chisel. Finer adjustments can be made with a file.

Once a leg has been fitted to its mortise, and the shoulders fit tightly, mark both parts so that they can be easily identified when it's time for gluing. The marking system I used on this stand is a simple but effective one. Using a punch (an awl or a nail will also work), I marked each tenon with one, two or three dots and identified its accompanying mortise in the same way on the end grain of the boss.

When the table is completed and the top is ready to be mounted to the hinge block, be sure to position the pedestal so that one of the legs projects directly backward. If the leg is placed forward, it will not only detract from the impact of the suspended oval top, but will also be prone to damage from room traffic and may trip passersby.

With a pair of dividers set to the radius of the boss, walk off six equal segments on the circumference of the boss. Then draw lines from the center to every other point.

Make a template for the sliding dovetails by copying the boss' penciled pattern, then cutting an outline of a mortise bisected by one of the lines.

Use the template to pencil in the mortises on the end of the boss and transfer the layout to the sides using a square.

With the pedestal held in a vise, cut the mortises with a dovetail saw and chisel out the waste.

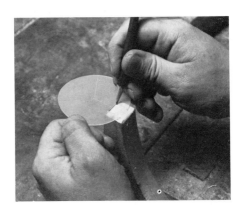 

Use the template to mark the tenon and the beveled shoulders on top of each leg (far left), and then use a square to continue the layout down both sides of the leg. With the leg in a vise, cut the tenon with a dovetail saw (left). The saw will not follow the curve of the template but will create beveled shoulders that fit tightly against the boss.

CANDLESTAND
Scale: ⅛ in. = 1 in.

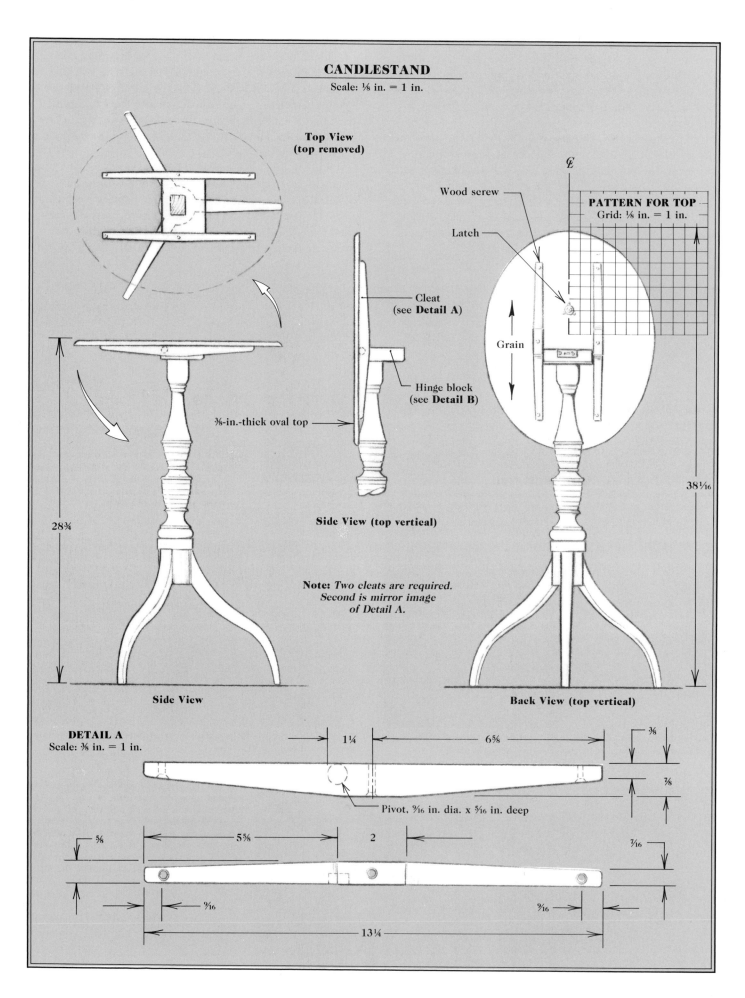

**Top View
(top removed)**

Wood screw

Latch

PATTERN FOR TOP
Grid: ⅛ in. = 1 in.

Cleat
(see **Detail A**)

Grain

Hinge block
(see **Detail B**)

⅜-in.-thick oval top

38¹⁄₁₆

28¾

Side View (top vertical)

Note: *Two cleats are required.
Second is mirror image
of Detail A.*

Side View

Back View (top vertical)

DETAIL A
Scale: ⅜ in. = 1 in.

1¼   6⅝   ⅜

⅞

Pivot, ⁹⁄₁₆ in. dia. x ⁵⁄₁₆ in. deep

⅝   5⅝   2   ⁷⁄₁₆

⁹⁄₁₆   ⁹⁄₁₆

13¼

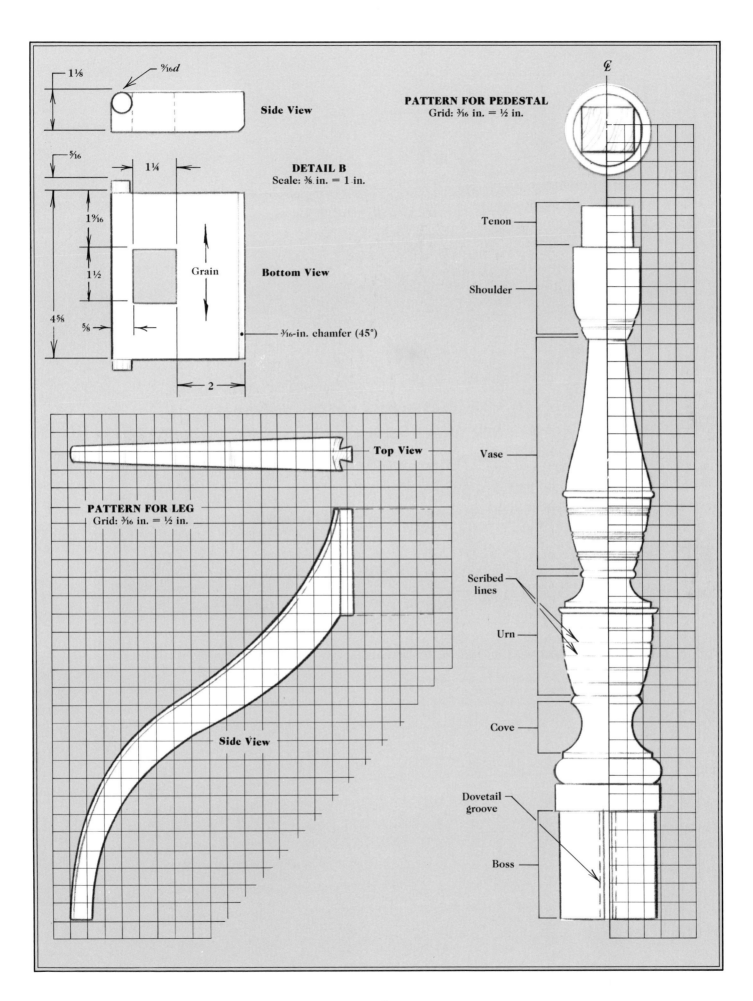

1⅛

⁹⁄₁₆*d*

Side View

PATTERN FOR PEDESTAL
Grid: ³⁄₁₆ in. = ½ in.

⁵⁄₁₆

1¼

DETAIL B
Scale: ⅜ in. = 1 in.

1⁹⁄₁₆

1½

Grain

Bottom View

4⅝

⅝

³⁄₁₆-in. chamfer (45°)

2

Top View

PATTERN FOR LEG
Grid: ³⁄₁₆ in. = ½ in.

Side View

Tenon

Shoulder

Vase

Scribed
lines

Urn

Cove

Dovetail
groove

Boss

This simple, dovetailed and veneered box has served numerous owners for about 160 years as an elegant storage chest for treasured objects. (Project: Jointed lid and "matched" veneers, p. 46.)

Lord Box

Chapter 5

The veneered box presented in this chapter is in reality a very well-designed and well-made piece of furniture. Like the display shelf (p. 126), this box is an ideal storage space for the small, cherished, personal objects we all have. The maker and original owner of this piece are not anonymous, however. The story of this box and how I came to own it is an interesting one, which I would like to tell.

Throughout the 19th century, the Federal-period house I now live in was occupied by the family of Ebenezer Lord. Lord was a successful cabinetmaker whose long career, begun around 1811, spanned the Federal, Empire and Victorian furniture periods. For more than 50 years, he and his apprentices supplied Portsmouth with wooden products that ranged from furniture to ships' figureheads.

Lord was also an important social and political leader in Portsmouth, but time gradually erased the town's memory of him and scattered his work. When we bought our house in 1976, I had never heard of Ebenezer Lord. Nor had the townspeople I questioned after establishing the house's chronology of owners in the county's Registry of Deeds. I spent the next few years working in various archives to rediscover the man who had so long been a part of this house and to reconstruct the network of journeymen and apprentices he had trained. While I learned a great deal about Lord from my research, examples of his work eluded me.

Then one evening Carol and I were visiting our lawyer and his wife. After dinner our host said to me, "Since you're interested in Portsmouth history, let me show you some papers I have." These were papers that he had found as a boy, while rummaging in the attic of his uncle's law office in search of stamps for his collection. He had stuffed the papers and their stamped envelopes into a wooden box that was also in the attic and somehow managed to keep these boyhood treasures all his life.

When I opened the box, I lost all interest in the papers it contained. My eye was seized by a penciled inscription on the inside of the lid, which read, "Susan B. Lord, New Year's Present, Portsmouth, N.H." This box had been presented to Susan Boardman Lord, Ebenezer's eldest daughter, who, I had learned in my research, always used her middle initial to distinguish herself from her mother, Susan Lord.

The box represented the first object I had ever been able to attribute to the shop of the man I had been studying for years. A number of other pieces made by Lord and his apprentices have since been identified in both public and private collections, but this box remains very special to me because it was also used in the house Carol and I now own.

Lord dealt in veneers as a sideline to his furniture business, advertising that he always had a large supply on hand. The pieces of veneer used on this box probably came from his own stock. I don't believe that the veneers were chosen randomly; in fact, I think they may even have been cut especially for this piece. (Remember that this was a presentation piece for Lord's daughter, and it is not likely to have been production work.) The carcase of the box is veneered with a very pale gold Honduras mahogany, whose heavy stripes run horizontally around the piece. In real contrast to the sides, the top is covered with a deep red-brown, San Domingo, crotch-grain mahogany with a swirling figure.

The effect of this design is intriguing. The stunning gold on the sides of the box makes the piece stand out dramatically in any room. The dark veneer on top produces a drama of its own, creating the illusion that the box may not really have a lid and that the viewer can look directly down into its contents. The swirling figure of the dark veneer on the lid suggests also that what is contained in the box is a liquid in a surreal state of flux.

The finishing on the piece enhances this illusion. The sides of the carcase were finished with a shellac, whose sheen is pleasant but not too glossy. In contrast, the top is French polished to a high gloss that makes it look like a sheet of tinted glass, through which one sees the sensuous form trapped inside.

Another curious visual effect of the veneer is created by the pronounced horizontal stripes on the carcase. Because the grain reflects light differently as one walks around the box, the figure appears to undulate.

To the left of the keyhole is a vertical line caused by deflection of the wood around a spike knot. When viewed obliquely from the right, the line is just barely visible. As one moves from right to left, this line becomes more and more obvious. And for the viewer who passes by the box at a normal gait, the veneer's horizontal stripes seem to shimmer and the vertical line magically appears. The same visual effect is achieved on all four sides of the box, since the four sheets of veneer are sister cuts from the same flitch and carry the same pattern.

It is the figure in the veneer that holds the secret of the box's success. Most Federal furniture that produces this illusion of movement does so with sweeping curves. Since such curves are obviously impossible on a rectangular box, the maker looked to another design element—a particular pattern of veneer—to achieve the desired effect. The creation of this illusion, however, depends not only on the figure of the wood but also on the viewer's movement past the box; the seated viewer will see none of its magic. I consider this design the product of genius. How else can one explain such complexity and sophistication in something as simple as a box?

After trying this piece in several spots in our home, Carol and I have decided that it is best displayed in our parlor. This room has a sunny southern exposure and, with the shutters open, plenty of light to reflect and ripple on the box's golden striped veneer. We usually set the box on the card table (p. 10), whose dark, San Domingo mahogany top provides a dramatic background to set off the light-colored sides of the box. The table and box have been given a space under a window all their own, and hardly a day goes by that I don't spend at least a moment letting my eye enjoy this box.

If you plan to make this box, I recommend that you invest some time and thought in choosing the veneers for it, since they account for the real visual impact of this piece. Without eye-teasing veneer, the object is just a plain wooden box.

The construction of the carcase and its lid is very simple. They are made of clear white pine and joined with through dovetails at the four corners. Both the top and bottom boards are merely glued and nailed in place. As woodworkers, we might be disappointed that more complex joinery was not used in a piece so visually complex. Yet the carcase is nothing more than a substrate for the veneers. The only requirement of the carcase is that it be stable, since wood movement due to seasonal changes in humidity could damage the highly figured skin that covers it.

While making the carcase, give some thought to what you will keep inside. The original box has an undivided interior space, but you can arrange this space any way you wish. You may want to have built-in dividers or even a miniature bank of drawers. None of these alternatives will affect the box's exterior.

Some hardware is required to duplicate this piece. There is a lock on the original Lord box, but it is not necessary to include one on yours. Do include the keyhole and brass surround, though, even if they do not service a lock. I also strongly recommend including the brass handles on either end. These three metal mounts (all of which are available from the hardware suppliers listed in the appendices) are a part of the idiom we associate with Federal furniture. A lock and handles immediately announce that this is not just a fancy wooden box. This is a piece of furniture.

Jointed lid and "matched" veneers

One of the interesting features of the Lord box is the way the pattern of the veneer continues across the joint of the lid onto the sides. Veneering the box and lid separately to achieve this effect would be extremely difficult. The method Ebenezer Lord used, however, is easy and effective: he constructed a closed box and then sawed it open, joining the lid to the base with hinges.

The box can be made of any stable wood, such as pine, basswood or tulipwood. The layout of the dovetails at the four corners is important. There is single half pin at the top of the sides. The first full pin is located approximately 7/16 in. from the top and is sufficiently large to allow the joint of the lid to be centered on it. The placement and size of this first full pin are critical since the lid, when cut later, should bisect this pin. The remaining height of the sides is comprised of two or three pins and tails—their exact number is impossible to determine without X-raying the box, as the carcase has remained so stable that the joints have not telegraphed through the veneer. The sawkerfs made when cutting the dovetails don't offer many clues either to the number of pins, since few of these kerfs extend into the box. I can only assume from standard practices and practical experience that the tails are cut on the ends of the box and the pins are cut on the front and back.

Using an electric stud finder, I found that the top and bottom were nailed to the carcase, with their edges flush with the sides. The slight stain in the joint reveals that the top and bottom were also glued in place. While drawn or cut finish nails can be used to secure the bottom on your box, it is best to use T-headed brads on the top, since they will leave no holes to be filled, which would later show through the veneer. Make sure that the brads used for the top are only 1 in. long, so that they will not extend into the joint of the lid.

Once the box is constructed, clean up the outside surface with a low-angle block plane. This tool, which the maker of the box would have called a miter plane, is less likely to tear end grain than is a smoothing plane, whose iron is set at 45°.

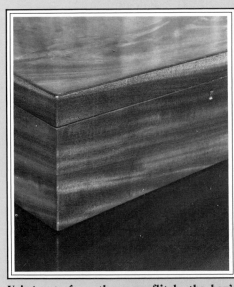

Using cuts from the same flitch, the box's maker "matched" the stunning mahogany veneer on the sides of the carcase by veneering a closed box and then sawing it open to create a lid.

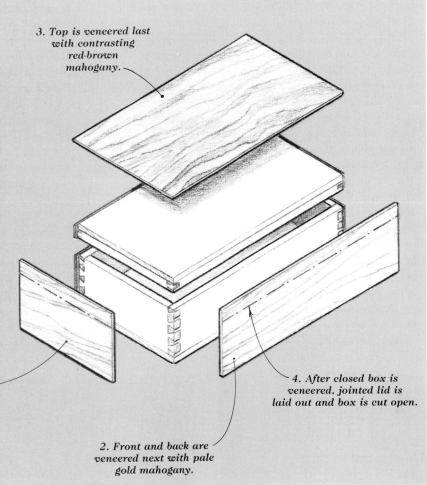

3. Top is veneered last with contrasting red-brown mahogany.

1. Ends of closed pine box are veneered first with pale gold mahogany.

2. Front and back are veneered next with pale gold mahogany.

4. After closed box is veneered, jointed lid is laid out and box is cut open.

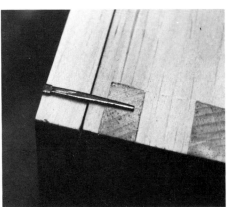

Make sure the layout of the dovetails allows enough space for you to center the joint of the lid on the first full pin. After completing the carcase of the box, nail on the top and bottom (left). Use 1-in.-long, *T*-headed brads on the top, which will not interfere with the lid joint (above).

The next step is to prepare the sheets of veneer. It is unlikely that you'll be able to duplicate the pattern of the original light-colored veneer, so simply select a flitch that interests you. Finding a sheet of dark, crotch-grain veneer like that used on the top of the box will probably be relatively easy. Once I had selected the veneers I wanted to use—mahogany for the sides and crotch-grain birch for the top (the bottom is not veneered)—I cut them on a bandsaw and thickness-planed them to 1/16 in.

The sheets of veneer can be applied to the box with contact cement, but I prefer hot glue. To prepare the veneer for gluing, first label each sheet as to its position. The order in which the sheets are applied is important. The two ends of the box should be veneered first to prevent the end grain on the sides of these sheets from showing on the front of the box. With the ends veneered, cut away any excess with a veneer saw and clean up the edges with a block plane. Next apply the front and back sheets of veneer and trim the edges with a veneer saw. You can plane the long edges where the front and back meet the top and bottom of the box, but use a veneer saw to trim the ends, as the plane could easily injure the adjacent veneer on the ends of the box. The four corners

on the original box are slightly rounded, probably the result of being cleaned up with very fine sandpaper.

Last to be applied is the top sheet of veneer. The edges of this sheet should also be cleaned up with a veneer saw and lightly sanded to finish them.

Once the veneer has been applied, lay out the joint for the lid by setting a marking gauge to 1¼ in. and scribing a line this distance from the top on all four sides of the box. Now secure the box in a bench vise, wrapping a towel around the box to prevent damage to the veneer. To cut open the box, I used a 14-point handsaw, which is fine enough to prevent tearout in the veneer.

After the lid has been separated, plane away the sawmarks on both edges. Be sure to plane from all corners toward the middle to prevent chipping the veneer.

If you've used pine or another light-colored wood for the carcase, you'll want to brush a thin red wash on the edges of the carcase and lid, as Lord did on the original box. I make an extra-thin batch of red milk paint for this wash, which eliminates the fine, light line that would appear around the joint of the lid and carcase, were the edges not stained. All that remains to complete the box is to mount the hinges, keyhole surround and handles.

Trim any excess at the ends with a veneer saw; clean up the edges with a block plane.

With the box veneered, scribe a line 1¼ in. from the top on all four sides of the box.

Cut the box apart along the scribed line, using a fine-toothed saw to prevent tearout of the veneer (above). Then plane away the sawmarks on the edges of the lid and carcase, working from the corners toward the center to avoid chipping (left).

— 48 —

LORD BOX

Scale: 3/16 in. = 1 in.

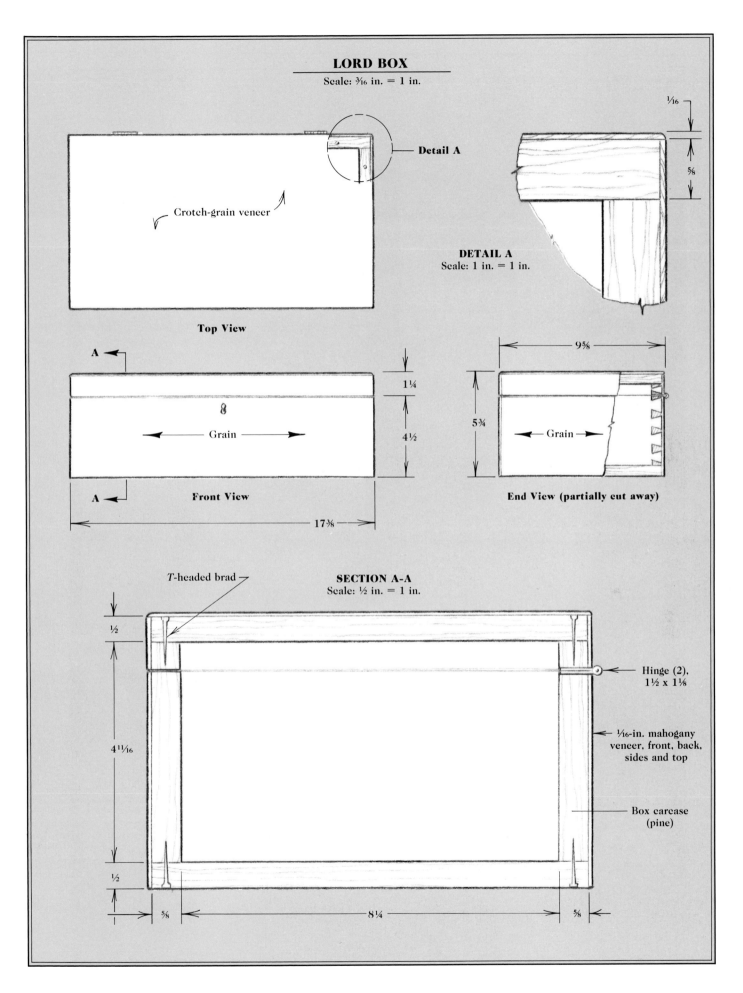

Crotch-grain veneer

Detail A

Top View

DETAIL A
Scale: 1 in. = 1 in.

1/16

5/8

Front View

A

A

Grain

1 1/4

4 1/2

17 3/8

End View (partially cut away)

9 5/8

5 3/4

Grain

SECTION A-A
Scale: 1/2 in. = 1 in.

T-headed brad

1/2

4 11/16

1/2

5/8

8 1/4

5/8

Hinge (2),
1 1/2 x 1 1/8

1/16-in. mahogany
veneer, front, back,
sides and top

Box carcase
(pine)

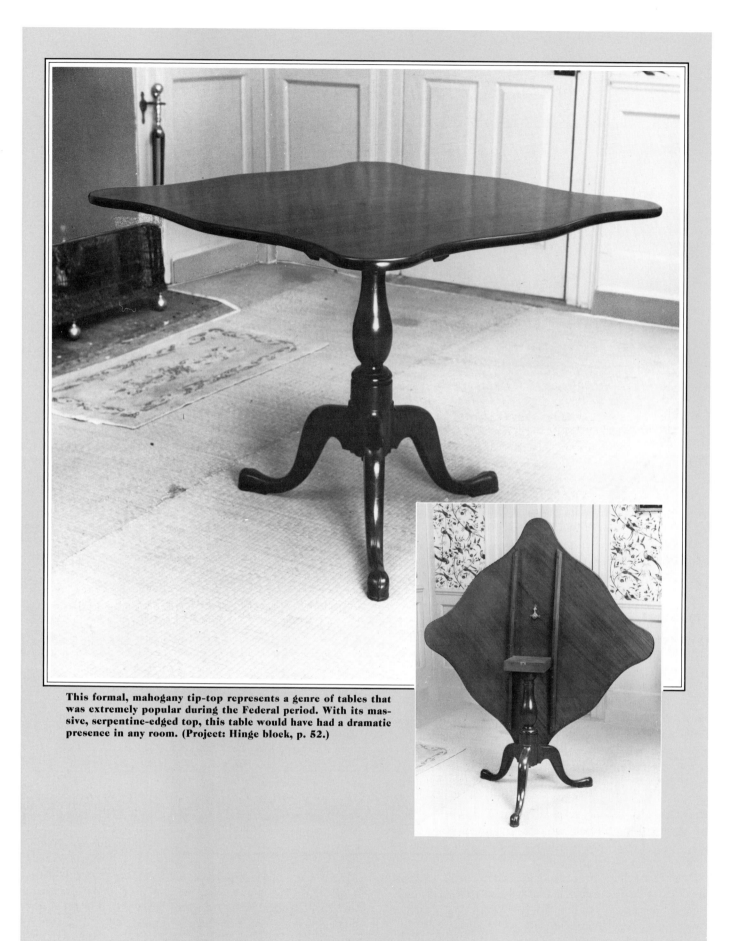

This formal, mahogany tip-top represents a genre of tables that was extremely popular during the Federal period. With its massive, serpentine-edged top, this table would have had a dramatic presence in any room. (Project: Hinge block, p. 52.)

Tip-Top Table

Chapter 6

This tip-top table offers a clever solution to the familiar problem of what to do with a tabletop when it's not being used. In similar fashion to the gateleg and Pembroke tables (pp. 90 and 156), the top on this table can be pivoted out of the way. Unlike the gateleg, though, this table doesn't fold up into a compact unit that can be stored unobtrusively against a wall. Instead, its hinged top swings into a vertical position, and the tip-top becomes a major piece of furniture that dominates the corner of the room it occupies.

The hinge mechanism on this table is the same device used on the candlestand (p. 38), but these tables are otherwise quite dissimilar. The candlestand is small and so versatile that it can be used in almost any setting, while this tip-top is so large that it functions very differently in a room. When its top is raised for dining, the table must be moved to a large, open area of the room. With its top positioned vertically, it stands 4½ ft. high and either dwarfs or competes with other furniture nearby. Thus, when not in use, this table demands a corner unto itself.

It is unusual for a piece of furniture to be so aloof. But, as with any special case, this one also presents some unique opportunities. Whenever I find a particularly striking piece of wood, I usually set it aside for a special project—which means that I generally end up with more special wood than special projects. If you are like me, take note. With its sensuous, serpentine edge, the top of this table commands attention and offers an ideal place to make use of some wide boards with a pronounced figure.

The original table is made of extremely dark San Domingo mahogany. We keep the piece in our parlor, which has beige woodwork and a paler beige background in the wallpaper. This large, dark table is the centerpiece of the light-colored room and is placed in the middle of the floor with its top positioned horizontally, ready whenever we want to dine in that room.

If you have a more somber setting in mind for your table, you might want to use a light-colored wood like curly or quilted maple, or even wavy birch. Whatever wood you select, make sure that you have enough to glue up a 36-in.-sq. top. I would suggest using the same species for the table's legs and pedestal, but you'll find these parts easier to make if you work with straight rather than wavy grain. Not only would a pronounced figure make it more difficult to carve the table's three feet and cut dovetail mortises in the boss of the pedestal, it would also be a waste of special wood since these parts are hidden when the top is displayed and in shadow when the piece is used.

The heavy base on this table is quite a contrast to the candlestand's thin pedestal and delicately tapered legs. The legs on the large tip-top must be sturdier both because of its size and because it is used differently. Meals are eaten at this table, and the weight of food, drink and tableware can be considerable. Furthermore, when diners rest their elbows on the edges of the top, its large overhang places their weight far away from the point of support in the center.

Although the table's legs are 1¾ in. thick at the point where they radiate from the boss, they are still attractive. Like the legs on the candlestand, those on this tip-top follow an S-shaped curve, in this case a cyma reversa, which runs in the opposite direction from the cyma recta curve found on the smaller stand. These two tables illustrate clearly the power of line to create feeling. One curve appears very delicate, the other robust.

The cyma reversa curve creates a distinct knee, rounded on its upper edge and flat underneath. From the knee the thick leg tapers to an ankle and from the ankle breaks into a pad foot. This foot, with a clear rib on its upper surface and a solelike platform on the bottom, is a survival feature from the Chippendale period. The upper pedestal, with a vase like that on a large Windsor-chair leg, identifies the table as a Federal piece, probably from the Boston area.

If you decide to make this table, I suggest assembling it with the third leg directed backward. Occasionally I've come across a large tip-top with the odd leg projecting forward, which makes the table look awkward and interferes with room traffic. The only advantage to positioning the leg forward is that the piece can be placed close to a wall. With the leg oriented to the back, as it is on this tip-top, the table stands nicely in a corner.

The weakest structural spot on such a large tripod table is the boss. It is common to find old three-legged tables on which the boss has split. This problem can usually be avoided by attaching a sheet-metal trifid support to the boss. This piece, which can be cut out of scrap metal, has three arms that radiate in the same pattern as the legs on the table. A small nail or screw is passed through the center of the support to hold it to the underside of the boss. Another nail or screw is driven at an angle toward the boss through each arm of the trifid piece and into the corresponding leg.

To keep the top from tipping over when weight is put on the wrong corner, both this table and the candlestand have a specially designed catch that locks the top in its horizontal position. If you plan to make this table, you'll want to order a reproduction brass catch from one of the suppliers listed in the appendices. Each catch comes with a keeper, and the pair must be carefully mounted. If the catch is fit too tightly against the hinge block, the sliding bolt cannot be easily disengaged. On the other hand, if the catch is positioned too far from the block, the bolt will not catch securely in the keeper—and everything on the table could end up in someone's lap.

The original table is finished with orange shellac, which complements the dark color of the mahogany. We keep the piece well waxed to protect the shellac from spills and we use a mat under hot dishes. If you want a more durable finish, try varnish or lacquer. I don't think these have the depth of shellac, but they are more resistant to wear and spills. The easiest clear finish of all to apply and care for is oil and wax, but their effect is too flat for my taste. The highlights that result from a hard, polished finish give the table a far richer look.

Hinge block

The hinge mechanism for raising the tabletop on both this table and the candlestand requires two cleats and a hinge block. The cleats on this table are made of mahogany, like the piece itself, while the hinge block is a native diffuse-porous hardwood that appears to be cherry or maple.

Using the same wood as you select for the table, make the cleats to the shape and dimensions shown in the drawing on p. 57, with the grain of the wood running in the direction indicated.

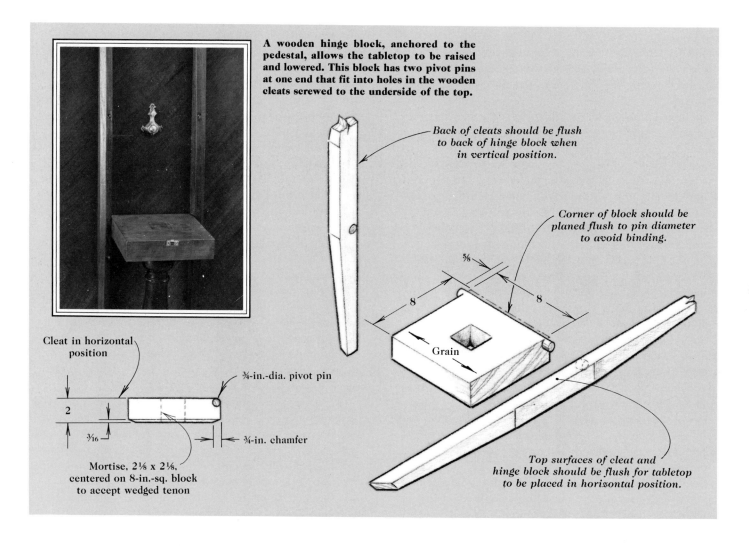

A wooden hinge block, anchored to the pedestal, allows the tabletop to be raised and lowered. This block has two pivot pins at one end that fit into holes in the wooden cleats screwed to the underside of the top.

Back of cleats should be flush to back of hinge block when in vertical position.

Corner of block should be planed flush to pin diameter to avoid binding.

⅝

8

8

Grain

Cleat in horizontal position

2

¾-in.-dia. pivot pin

³⁄₁₆

¾-in. chamfer

Mortise, 2⅛ x 2⅛, centered on 8-in.-sq. block to accept wedged tenon

Top surfaces of cleat and hinge block should be flush for tabletop to be placed in horizontal position.

To make the hinge block, first cut a piece to the overall dimensions, 9¼ in. by 8 in. Now grip the block in a vise, end grain up, and measure in ⅜ in., the radius of the wooden pivot on which the block turns, from both the long and short faces. Where these two measurements intersect will be the center of the pivot pin. Use this center to scribe a circle with a pair of dividers set to ⅜ in. This circle should touch or nearly touch both faces of the block. If yours is not quite flush with one face, as is the case with mine, you can remove the excess wood later.

Remove the block from the vise and use a square to mark a line all the way around the edge of the block, ⅝ in. in from the edge, or the depth of the pivot pin. Then use the square to transfer the diameter of the pivot from the end of the block to the adjacent sides. These lines indicate the waste to be removed. Replace the block in the vise, end grain up, and cut along the inside line just behind the pivot with a backsaw. Then remove the largest area of waste with a cross-cut panel saw and the smaller area just below the pivot with the backsaw to leave a protruding cube with a circle drawn on its end grain. Undercut the cube's corners with the backsaw, and shave the waste away with a fishtail gouge or chisel. Smooth away the facets left by the gouge with a file, leaving the pivot slightly oversized for now. Follow the same process to make the wooden pivot at the other end of the block.

To lay out the wooden pivot, scribe a circle on one corner of the hinge block with a pair of dividers set to a ⅜-in. radius (left). After marking off the waste areas, make the first cut behind the pivot with a backsaw (below). Cut away the large waste area using a panel saw.

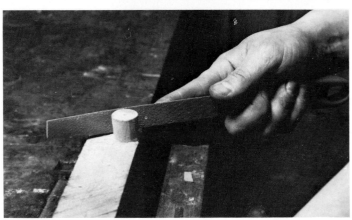

With most of the waste removed, undercut the pivot's corners with a backsaw (top left), then rough-shape with a fishtail gouge (above). Round the faceted edges of the pivot with a file, leaving the pivot slightly oversized for later adjustment (left).

Round the edge of the block between the pivots with a block plane, making sure to plane away any excess from the edge so that the pivot pins and edge form a continuous surface.

Place the pivot hole as close as possible to the upper edge of the cleat, using a block of wood to bolster the thin area while drilling the hole.

After fitting the pivot, sight along the rounded edge of the block and rotate the cleat to find high spots on the block that need to be removed. If necessary, plane the block or the cleat so they are flush.

Now clamp the hinge block in a vise with its upper surface facing out and the pivots parallel to the benchtop. Round the square corner on the edge between the pivots with a block plane, leaving it slightly larger than the pivots' diameter. You may have to further adjust this edge later.

The next step is to drill the pivot hole in the cleats. Lay one of the cleats on the bench, and with dividers set to ⅜ in., scribe the pivot hole with its center 3⅝ in. off the cleat's centerline and so that its diameter is almost tangent to the cleat's upper edge. Then secure the cleat in a vise and clamp a scrap block adjacent to where the hole will be drilled. This scrapwood will bolster the thin edge of the cleat and prevent the drill bit from splitting the edge loose. Use a ¾-in. bit to bore the ⅝-in.-deep pivot hole, placing the lead of the bit on the centermark of the hole and using a square to keep the brace and bit vertical.

Once the pivot hole is drilled, test-fit the pivot. If it is too tight, use a file to adjust the pivot pin. Once you have a satisfactory fit, assemble the cleat and pivot. Now sight along the edge of the block while rotating the cleat to determine if there are any high spots on the hinge block that need further shaving. If the pivot pins, end of the hinge block and back edges of the cleats are not flush, the tabletop cannot be placed in a fully vertical position. Once everything fits, mark the cleat and pivot as a pair to prevent confusion when they are later assembled.

Next set the cleat parallel to the block's upper surface. The pivot pins, top of the block and upper edges of the cleats should be flush in order for the tabletop to be placed in its full horizontal position. If they are not, plane the block or the upper edges of the cleats to adjust them.

Repeat the above steps to make the second pivot hole. After testing the fit of this pivot in its hole, remove the cleat and bevel the bottom edges of the block in the same way as for the lid of the candle box (p. 132). Once the hinge block and cleats are finished, attach the pedestal to the block with a wedged through tenon, and screw the cleats to the underside of the top.

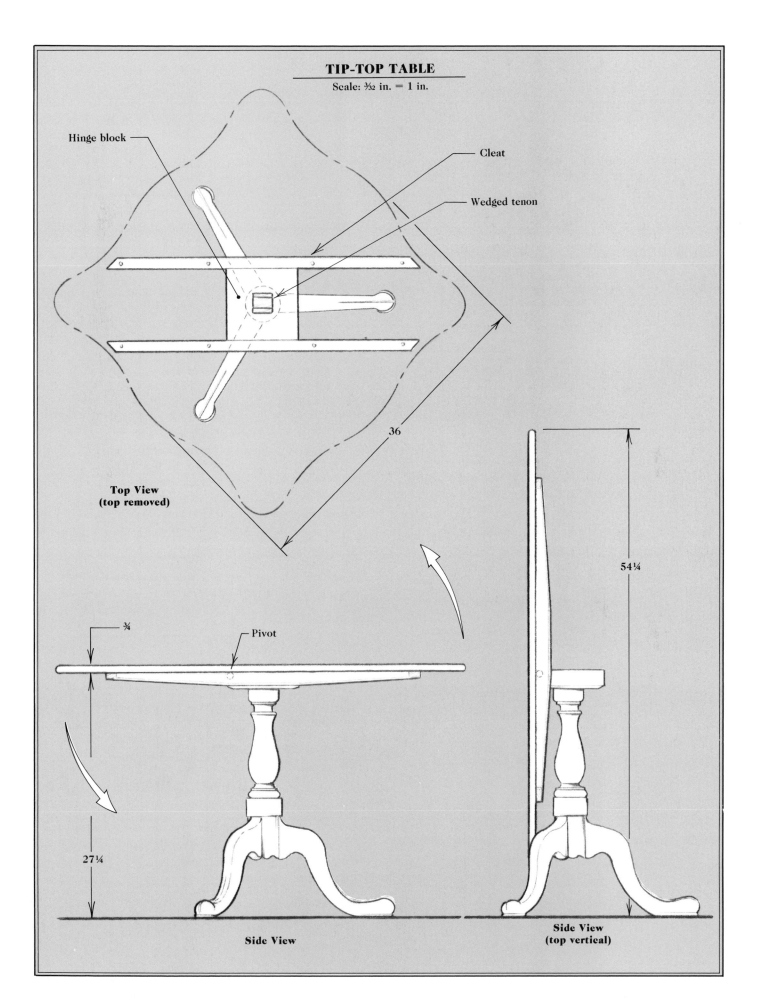

TIP-TOP TABLE

Scale: ³⁄₃₂ in. = 1 in.

Hinge block

Cleat

Wedged tenon

36

Top View
(top removed)

54¼

¾

Pivot

27¼

Side View

Side View
(top vertical)

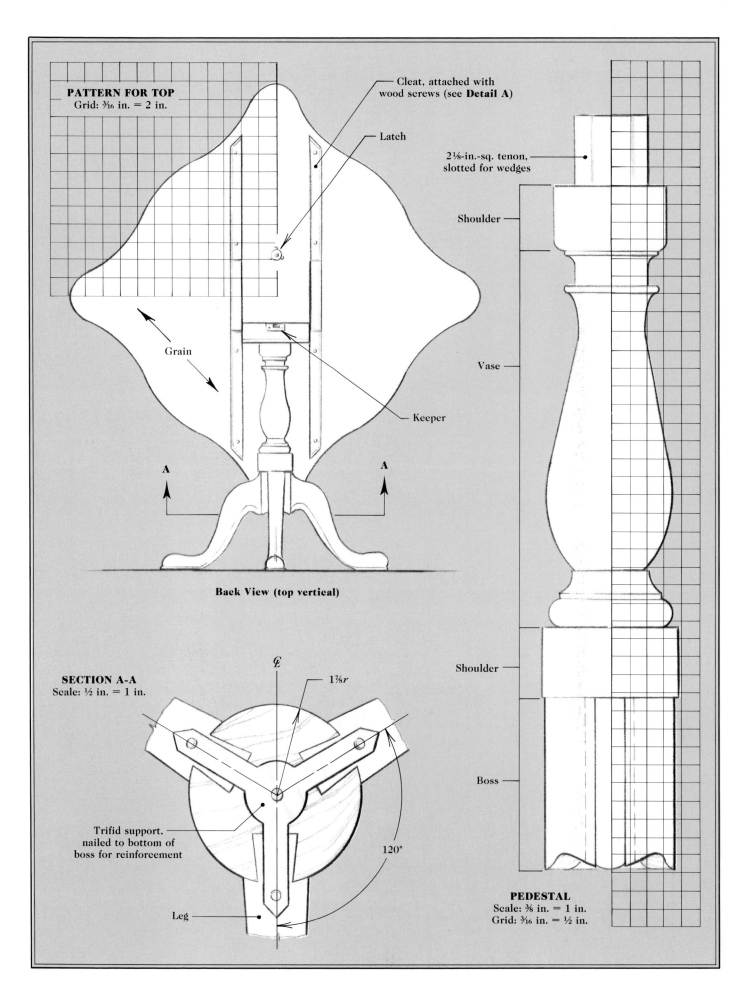

PATTERN FOR TOP
Grid: ³⁄₁₆ in. = 2 in.

Cleat, attached with
wood screws (see **Detail A**)

Latch

Grain

Keeper

2⅛-in.-sq. tenon,
slotted for wedges

Shoulder

Vase

A   A

Back View (top vertical)

Shoulder

SECTION A-A
Scale: ½ in. = 1 in.

℄

1⅛r

Boss

Trifid support,
nailed to bottom of
boss for reinforcement

120°

Leg

PEDESTAL
Scale: ⅜ in. = 1 in.
Grid: ³⁄₁₆ in. = ½ in.

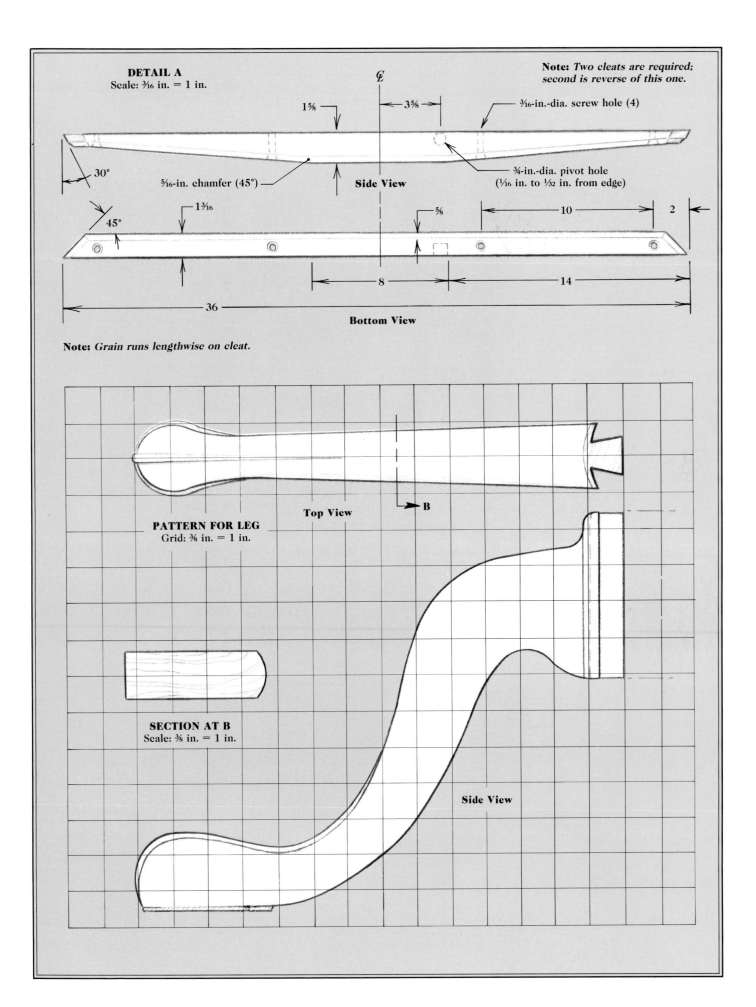

DETAIL A
Scale: ³⁄₁₆ in. = 1 in.

Note: *Two cleats are required; second is reverse of this one.*

1⅝

3⅝

³⁄₁₆-in.-dia. screw hole (4)

30°

⁵⁄₁₆-in. chamfer (45°)

Side View

¾-in.-dia. pivot hole
(¹⁄₁₆ in. to ¹⁄₃₂ in. from edge)

45°

1³⁄₁₆

⅝

10

2

8

14

36

Bottom View

Note: *Grain runs lengthwise on cleat.*

Top View

B

PATTERN FOR LEG
Grid: ⅜ in. = 1 in.

SECTION AT B
Scale: ⅜ in. = 1 in.

Side View

This elaborate secretary is actually two basic pieces of furniture—a chest of drawers with a cupboard-bookcase sitting on top. (Project: Muntins, p. 61.)

Secretary

Chapter 7

This combination desk-bookcase is called a secretary. It is one of a group of about a dozen similar Federal-period secretaries in public and private collections around the country that are believed to have been made in Portsmouth. Although Portsmouth was a major Colonial and Federal-period cabinetmaking center, little is known about the furniture manufactured here, and only a surprisingly small amount of surviving furniture can be attributed with confidence to this city's cabinet shops. Several of the secretaries in this group were branded with the names of people known to have lived in Portsmouth during the early 19th century, but these people were probably the owners of these pieces, not their makers. The secretary in this group that, in time, may become the Rosetta stone for identifying more secretaries and other Portsmouth furniture bears a handwritten inscription stating that it was made by Ebenezer Lord, the cabinetmaker who throughout much of the 19th century owned the house my wife and I now own. A second inscription on that piece dates it to 1811 and identifies the shop where Lord worked as a journeyman.

On all of these related secretaries, the cupboard-bookcase doors have two, three or four long windows, each topped by a Gothic arch. Although this motif is the visually dominant feature of these pieces, it was used by cabinetmakers working in many other cities, too, and cannot alone be used to link these secretaries to Portsmouth. This conclusion is instead based on a combination of similarities among the pieces, such as construction techniques and the choice of moldings, skirts and veneers.

Like the mirror (p. 20), this secretary is an architectural piece of furniture, meaning that it bears elements borrowed from classical Greek architecture. It has both an entablature (the elements immediately above the column on a Greek temple) and a pediment above it. The entablature is modified by the elimination of its lowest element, the architrave, which is normally positioned beneath the cornice and the frieze. The cabinetmaker probably dispensed with the architrave because the piece would usually have been placed in a formal room. Such a room almost certainly would have had a large cornice molding at the intersection of the walls and ceiling, which would not have included an architrave. (This element was commonly reserved for use as a casement around doors, windows and fireplaces.) Because this piece stands quite tall, the effect of this design is particularly successful. The cornice and veneered frieze on the secretary fall just below the same elements of the wall's molding, echoing their architectural counterparts.

Like most cornices, that on the secretary is a combination of several different molding profiles. The cabinetmaker used shapes popular in interior woodwork of the period, since he couldn't be sure what the makeup of the cornice would be in the room that would house the secretary. The lower molding of the cornice on this piece, called a cove and bead, was a common Federal shape used both on the cornice in a room and as a backband on architraves. The uppermost molding is a quarter-round, which, like the secretary's frieze, is faced with cross-banded veneer. Such cross-banded veneer, which is veneer set at a right angle to the substrate, was a common technique in Federal-period cabinetwork.

At first glance, the secretary appears to be an extremely complicated piece of furniture, but actually it is simply a clever combination of several basic elements. It is essentially two separate pieces of furniture: a chest of drawers, and a two-door cupboard-bookcase that sits atop it. The chest of drawers and the cupboard are simple, dovetail-joined, rectangular boxes with solid mahogany sides and pine tops and bottoms. These two boxes, open front and back, are positioned vertically. Backboards fill the rear side of both, and doors or drawers the front.

The top of the chest is made up of two distinct areas, one that slopes forward to create a writing desk and a second horizontal surface that supports the cupboard. Nailed in place over the upper row of dovetails in the chest is a cove molding that forms a lip and holds the cupboard in position. The pine carcase of the entablature that tops the cupboard is also a dovetailed box. This box is open top and bottom, positioned horizontally, and largely covered with mahogany veneer.

The secretary's visual statement seems equally complex at first glance, but this, too, can be broken down into basic design elements. A combination of several features, such as the skirt, cornice and shape of the feet, relates this secretary to the others made in Portsmouth. Yet the use of color, texture and pattern in the piece is an expression of the individual cabinetmaker.

Like the architectural mirror, this piece makes use of two tones of mahogany, but does so for different reasons. On the secretary the cabinetmaker used dark, crotch-grain, San Domingo mahogany on the skirt, outer face of the writing desk, frieze, center plinth on the pediment, and drawer fronts. He then used a light Honduras mahogany on the feet, sides of the lower carcase, dividers around the small drawers, finials and outer plinths on the pediment, and cove molding separating the upper and lower sections of the piece. This use of light mahogany perhaps resulted from the maker's solution to a problem that arose in designing the secretary's French feet. These feet are sufficiently strong to support the piece, even when it is loaded with books, but their proportion is troublesome. The bottom of the secretary is the same size as an ordinary chest of drawers, with its feet in matching scale. Since the entire piece is more than twice as tall as a normal bureau, though, feet that are appropriately sized for the base seem tiny on the full piece. By making the feet of a lighter-colored wood, the craftsman visually exaggerated them without actually increasing their size.

This solution, however, had to be integrated into the overall design of the secretary. The cabinetmaker therefore extended the motif of light-colored wood throughout, visually tying the piece together while also downplaying its component construction. Surrounding the two small drawers with a band of lighter wood, for example, not only sets off the darker drawer fronts but also smooths the transition from the lower chest to the cupboard-bookcase.

The cabinetmaker's use of bookmatched veneers on the fronts of the four large drawers is especially worthy of note. Bookmatched veneers were commonly used on wide, flat surfaces in Federal furniture, but here the results are exceptional. The drawers are faced with adjacent sister cuts from the same flitch, which was taken from the base of a limb. The resulting shape of the figure is a pronounced whorl. When bookmatched, the veneer displays the whorl not only as a mirror image but also as positive and negative images. On the left side of the drawer fronts the red-brown whorl is surrounded by a dark background. On the right side the mirror-image whorl is dark and set against a red-brown background.

At first glance, few people notice this unusual use of veneer. The effect is necessarily subtle, as the purchaser would undoubtedly have been uncomfortable with a piece that did not observe the rigid symmetry expected on furniture of the period. With this positive/negative image, however, the cabinetmaker cleverly violated the rule of symmetry without creating offense.

All four edges of the large drawer fronts are ornamented with cock beading, a raised lip made of a thin, separate strip of wood set into a shallow rabbet. This detail, discussed at length in the chapter on the chest of drawers (p. 170), protects the fragile veneer from chipping, helps articulate the facade of the drawer fronts and keeps the front of the carcase from reading as a simple plane.

The brass pulls on the drawers are called rosettes. Generally identified with the Sheraton style, they seem to contradict the presence of the French feet, which are associated with the Hepplewhite style. Yet this apparent contradiction confirms that any attempt to rigidly date or classify furniture by a single feature will often be inaccurate. The presence of the rosettes makes me suspect that this piece dates to around 1815, when the Sheraton style was popular in Portsmouth. This would place its date of manufacture a couple of years after the only two dated secretaries in the Portsmouth group were made.

The secretary's cupboard-bookcase was intended to store books and other treasured possessions. It is not surprising that one of the most elaborate pieces of furniture in a Federal house would have been made for this purpose. At the time, books were still very expensive and were highly regarded. Probate household inventories often noted the number of books owned by the deceased, and sometimes even listed them by title.

The books and other items stored in the bookcase were not always on display. The back side of glass-paned secretary doors was often covered with curtains tacked to the doors' stiles and rails. Tack holes on the top and bottom rails of the doors on this secretary confirm that these doors were at one time curtained.

Because the stored books and objects would vary in size, the shelves in this and the other Portsmouth secretaries were adjustable. They could be fit into any of eleven closely spaced dadoes cut in the insides of the bookcase carcase and in both sides of the central divider.

The original crown glass remains in the bookcase doors and is typical of sheet glass available in the Federal period. The panes were cut from a large, flat disc made by spinning molten glass. This process resulted in the imperfections that give the glass its texture. Looking through the panes at close range, one sees no obvious distortion. Because of the imperfections, however, light reflected from the glass ripples like the surface of a pond disturbed by a slight breeze. This same crown glass is used in all the window sash in the parlor and elsewhere in our house, and it protects the Federal-period prints on the parlor walls and shelters the candle in the lantern hanging in the center of the room. On a sunny day or by evening candlelight, a visitor to the parlor is greeted with a subtle light show of reflections off the room's crown glass.

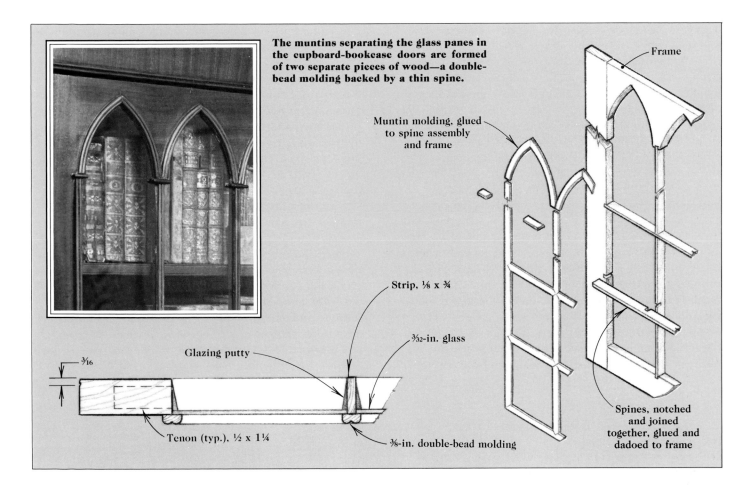

The muntins separating the glass panes in the cupboard-bookcase doors are formed of two separate pieces of wood—a double-bead molding backed by a thin spine.

Frame

Muntin molding, glued to spine assembly and frame

Strip, ⅛ x ¾

³⁄₃₂-in. glass

Glazing putty

³⁄₁₆

Tenon (typ.), ½ x 1¼

⅜-in. double-bead molding

Spines, notched and joined together, glued and dadoed to frame

The other secretaries in the Portsmouth group are of interest because they illustrate how Federal-period production cabinetmakers variously adapted a design. This secretary, which is 7 ft. 9 in. tall, fits comfortably in our parlor, where the ceilings are 8 ft. 2 in. But because many Federal-period homes would have had lower ceilings, cabinetmakers would often have been called upon to shorten this design. This was sometimes done by placing the two small drawers in the bottom of the bookcase behind the doors instead of beneath them. It was also common to reduce the height of the frieze by about an inch so that the entablature remained in proportion. With these two changes the secretary lost about six inches overall, and another four inches could be removed by eliminating the center finial. All these adaptations lowered the height of this design to as little as 6 ft. 11 in. If you want to make a scaled-down version of this secretary for your home, these same changes will work for you, too.

One other minor change you might want to make in reproducing this piece involves the writing desk. The sloping surface on the chest of drawers is a folded lid that lowers onto two sliding supports flanking the top drawer and opens to create the desk. The ample work area is covered with lightweight, green wool fabric, which was quite serviceable when quill pens were used for writing. Now that quills have been replaced by ball-point pens, which require more pressure for writing, I would suggest that you replace this rather delicate fabric with a sturdier material such as fine leather or high-quality felt.

Muntins

The individual panes of glass in the secretary doors are separated by a web of shaped wooden strips called muntins. These muntins form two lower tiers of small panes and an upper tier of elongated panes topped by Gothic arches. Like window-sash muntins, those in the secretary are T-shaped in cross section. Window-sash muntins, however, are normally made of a single piece of wood, while those in this secretary are built up of two separate strips. Here, the visible molded surface forms the top of the T; the bottom is a thin spine, which forms a rabbet on either side. The edges of the glass panes fit into these rabbets and are held in place by glazing points and glazing compound.

Make each door frame before making the muntins, using mahogany throughout. Cut the stiles and rails to the dimensions shown in the plans, copying the Gothic arches in the top rail. The edges of these arches will be covered by a molding in front and a bead of putty behind, so you need not labor over cleaning up the sawn edges. Join the frame with mortise-and-tenons, and test-fit the stiles and rails, but do not glue them yet.

The spines of the muntins in each door are made of ⅛-in. by ¾-in. stock. Their ends are set into dadoes cut into the inside edges of the door frame. Where the vertical and horizontal spines cross, matching notches are cut into each piece to form a bridle joint. I made the spines by ripping thin slices off a ¾-in. mahogany board and planing them to thickness. After each slice, I rejointed the board so that each new piece cut would have one finished side.

Cut the dadoes in the door frame with a dovetail saw and remove the waste with a ⅛-in. chisel. Remember that these dadoes will be covered by the applied molding, so don't make them any deeper than half the width of the molding, or 3/16 in. Now mark and cut the spines to length and test-fit each piece.

To locate the intersections of the horizontal and vertical strips, first partially insert the vertical strips into their corresponding dadoes, pushing them slightly below the surface of the door frame. Then set the horizontal strips in their dadoes. The lower corners on each end of the horizontal strips will just catch in the frame, but the assembly is stable enough to allow you to mark the joints.

Using a mat knife as a scribe, begin marking the joints on the vertical strips on both sides of the horizontal strips. Then remove the two vertical strips and use a square to scribe the joints down their sides. Place these strips together to line up the marks on their upper edges, put them in a vise, and make the cuts with a dovetail saw, being careful to cut only about ⅜ in. deep. Working with the two strips together makes them stiffer and less liable to break while being sawn. It also helps ensure that the

four joints will be uniform. After removing the waste with a chisel, test the width of each slot by inserting one of the horizontal strips.

Reposition the vertical strips in the door frame, this time letting them sit flush. Set the horizontal strips in place and push them down into the slots in the vertical pieces and dadoes. The horizontal strips will now sit halfway into the verticals and can be adjusted with the help of a square until each opening is square. When you are satisfied, mark the positions of the vertical strips on the horizontals. Then remove the horizontals and cut the slots in them the same way as for the verticals. This will produce two halves of a bridle joint, which should assemble perfectly.

Before proceeding to make the moldings for the front of the muntins, glue the mortise-and-tenon joints of the door frame and set the door aside to dry. The muntins' front moldings are reeded, a common motif on Federal furniture, which I produced with the same 3/16-in. plane used to reed the front legs of the Fancy chair (p. 100). If you cannot find one of these wooden planes, try a Stanley #45 or #55, or a multi-plane.

Assemble the spines in their dadoes and mark on the vertical strips where the horizontals and verticals intersect (left). Cut the notches in the two vertical spines at the same time (above).

Reassemble the spines in the door with the horizontals in the notches just cut, check that the horizontals and verticals are square, and mark the corresponding slots to be cut in the horizontal spines.

For the moldings, I simply made a series of reeds on a flat board. Begin by planing a piece of mahogany to ³⁄₁₆ in. thick. Be sure to select straight-grained wood, as a pronounced figure would tear. To make the reeds, roll the plane slightly to the left so that one leg of the cutter is set over the arris, while the other rides on the surface of the wood. Take a first pass, which should produce a groove in which the plane will track. Several more passes will be required to fully develop the reed. My wooden plane has a stop that will eventually ride on the surface of the board and automatically cease the cutting action.

Set the left leg of the cutter in the groove just cut and use it as a track to cut the next reed. Repeat this process across the mahogany until you have enough molding material. If you experience tearout, turn the mahogany around and start to reed from the other direction. When you have finished the reeding, use a mat knife to cut the mahogany into strips of two reeds each. Clean up the rough edges of the strips with a block plane.

When the molding is applied to the door frame, the V-groove between the two reeds should be placed exactly over the inside edge of the stiles and bottom rail. Position a piece of molding on one of the stiles, leaving excess length at the top and bottom. Mark where the bottom rail intersects, then scribe a miter and make the cut. (I find it is easier to do this with a mat knife than with a dovetail saw.) Repeat these steps for the other vertical strip.

Next miter one end of the molding strip for the bottom rail and lay this strip in place along with the corresponding vertical molding. If the two miters do not meet perfectly, use a low-angle block plane to make adjustments. I hold the plane in one hand with its heel against my sternum. Holding the molding in my other hand, I draw the miter across the mouth of the plane, removing wood only where necesary in tissue-paper-thin shavings.

When the miter is complete, set the two pieces in place. Position the other vertical molding and rest its miter over the end of the horizontal—this is more accurate than measuring. Mark and cut the second miter on the bottom strip and use the block plane to adjust the fit.

With these three molding strips fitted and in place, position the grid of ¹⁄₈-in. spines in the dadoes and mark where the molding strips intersect the spines. At the same time mark the finished height of the two vertical molding strips. Remove the three molding strips and lay out the indented V of the double miter at each of the six intersections. I cut these with a dovetail saw and cleaned them up with a chisel. Next cut the reeded molding for the perimeter strips to length. Spread glue on the backs of the strips and clamp them in place on the frame.

The ten short horizontal and vertical sections and the two longer sections of molding that will cover the spines are all joined with four four-way miters. These occur at the corners of the middle pane on the second row. Each of the short pieces needs to have two 45° cuts at each end. I scribed the cuts with a mat knife and miter square but cut them with a dovetail saw. Be sure to cut to the outside of the scribe mark, which will leave a little excess wood for adjustment. Test the fit of these pieces with one another

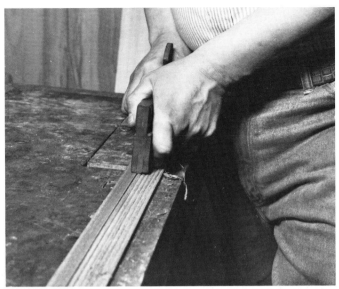

Use a ³⁄₁₆-in. center-bead molding plane, inclined slightly to the left, to cut a series of reeds on a flat board. The plane tracks in the groove of one reed to produce the adjacent reed. After the reeding is complete, cut the board into strips two reeds wide.

Use a low-angle block plane to fine-tune the miters cut on the ends of the molding strips.

and the muntins on the frame and make any corrections with the block plane. Then glue the spines in place and glue the reeded moldings to the spines.

The transition from the vertical muntins to the curved molding around the arches is made by a short, single horizontal bar. This bar, produced with the reeding plane, is made from $7/16$-in. mahogany stock so that it projects above the muntins. Note that the two middle bars are longer than the outer ones to accommodate the two curved muntins that meet above them. Cut the bars to length and round both ends with sandpaper.

Cut the six curved moldings to the shape and dimensions shown in the drawing on p. 67. I cut them out with a coping saw and cleaned up their curved edges with the same small spokeshave used on the concave edges of the seat on the rod-back Windsor chair (p. 118).

To reed the curved moldings, I used the same scratch tool as for the simulated cock beading on the chest of drawers (p. 170), cutting a line parallel to the two curved edges. First, however, you need to round the fence of the wooden block to allow the tool to follow a concave surface. Then turn the wood screw to set the width of the cut to exactly one-half the width of the six curved pieces. I shaped the cleft of the molding with the same small V-shaped parting tool used to reed the arm post of the sofa (p. 30). Note that when the grain of the piece changes, you will need to change the direction of your cut to prevent splintering. Smooth out the cut with a small piece

of sandpaper, folded so that it abrades both sides at once, and finally sand the outside edge to round it.

Now assemble the arched muntins to test their fit both at the top of the arch and at the horizontal transition bar. When you are satisfied with the fit, glue the muntins in place and clamp them till dry.

Duplicating the original crown glass in the secretary's doors will be difficult, although you may find an antique or architectural salvage dealer who will sell it by the pane. Cylinder glass will be easier to find, since window glass continued to be made by this process into the 20th century.

The rectangular panes can be easily sized, but a $1/4$-in.-thick wood template should be made for the arched panes. Test the template's fit in the arched openings. It should not be too tight, as glazing or the wood's seasonal movement could break a tight-fitting pane. Using a good-quality, diamond-pointed glass cutter and wearing gloves, score the pane around the outline of the template, hold it over the corner of a table and snap off the waste.

Set the glass in the door and hold it in place with glazier's points. (The push points available at hardware stores are too large.) Points of any size can also be made, like those on the original secretary. Small metal triangles were cut from sheet iron with shears and then carefully pushed in place with the bit of a screwdriver. For glazing, I prefer a compound sold under the brand name "Old-Fashioned Putty," which is made of linseed oil and whiting and is not as dry as other varieties.

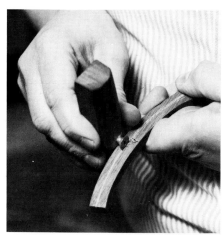

Once you are satisfied with the fit of the curved muntins, assemble and glue them, clamping them in place while they dry.

With a scratch tool, begin reeding the curved molding strip by cutting a groove parallel to the edge of the strip (above left). Then use a small V-shaped parting tool to round the initial groove made by the scratch tool (left).

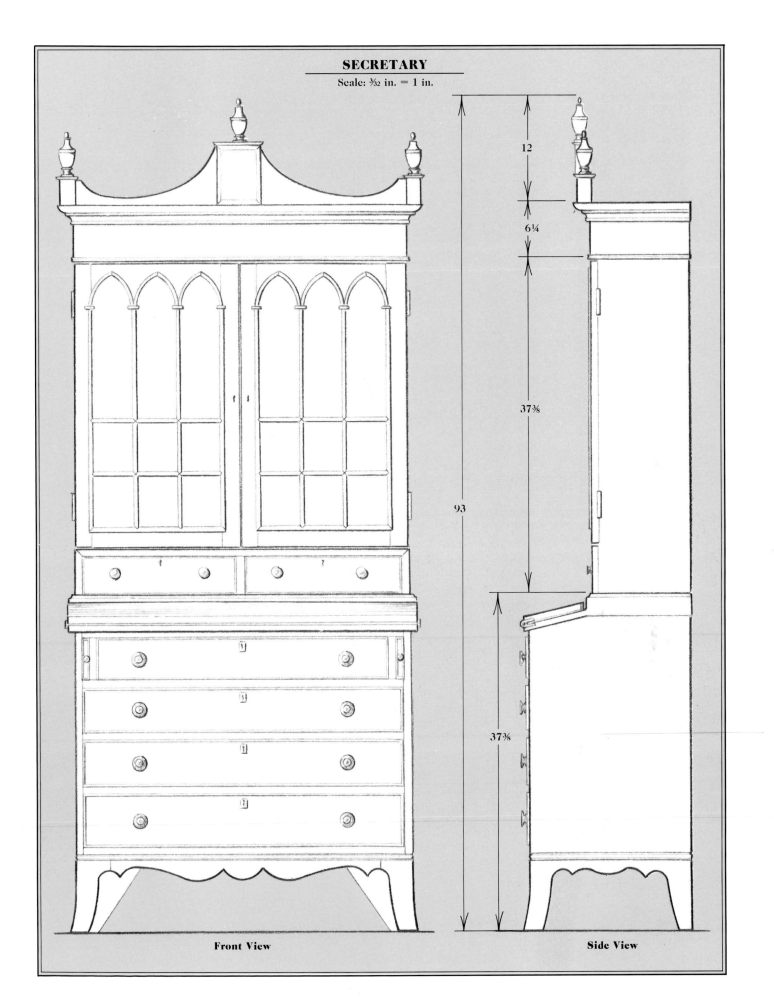

SECRETARY

Scale: ³⁄₃₂ in. = 1 in.

12

6¼

93

37⅜

37⅜

Front View

Side View

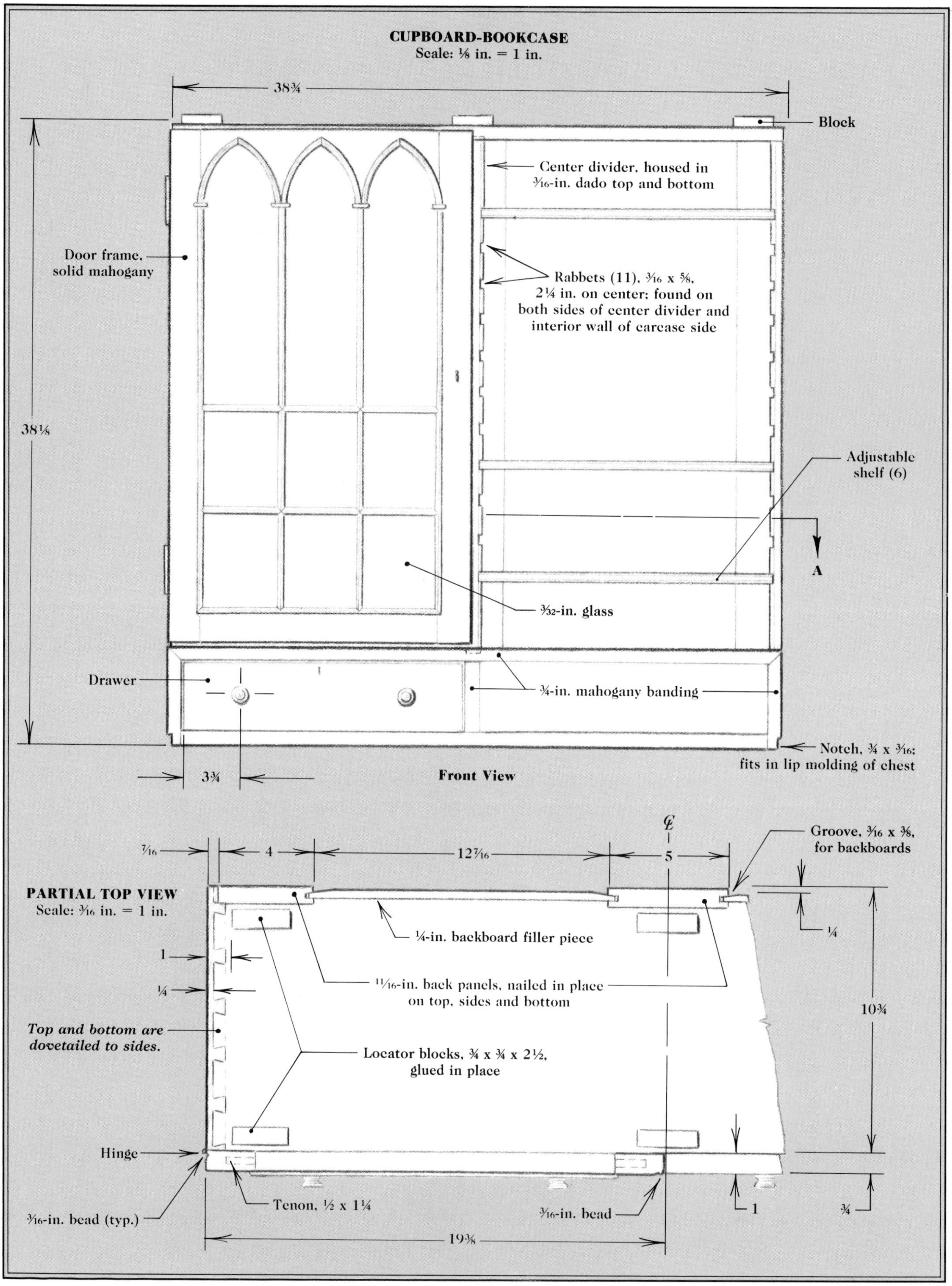
CUPBOARD-BOOKCASE
Scale: ⅛ in. = 1 in.
38¾
Block
38⅛
Center divider, housed in 3⁄16-in. dado top and bottom
Door frame, solid mahogany
Rabbets (11), 3⁄16 x ⅝, 2¼ in. on center; found on both sides of center divider and interior wall of carcase side
Adjustable shelf (6)
A
3⁄32-in. glass
Drawer
¾-in. mahogany banding
Notch, ¾ x 3⁄16; fits in lip molding of chest
3¾
Front View
PARTIAL TOP VIEW
Scale: 3⁄16 in. = 1 in.
7⁄16
4
12 7⁄16
5
Groove, 3⁄16 x ⅜, for backboards
¼
¼-in. backboard filler piece
1
¼
11⁄16-in. back panels, nailed in place on top, sides and bottom
10¾
Top and bottom are dovetailed to sides.
Locator blocks, ¾ x ¾ x 2½, glued in place
Hinge
Tenon, ½ x 1¼
3⁄16-in. bead (typ.)
3⁄16-in. bead
1
¾
19⅜

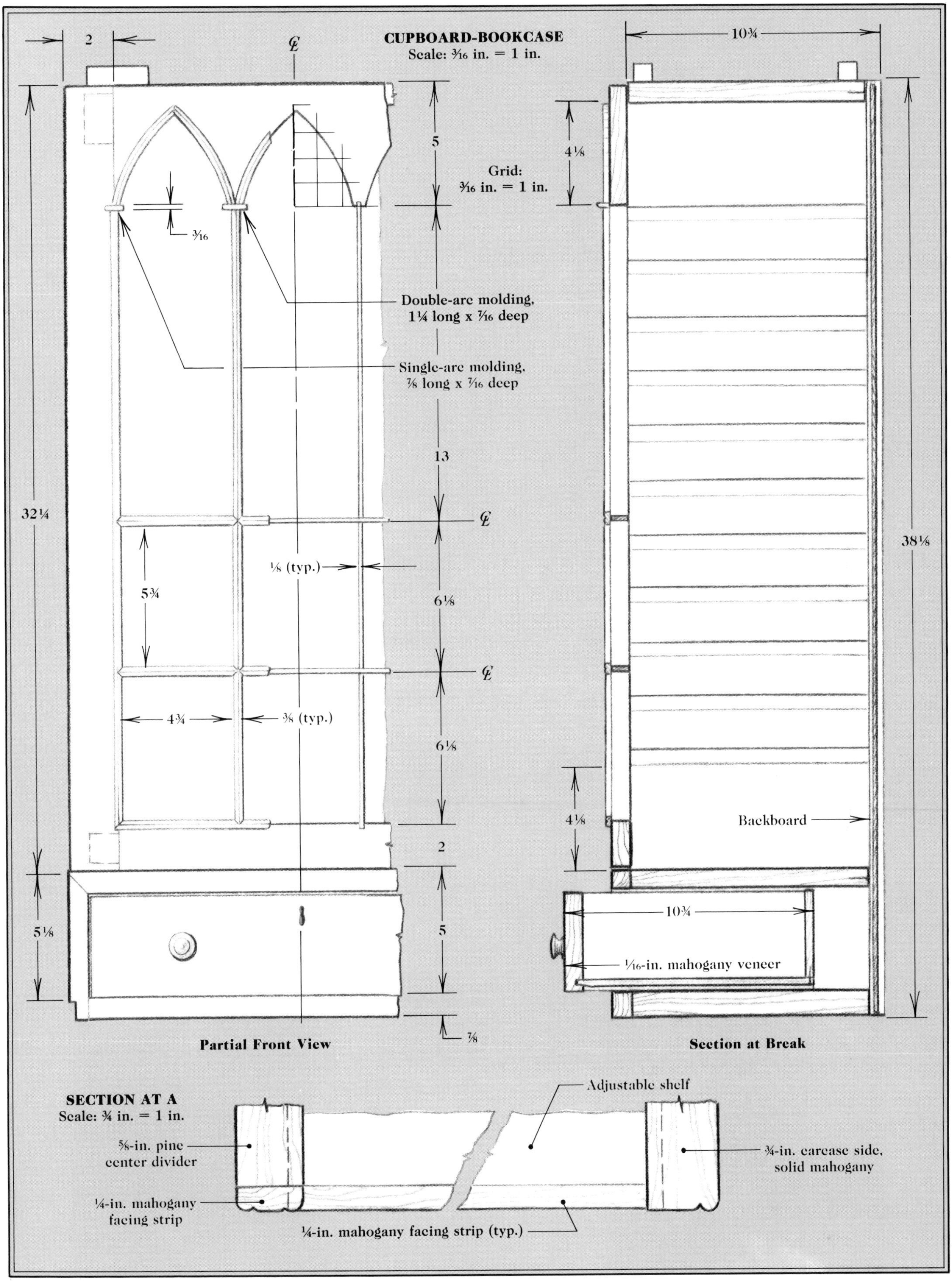
CUPBOARD-BOOKCASE
Scale: 3⁄16 in. = 1 in.
Grid:
3⁄16 in. = 1 in.
2
℄
5
3⁄16
Double-arc molding,
1¼ long x 7⁄16 deep
Single-arc molding,
⅞ long x 7⁄16 deep
13
℄
32¼
⅛ (typ.)
5¾
6⅛
℄
4¾
⅜ (typ.)
6⅛
2
5⅛
5
⅞
Partial Front View
10¾
4⅛
38⅛
4⅛
Backboard
10¾
1⁄16-in. mahogany veneer
Section at Break
SECTION AT A
Scale: ¾ in. = 1 in.
Adjustable shelf
⅝-in. pine
center divider
¾-in. carcase side,
solid mahogany
¼-in. mahogany
facing strip
¼-in. mahogany facing strip (typ.)

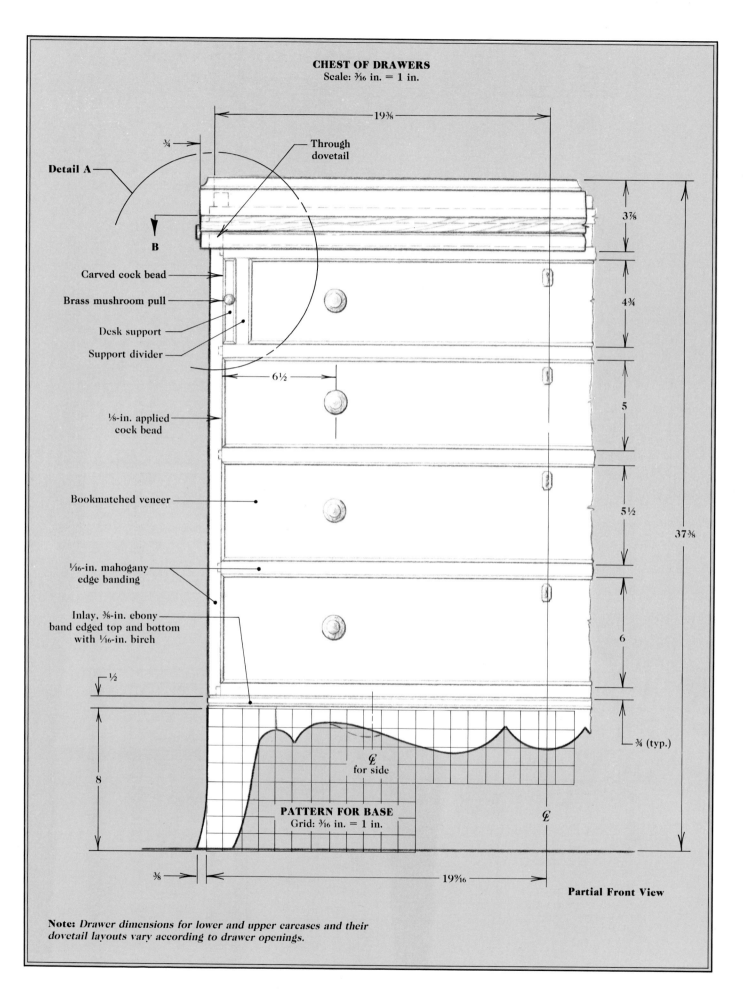

CHEST OF DRAWERS
Scale: ³⁄₁₆ in. = 1 in.

19⅜

¾

Detail A

Through
dovetail

B

3⅞

Carved cock bead

Brass mushroom pull

Desk support

Support divider

4¾

6½

⅛-in. applied
cock bead

5

Bookmatched veneer

5½

¹⁄₁₆-in. mahogany
edge banding

Inlay, ⅜-in. ebony
band edged top and bottom
with ¹⁄₁₆-in. birch

6

37⅜

½

¾ (typ.)

℄
for side

8

PATTERN FOR BASE
Grid: ³⁄₁₆ in. = 1 in.

℄

⅜

19⁹⁄₁₆

Partial Front View

Note: *Drawer dimensions for lower and upper carcases and their
dovetail layouts vary according to drawer openings.*

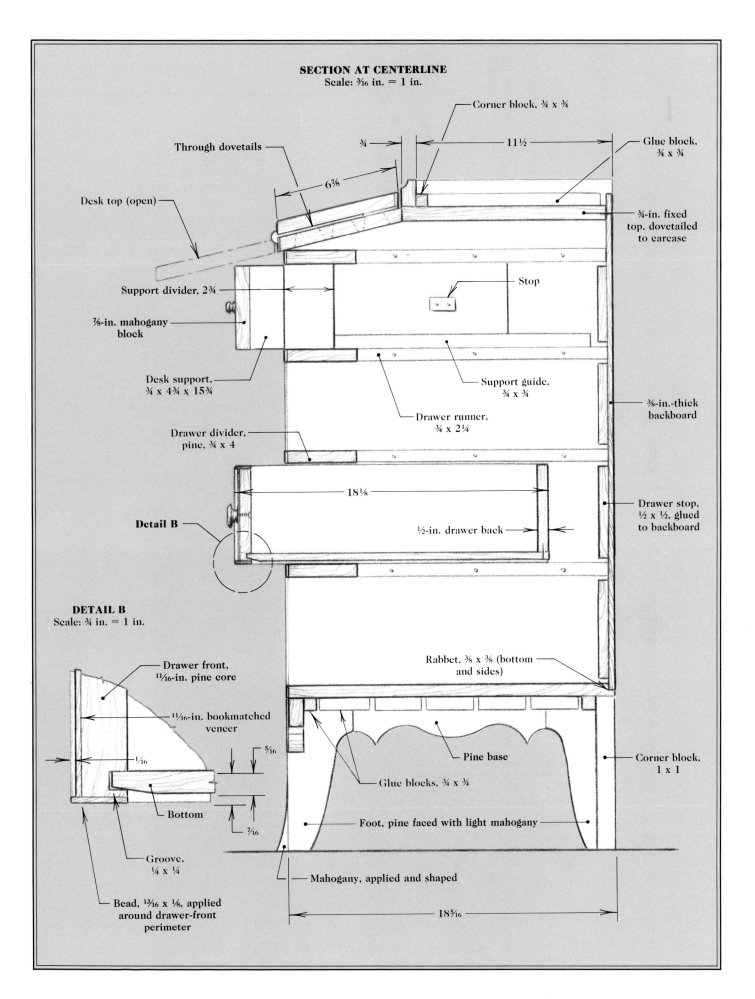

SECTION AT CENTERLINE
Scale: ³⁄₁₆ in. = 1 in.

Corner block, ¾ x ¾

Glue block, ¾ x ¾

Through dovetails

6⅞

¾

11½

Desk top (open)

¾-in. fixed top, dovetailed to carcase

Support divider, 2¾

Stop

⅞-in. mahogany block

Support guide, ¾ x ¾

Desk support, ¾ x 4¾ x 15¾

Drawer runner, ¾ x 2¼

⅜-in.-thick backboard

Drawer divider, pine, ¾ x 4

18⅛

Detail B

½-in. drawer back

Drawer stop, ½ x ½, glued to backboard

DETAIL B
Scale: ¾ in. = 1 in.

Drawer front, ¹¹⁄₁₆-in. pine core

Rabbet, ⅜ x ⅜ (bottom and sides)

¹¹⁄₁₆-in. bookmatched veneer

⁵⁄₁₆

¹⁄₁₆

Bottom

Pine base

⁷⁄₁₆

Glue blocks, ¾ x ¾

Corner block, 1 x 1

Groove, ¼ x ¼

Foot, pine faced with light mahogany

Bead, ¹³⁄₁₆ x ⅛, applied around drawer-front perimeter

Mahogany, applied and shaped

18⁵⁄₁₆

TOP VIEW AND SECTION AT B
Scale: ⅛ in. = 1 in.

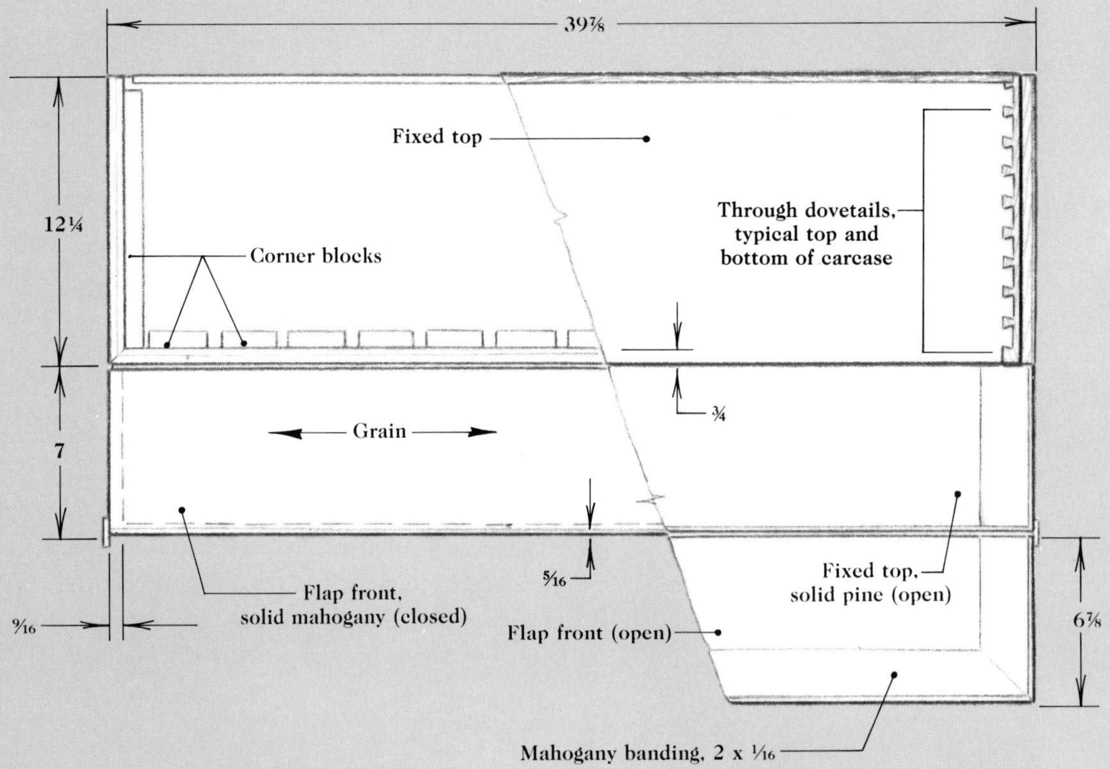
39⅞
12¼
7
Fixed top
Through dovetails, typical top and bottom of carcase
Corner blocks
Grain
¾
5/16
9/16
Flap front, solid mahogany (closed)
Fixed top, solid pine (open)
Flap front (open)
6⅞
Mahogany banding, 2 x 1/16

Note: *Phantom line indicates carcase below.*

DETAIL A
Scale: ⅜ in. = 1 in.

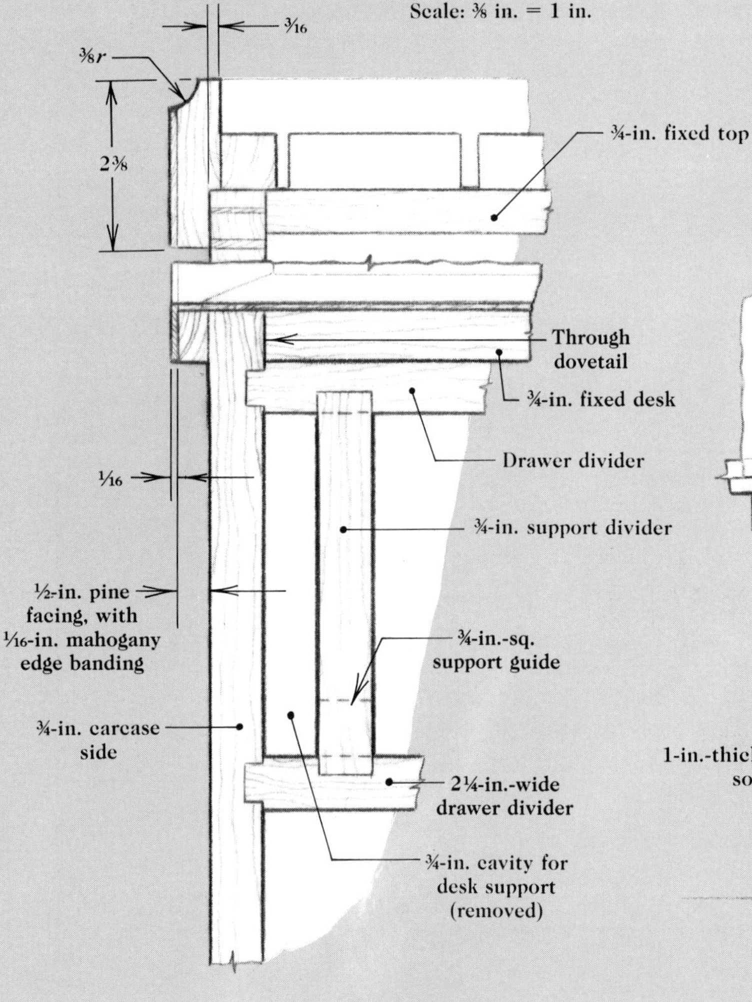
3/16
⅜r
2⅜
¾-in. fixed top
Through dovetail
¾-in. fixed desk
Drawer divider
1/16
¾-in. support divider
½-in. pine facing, with 1/16-in. mahogany edge banding
¾-in.-sq. support guide
¾-in. carcase side
2¼-in.-wide drawer divider
¾-in. cavity for desk support (removed)

PARTIAL BACK VIEW AT BASE
Scale: ¼ in. = 1 in.

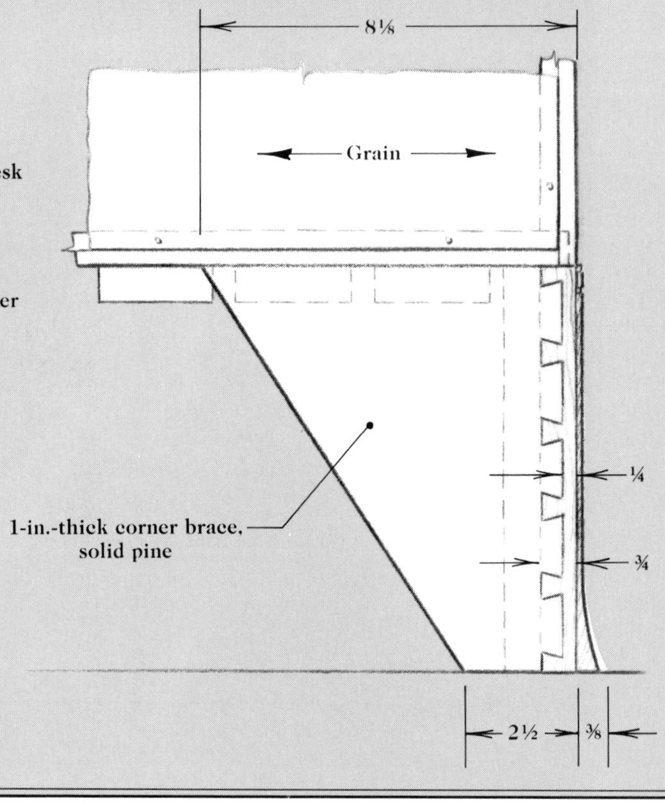
8⅛
Grain
¼
¾
1-in.-thick corner brace, solid pine
2½
⅜

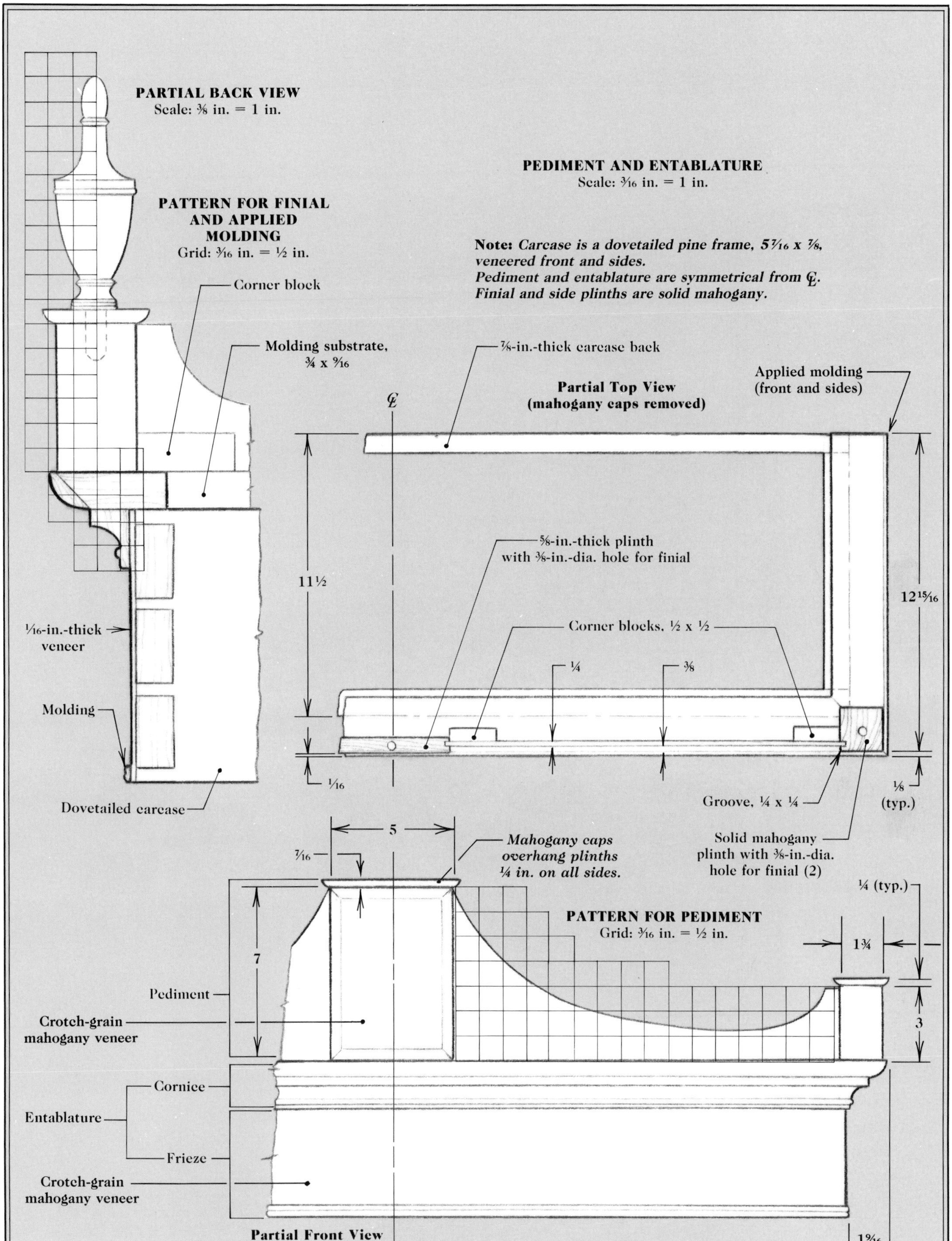
PARTIAL BACK VIEW
Scale: ⅜ in. = 1 in.
PATTERN FOR FINIAL AND APPLIED MOLDING
Grid: 3⁄16 in. = ½ in.
Corner block
Molding substrate, ¾ x 9⁄16
1⁄16-in.-thick veneer
Molding
Dovetailed carcase
PEDIMENT AND ENTABLATURE
Scale: 3⁄16 in. = 1 in.
Note: Carcase is a dovetailed pine frame, 5 7⁄16 x ⅞, veneered front and sides.
Pediment and entablature are symmetrical from ℄.
Finial and side plinths are solid mahogany.
⅞-in.-thick carcase back
Partial Top View
(mahogany caps removed)
Applied molding
(front and sides)
℄
11½
12 15⁄16
⅝-in.-thick plinth
with ⅜-in.-dia. hole for finial
Corner blocks, ½ x ½
¼
⅜
1⁄16
⅛
(typ.)
Groove, ¼ x ¼
Solid mahogany
plinth with ⅜-in.-dia.
hole for finial (2)
5
7⁄16
Mahogany caps
overhang plinths
¼ in. on all sides.
¼ (typ.)
PATTERN FOR PEDIMENT
Grid: 3⁄16 in. = ½ in.
1¾
7
3
Pediment
Crotch-grain
mahogany veneer
Cornice
Entablature
Frieze
Crotch-grain
mahogany veneer
Partial Front View
19⅜
1 9⁄16
(typ.)

THE
DINING ROOM

With salmon-colored walls and burgundy woodwork, the colors of our dining room are its most striking feature. These are the room's original colors, I was surprised to discover when restoring it several years ago. The painters had been consistent with the general decorating scheme in the other formal areas of the house, where the walls were papered and the woodwork painted a darker shade of the background color in the wallpaper. Although the dining-room walls are painted rather than papered, the pairing of two shades of one color repeats the effect found in the parlor, bedchamber and front hallway.

The floor in this room was originally unfinished, but at my wife's request I painted it with a checkerboard pattern of 12-in. black squares over a white base. This was a common treatment in American homes from the 17th to the mid-19th century. Together, the checkerboard floor and two-tone red walls make a very bold color scheme, which is in character with the Federal period, even if it's in marked contrast to the more sedate parlor next door.

The dining room's woodwork is simpler and less abundant than that in the parlor. The fireplace mantel, though similar to the parlor's, is smaller and more restrained. A prominent detail on the mantel is the cornice's denticulated bed molding, which echoes a row of dentils under the crown molding in the room's cornice. The walls also have a projecting chair rail to protect the plaster from being damaged by the ten Fancy chairs that ring the room. Although the window casements are rabbeted to allow for hinged shutters, shutters were never installed. The amount of light entering the room is regulated by curtains.

The largest piece in the room is the sideboard. Accompanying it are a very large, mahogany gateleg table, and a marble-topped table, called a mixing table, for preparing alcoholic beverages (even a small spill of alcohol would spot a shellac finish). A dumbwaiter serves as a display stand but is pulled up to the table and used for serving when we are dining.

In typical Federal fashion, we place the furniture against the dining-room walls when the room is not in use, leaving the center of the room clear. The chairs symmetrically flank each table in imitation of dining-room furniture arrangements found in both the Sheraton and Hepplewhite pattern books (see p. 2).

Our dining room has an interesting period in its history. In 1915 the house was sold for the first time outside the Seaward-Lord families. The new owner repaired watches and clocks and used this room as his shop. A 1920s sketch of our street shows a sign hanging by the front door advertising this business. After we bought the house, I found that sign in the cellar.

A vital part of a Federal-period household, trays transported meals and tea each day from the kitchen to a more comfortable or more formal setting. (Project: Edge banding, p. 77.)

Tray

Chapter 8

I n Federal-period homes, food was cooked in the kitchen but often eaten in another room. Because of the kitchen fireplace's large opening (intended to give the cook better access to the fire and kettles), considerable heat was drawn up the flue in winter, so meals were served in the dining room or parlor where the fire could be kept burning vigorously. In summer, the small bed of coals kept constantly burning in the kitchen fireplace made the room so hot that housewives would certainly have appreciated Harry Truman's admonition to get out of the kitchen (even if their lot in life precluded following his advice). Since Federal-period Americans also regularly enjoyed taking tea and always did so in a more formal setting than the kitchen, this meant that food was carried several times a day from the kitchen to another room. Each household was therefore equipped with several trays, or, as they were then called, waiters (five are listed in the 1805 inventory of our house).

The most common type of tray was made of tin-coated sheet iron and was produced in factories at Pontypool or Usk, Wales. These trays were brightly painted and decorated. The technique used was called japanning, which consisted of several layers of varnish applied over paint, and which produced an attractive, durable and waterproof surface. Mass production and the low wages paid to the women decorators made these metal trays inexpensive. Wooden trays like this one required more time to produce and were therefore more costly and less common. When a cabinetmaker did make a wooden tray, it was intended for formal use, and mahogany was the usual material.

As a woodworker, I have a special fondness for this tray. Most wooden trays of the Federal period had cast-brass handles and a pierced-metal gallery, or rim, that too was often of brass. The maker of this tray was clever enough to make these elements almost entirely of wood. Not using

metal created some problems, however, the principal one being how to make wooden handles. Normally these cast-brass parts were U-shaped and had threaded ends which could be inserted into holes in the tray's wooden bottom and secured with nuts.

The maker of this tray carved each U-shaped handle from a single piece of wood and oriented the grain to run vertically in the horizontal handhold. To minimize the weakness in this short-grain section, he made this area thicker than the rest—in addition to the structural advantage, it also makes sense that the handle be rounder and thicker where it will be grasped. The long-grain legs of the handles could be made thinner because they are inherently stronger than the horizontal piece. The fact that the original handles have survived 180 years of use proves the practicality of this solution.

The metal strip that was commonly used as the gallery on wooden trays offered strength and durability, was easier to install than wood, and could be stamped or pierced to make its surface more interesting. The problem with making the gallery of a heavily figured wood like mahogany is that it does not bend well and in thin strips is fragile. A light blow to such a thin wooden edge will bruise or chip it.

The imaginative solution the maker employed in this tray was to laminate four $\frac{1}{16}$-in.-thick strips of veneer to form the gallery. This takes advantage of the aesthetic qualities of wood while overcoming its weaknesses. The innermost strip is 1½-in.-wide mahogany edge banding, which is cut so that the grain runs across, rather than the length of, the strip. This means that the strip's upper edge is end grain and very fragile. The next layer appears to be a combination of birch (or some other diffuse-porous hardwood) and brass. The birch forms the lower portion of this layer and a strip of brass the same thickness as the wood has been set in to form the exposed edge. The wood is visible only from the bottom, where it is too thin to be

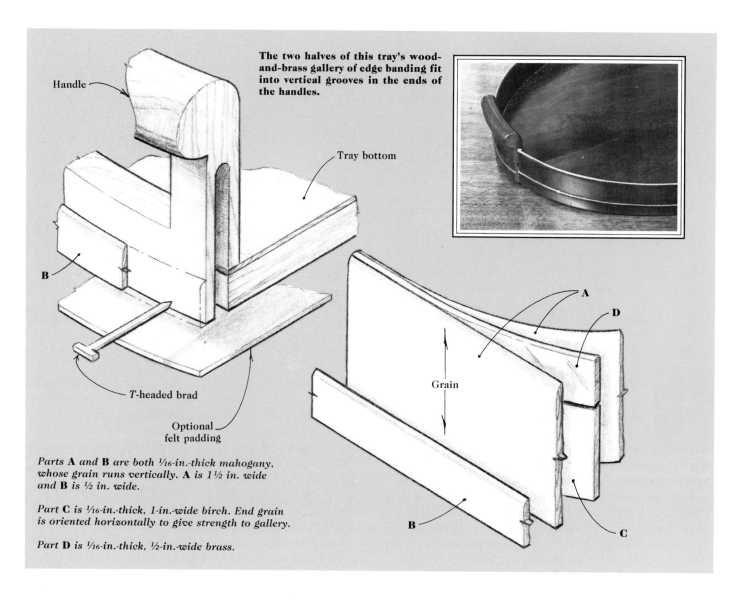

Handle

The two halves of this tray's wood-and-brass gallery of edge banding fit into vertical grooves in the ends of the handles.

Tray bottom

B

T-headed brad

Optional
felt padding

A

D

Grain

B

C

*Parts **A** and **B** are both ¹⁄₁₆-in.-thick mahogany, whose grain runs vertically. A is 1½ in. wide and B is ½ in. wide.*

*Part **C** is ¹⁄₁₆-in.-thick, 1-in.-wide birch. End grain is oriented horizontally to give strength to gallery.*

*Part **D** is ¹⁄₁₆-in.-thick, ½-in.-wide brass.*

positively identified. Nor is it possible to determine where the brass ends and the wood begins because the joint is covered on both sides, but I suspect that the brass is about ½ in. wide. The third strip is 1½-in.-wide mahogany veneer, identical to the first. The upper edge of the sandwich created by these three layers of veneer is rounded, exposing the brass just a hair above the mahogany edge banding that flanks it. The brass protects the fragile end grain of the mahogany and also takes on a light gold color when polished, creating an interesting highlight against the dark wood.

The fourth layer of veneer is ½-in.-wide mahogany edge banding, laid over the lower part of the third layer. A strip of the same width and thickness was applied to the outside bottom edge of the handles after assembly. These ½-in.-wide strips create a stepped lower edge, which is visually more interesting than a straight, unbroken line would be.

The bottom of this tray is oak, veneered with mahogany. This seems strange because even though during the Federal period mahogany was a more costly wood, the labor needed to veneer the bottom would have exceeded the cost of a short, solid mahogany board. I would make the bottom out of a single ⅜-in.-thick piece of mahogany.

The construction of the tray itself is simple. The laminated gallery and the handles are butted against the edge of the oval bottom board. Two ³⁄₁₆-in.-deep vertical grooves are cut into the ends of the handles, and the ends of the gallery are set into these grooves. No nails were used to secure the gallery of my original tray. It was simply glued in place. This produced a less-than-reliable glue joint, however, since glue does not adhere well to the end grain at the ends of the oval bottom. The maker of this tray solved the problem by securing the handles to the bottom with brads, which are hidden by the outer strip of edge banding.

When deciding how to finish the tray, keep in mind that it may often be used for transporting vessels that contain liquids and hot food. The original is finished with shellac, so we keep it well waxed and always use an insulating pad when carrying anything hot. I would finish a new tray with varnish or lacquer, however. Glue a layer of felt or small felt pads to the bottom surface of the tray to prevent it from scratching tabletops.

Edge banding

To cut the edge banding for the gallery, you need about 1½ sq. ft. of veneer, ¹⁄₁₆ in. thick. The original is made of San Domingo mahogany, but you could use almost any veneer you prefer. You also need two veneer strips at least 26 in. long for the core. I used birch, but any type of veneer will do, as it is never seen. You can buy veneers, but I make my own by resawing scrap. I joint one edge of the veneer on a shooting board, as shown at right. Be sure to joint a side that is edge grain, not end grain. If you need to joint more than one sheet, lay them together and tap their edges on the benchtop to align them before inserting them in the shooting board.

Since the gallery is to be fitted into the handles at either end of the tray, you will be creating two lengths of laminated edge banding, each about 26 in. long (allowing a little extra for waste). In addition to the sheets of veneer, you will also need two strips of brass, ½ in. wide by ¹⁄₁₆ in. thick, at least 26 in. long. Brass can be purchased from many industrial suppliers. Ask if they have a 3-ft. shear, and have them cut the strips to width—this will save you a lot of work. Rough both sides of the brass with 80-grit sandpaper so that glue will bond well to it.

To cut the banding, lay a sheet of veneer on a smooth surface. Put the jointed edge against a large square so that the blade of the square runs across the grain of the veneer, and with a mat knife square the end of the sheet. Now measure in 1½ in. from this newly cut end and use the square and mat knife to cut off a strip of banding the width of the sheet of veneer. Repeat this process until you have enough strips to total more than the 104 linear inches needed for the first and third layers of the tray's gallery. Next cut about 52 in. of ½-in.-wide banding for the lower lip, or fourth layer, that will circumscribe the bottom outside edge of the tray.

Joint one edge of the internal layer of birch veneer on the shooting board. To strengthen the banding, the grain in the birch has to run parallel to the tray bottom rather than perpendicular to it, so here you will be cutting with the grain. Cut two 26-in.-long strips of 1-in.-wide birch veneer, being careful that the knife does not get caught and follow the direction of the grain instead of the edge of the square.

At this point you will have all the strips of veneer needed to make up the gallery. On the strips of mahogany edge banding, only one end is now square with the two edges, so use the square and mat knife to trim the second end square as well. To get lengths of edge banding long enough to make one-half of the gallery, you will probably need to join two or more strips together for each of the first, third and fourth layers. (My strips were 10 in. long, so I used three pieces for each layer and trimmed off the excess after the lamination was glued together.) Butt the pieces together to check the tightness of each joint, and if need be, recut the ends square. Then tape the pieces together with masking tape to make four 1½-in.-wide lengths of edge banding and two ½-in.-wide lengths.

You can make a simple shooting board to joint the veneer strips by tacking two straight strips of ¾-in. board, about 3 in. wide by 36 in. long, to a wide base. Slip the veneer (making sure to align the edges if you're jointing more than one strip at a time) between the narrow pieces of plywood and clamp it in place by hammering the nails partway into the base.

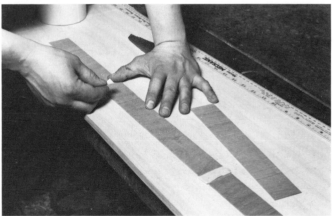

Use a large square and a mat knife to cut a second edge on the veneer, this one end grain and at a right angle to the first edge (top). Cut enough 1½-in.-wide strips to make up the first and third layers of edge banding for the gallery of the tray—about 104 linear inches. Then butt the strips together end-to-end to get the lengths you need for each half of the gallery, and tape the pieces together (bottom).

The sandwich formed by the 1½-in.-wide mahogany and the birch-and-brass core will be glued up first; the ½-in.-wide edge banding will be added later. Although the strips are already cut to width, you should do a trial run to familiarize yourself with the relationship of these layers while they're dry. This way, when everything is wet with glue, you will be able to work with speed and confidence. Begin by laying one of the wide mahogany strips taped-side-down on a smooth surface, and place a strip of brass on it. The brass may not have a perfectly straight edge, so when positioning it be sure that its upper edge does not dip below the edge of the mahogany at any point, even if in some places it projects more than in others. Lay a strip of birch beside the brass to make up the rest of the second layer. Now add another strip of mahogany over this core.

Now you are ready to glue these laminations together. I used white glue, but you can use any glue you prefer. Gather the clamps you will need, and also two pieces of wood to clamp the gallery between while the glue dries. The exact dimensions of these cauls are not critical, but the pieces must be wider than the gallery and slightly longer. They should also be thick enough (at least ¾ in.) so that they won't bend. Lay one of the cauls on the benchtop and cover it with a sheet of waxed paper to prevent glue squeeze-out from adhering the gallery to the board (the waxed paper itself will not stick to the glue).

Disassemble your test lamination and spread glue on the untaped side of the innermost strip of mahogany. Lay this piece taped-side-down on the waxed paper, making sure that neither the ends nor edges overhang the caul. Lay the brass on the glued surface, once again making sure that its upper edge no where dips below the upper edge of the mahogany. Next lay in the birch. Now spread glue on the inside surface of the third layer of edge banding and lay it glued-side-down on the brass and birch, making sure the edges of all the layers are aligned. Place another sheet of waxed paper on top of the sandwich and set the second caul over this. Position clamps evenly along the two cauls to ensure even pressure.

When the glue is dry, unclamp the boards and remove the tape. Place the lamination in a vise with the brass edge facing up. If the brass protrudes in places, joint it with a file, holding the file at an angle to the edge of the brass. This is known as drawfiling and will remove the metal quickly and easily. When the brass is flush with the mahogany, use the file to bevel both edges and remove the arris from the wood. This will leave the brass protruding slightly so that it takes the force of any blow to the banding. Now sand the file marks out of both the mahogany and the brass.

The final element to be added to this sandwich is the ½-in.-wide outer strip of mahogany veneer. Apply glue to the untaped side of this strip and position it flush with the lower edge of the wider lamination. As before, clamp the veneers between two boards protected with waxed paper. When the glue is dry, unclamp and remove the tape. Joint the bottom edge of the gallery on the shooting board.

Now bend the gallery pieces around the tray bottom, and with a mat knife trim the ends of the laminated strips where they will fit into the handles. The knife will cut only the wood, not the brass, so peel away the excess wood and cut the metal with a hacksaw. Even though the mahogany itself is very fragile, the entire sandwich is quite flexible because of the strength of the brass-and-birch core.

Apply glue to the outside edge of the tray bottom and clamp the gallery in place with a band or bar clamp. Slip the handles into place, their two grooves fitting over the ends of the gallery. Attach each handle with two 1-in.-long T-headed brads. Finally, glue the outer ½-in.-wide strips of mahogany edge banding on the bottom of each handle.

Place the sandwich of veneers on a board between sheets of waxed paper. Clamp another board on top, applying uniform pressure along the length of the lamination until the glue sets.

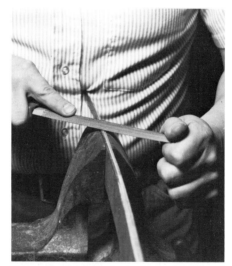

Where the brass projects above the edge of the mahogany, joint it by drawfiling. Then file away the arris of the mahogany on either edge of the brass. Sand the file marks and polish with 000 steel wool.

The upper edge of the gallery should be slightly domed so that the brass will protect the fragile end grain of the mahogany.

TRAY

Scale: ¼ in. = 1 in.

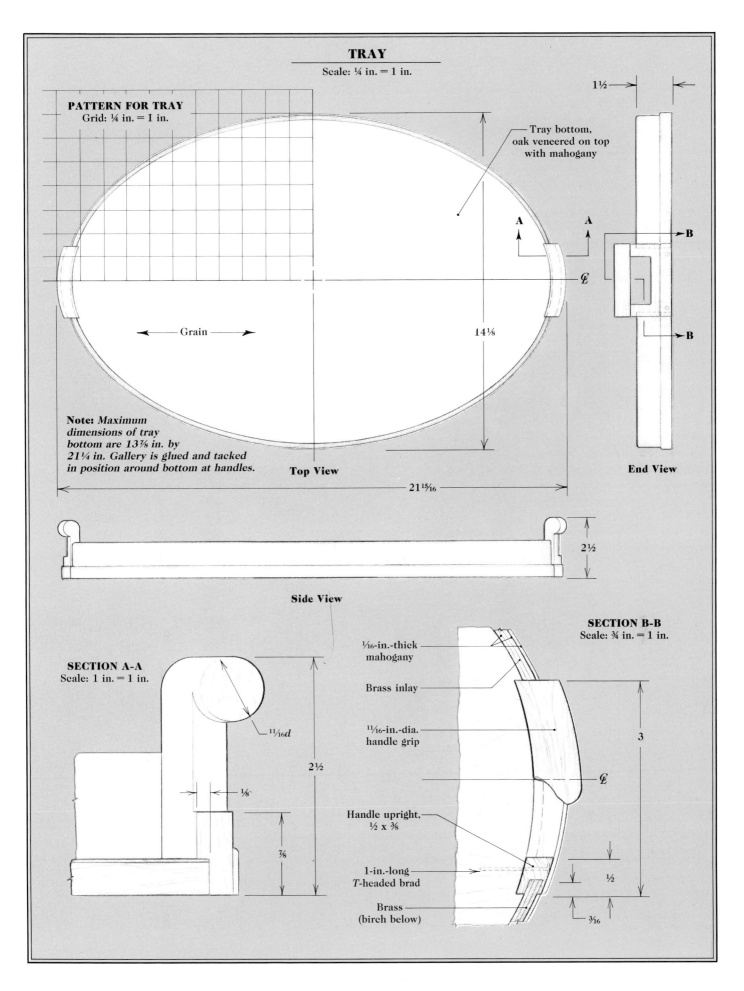

PATTERN FOR TRAY
Grid: ¼ in. = 1 in.

Tray bottom,
oak veneered on top
with mahogany

A   A

B

CL

← Grain →

14⅛

B

1½

Note: *Maximum
dimensions of tray
bottom are 13⅞ in. by
21¼ in. Gallery is glued and tacked
in position around bottom at handles.*

Top View

21¹⁵⁄₁₆

End View

2½

Side View

SECTION A-A
Scale: 1 in. = 1 in.

¹¹⁄₁₆*d*

2½

⅛

⅞

SECTION B-B
Scale: ¾ in. = 1 in.

¹⁄₁₆-in.-thick
mahogany

Brass inlay

¹¹⁄₁₆-in.-dia.
handle grip

Handle upright,
½ x ⅜

1-in.-long
T-headed brad

Brass
(birch below)

3

CL

½

³⁄₁₆

The maker of this formal Hepplewhite dining chair chose to restrain the chair's ornament and concentrate his efforts on the
elaborate splat, whose shape is actually an amalgam of designs
from both Hepplewhite's and Sheraton's pattern books. (Project:
Angled mortise-and-tenons, p. 83.)

Hepplewhite Chair

Chapter 9

This chair has an interesting story. I was antiquing one day with some friends in a town near Portsmouth. We stopped at a shop housed in a barn, and high in the old hay loft, amidst a clutter of nondescript castaways, I found this chair. The dealer announced condescendingly that it was just a reproduction, which was obvious, he said, because it was so light in weight. I examined the chair and was certain he was wrong. It looked to be of good-quality Federal-period workmanship and a nice example of a style often made in Rhode Island and Connecticut between 1790 and 1800. An exceptionally delicate chair, it was light in weight because it was made of Honduras mahogany. I purchased it, thinking that, if I were right, its low price would compensate for the dealer's insinuation that my knowledge of Federal-period chairs was inadequate.

Since we were in a small car, I was forced to ride home with the chair upside down in my lap. With the bottom of the chair staring up at me, I noticed a piece of paper inserted under the upholstery webbing. Its contents made me crow my vindication. The note, which was dated September 27, 1938, and signed Emily W. Tapley, read: "This chair came from the Reade House at 41 Main Street, Dover, N.H. It was inherited by my aunt Susan Tapley Moulton, who had spent much of her early life with her Reade aunts, in the old house, as her father, John Tapley, died when she was only 2 years old. She gave the chair to my sisters and me a few years before she died. There were six chairs of this set. One other Aunt Susan gave to Mary Reade Welch and it is now the property of John Tapley Welch of Dover, N.H. The other 4 were sold after Aunt Susan's death to a dealer in antiques in Boston. The Reade household was broken up in 1855. I do not know how long the chairs had been in existence before that date."

A couple of years passed, and one day the curator of the New Hampshire Historical Society came to our house to examine some furniture he thought he might like to include in an exhibition of New Hampshire cabinetmaking. I drew his attention to the chair, noting that it was probably made in southern New England but had an interesting New Hampshire history. As he read the note, he could not contain his excitement. He explained that he was doing the research necessary to have the Reade House listed in the National Register of Historic Places.

He told me much about the chair's original owner, Michael Reade, a successful lumber merchant who had built the Reade House. One of Reade's daughters had married a Tapley. To further verify the note, the curator sent me a copy of the inventory of Reade's estate taken in 1820 after his death. His household contents included a set of six mahogany dining chairs. This was undoubtedly one of them.

One might wonder why Reade would own chairs that were stylistically related to southern New England when the major cabinetmaking center of Portsmouth was only ten miles away. The reason may have been that Federal-period cabinetmakers were extremely productive and frequently shipped their surplus furniture on vessels sailing from every major port to wherever American ships traded. It is also possible that Reade's chairs were made locally by a man who had trained in southern New England and who retained a preference for this style of chair.

Whoever the chairmaker, this piece is an exceptional accomplishment. It is a restrained chair, yet its aesthetic statement is neither subdued nor static. At first glance, one might assume that it was made by a rural craftsman who was either unable to accomplish more demanding ornament or who did not know how to use such decoration. The shape of the splat, however, is an amalgam of several designs from the two most important furniture pattern books of the day—*The Cabinet-Maker and Upholsterer's Guide* by George Hepplewhite and *The Cabinet-Maker and Upholsterer's Drawing-Book* by

Thomas Sheraton—indicating that the cabinetmaker was familiar with high Federal style. On this chair, he masterfully chose to make the splat the dominant element. This detail is an exuberant burst of emotion that is the result of four strong verticals, each of which quickly draws the eye upward like a fireworks display.

Even though the work on the splat may have been subcontracted to a special carver, the decision to include it in the chair was the maker's. I have no doubt that the chair's simplicity results not from a lack of skill on the part of the craftsman but from other considerations. It may be that the chair's restrained design was determined by how much Michael Reade was willing to pay for his set. Were this the case, the design of the chair is particularly noteworthy, since it is usually much easier to feign success with an elaborate piece of furniture than with a very simple one.

Whether or not the chairmaker was working with such limitations in crafting this chair, he could have opted to use a number of typical Federal-period chair embellishments, such as molded front legs, stringing, inlay, veneer, a serpentine front rail and decorative rows of brass tacks. He could have kept the cost low by using several of these possibilities and executing them halfheartedly, but he was too much of a craftsman to produce something mediocre. Instead, he chose to include one finely executed feature, the splat, and by extension the floral cartouche on the crest rail, making these the focal points of the chair. Everything else that might compete with the splat was eliminated. Even the covering of the seat, which is original, seems to have been selected with this in mind.

The only other ornament the maker used on the chair is as purposeful as his decision to emphasize the splat. Aware of the Federal-period custom of lining up dining chairs against the wall so that, when not in use, they were seen from the front, he outlined the entire front of the chair by molding the edges of the front legs, seat frame, stiles and crest rail. The profile used on the straight edges of the legs and seat frame is an ovolo, a quarter-round set off by a fillet on either side. This ovolo is seen as a series of three straight, parallel lines—concave, convex and concave. The molding used on the curved edges of the stiles and crest rail is composed of two reeds separated by a V-groove. This molding has the opposite profile—convex, concave, convex—but from the front the three curvilinear elements are likewise read as tight, parallel lines.

In eliminating so many of the embellishments that normally ornamented Federal-period dining chairs, the maker risked creating what appeared to be a stripped-down version of this type of chair. To prevent this possibility, he reduced the chair's overall scale, making it appear even more delicate than most of its contemporaries. Indeed, this chair weighs only ten pounds and is reduced to six with the seat removed. Yet strength was not sacrificed. This chair has been in use for about 180 years, and we know that its five companions survived until at least 1938.

The chair's construction is as straightforward as its design. It is joined throughout with mortise-and-tenons, which was one of two popular methods of joining Federal-period chairs. Produced mainly by cabinetmakers, joined chairs used parts cut or shaped from sawn lumber for their rectangular mortise-and-tenons. These chairs are usually distinguished not by individual type but by general style or period—Chippendale, Hepplewhite or Sheraton, for example.

In contrast to joined chairs, socketed chairs were constructed with turned or whittled tenons fit into drilled, round holes. These chairs relied heavily on parts made from unseasoned stock, riven directly from a log and turned on a lathe. Socketed chairs like ladder-backs, Fancies and Windsors were usually produced by specialized chairmakers.

This Hepplewhite chair is made of Honduras mahogany. If you choose to reproduce it and want to make the chair in another wood, cherry would work well, though I would darken it with potassium permanganate before finishing it. I would suggest avoiding maple or birch, which are too light in color for this piece.

The splat can be cut out with a fine-tooth coping saw or jigsaw with about 20 points per inch, and the edges of the cutouts can be cleaned up with a file. The splat is mortised into the bottom of the crest rail and into a projection above the rear seat rail called a shoe.

The ovolo molding and double reed are cut after the completed chair frame has been test-fitted and disassembled. The ovolo molding can be cut with a molding plane or a router. For the double reed run around the stiles and crest rail, it's important that the center V-groove run perfectly parallel to the curved edges of the chair. The double reed can be cut with the same scratch tool used for making the simulated cock beading on the chest of drawers (p. 170) if you adjust the tool to follow a curved line by rounding the face that serves as a fence. After cutting the V-groove about 1/16 in. deep, back the screw out of the scratch tool with a screwdriver to double the width between the head and the fence. Doubling this distance positions the screw to mark the inside edge of the inside bead. Thus, when drawn around both edges of the stiles and crest rail, it scores another line parallel to the first. This second line undercuts the inside edge of the inside reed, making it easier to remove the wood in between. After the two lines have been incised around both edges of the stiles and crest rail, chisel out the wood in between to a depth of 3/32 in.

On many Federal-period chairs, the upholstery covers the seat rails. This chair, however, was constructed with a separate, removable seat, called a slip seat. The slip-seat frame, which is probably made of maple or birch, fits between the rails and is covered by the upholstery, leaving a border of mahogany exposed around the fabric.

The chair seat is stuffed with horsehair and covered with a 19th-century fabric known as haircloth, which is made from dyed horsehair woven on a loom. The resulting cloth has a slight sheen that resembles satin, but its texture and toughness are akin to the woven plastic webbing used on modern, aluminum-framed lawn chairs. This fabric is so durable that I am not surprised to find this original seat cover still intact.

Since I doubt that haircloth is still available, you will likely need to select a modern fabric if you decide to make a set of these chairs. In choosing a fabric, think about the visual interaction between the covering and the rest of the chair. The original haircloth is a dark gray-brown, which, I think, was selected for its subtlety. The chair could not carry a printed, striped or boldly colored cover.

I want to include one last observation about this chair before moving on to discuss its joinery. This is a formal chair, intended for use in the parlor or dining room, rather than in the kitchen where it would get hard wear. The fact that it is still intact is proof that the chair is not fragile. It is not as strong as a Windsor or a ladder-back chair, however—nor was it meant to be. If you make a set of these chairs, it's important to discourage guests, children and even yourself from lounging in them or rocking back on the rear legs. The latter is a recipe for disaster.

Angled mortise-and-tenons

The individual parts of this chair are easy to make, but cutting its numerous mortise-and-tenons, few of which are at right angles, is a fairly complex process. In a sense, the joinery is the chair's very essence, but it's so involved that to fully discuss all of the different joints would require more space than is available here. The following explanation of how to cut one of the compound-angled joints, however, will give you the basic information needed to cut the others. Because of this joinery's complexity, I strongly urge that before beginning a set of chairs, you make a mock-up in a soft, easy-to-work wood like pine.

The work of cutting the angled mortises, whether on a drill press or by hand, will be much easier if you use special cradles to hold the part being mortised at the desired angle in relation to the drill-press table or to the top and front edge of the workbench. My cradles are maple, glued up in blocks about 8 in. long by 4½ in. wide by 6 in. high. A trough is cut into the upper surface of each block, matching the width of the part being mortised and the angles of the mortise. This trough holds the part at the desired angle and keeps it from rocking out of alignment when the mortise is roughed out. Since I don't own a drill press, I've shown here how to rough out the mortises by hand with a bit and brace, gripping the cradle in the jaws of the front vise on my bench. I aligned the bit vertically by sighting along a try square, as shown in the chapter on the gateleg table (p. 90).

Making the cradles requires some thought and effort, but since they are merely holding devices, only the angles of the trough's walls need be precise. You can accurately cut the beveled sides of the trough by tilting the blade of a tablesaw to the necessary angle. The flat-bottomed trough of the cradles needed for the front legs can be chiseled with a firmer chisel to the depth of the sawcuts and then finished with a rabbet plane. The bottom of the trough for the back-leg cradles is more difficult to make, as it has to be shaped to the contour of the curved rear surface of the legs. This, too, can be done with a firmer chisel. If you plan to make a set of these chairs rather than just one, these cradles will save a lot of time.

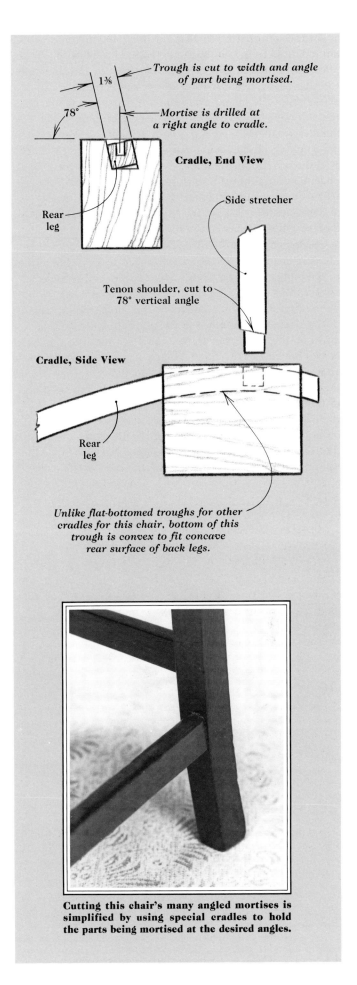

Trough is cut to width and angle of part being mortised.

1⅜

78°

Mortise is drilled at a right angle to cradle.

Cradle, End View

Rear leg

Side stretcher

Tenon shoulder, cut to 78° vertical angle

Cradle, Side View

Rear leg

Unlike flat-bottomed troughs for other cradles for this chair, bottom of this trough is convex to fit concave rear surface of back legs.

Cutting this chair's many angled mortises is simplified by using special cradles to hold the parts being mortised at the desired angles.

For the information on making and using these cradles, I am indebted to my good friend Al Breed of South Berwick, Maine, who makes joined chairs in both Queen Anne and Chippendale styles. Whether or not such cradles were used before the invention of the drill press is unknown, and if any have survived, I am unaware of them. Such devices would have served no purpose after the style of chair for which they were made went out of fashion. Each cold day would have imperiled their existence—most were probably burned in the shop stove.

Before proceeding further, let's establish how the mortises and the tenons are angled on this chair. If you look at the shoulders of the tenon at the back of the side stretcher, you'll see that it is beveled in two directions. Looking at the side of the chair, the shoulder of the tenon is angled backward from the upper corner to the lower corner. This angle, which I'll call the vertical angle, would be measured by laying a bevel square along the top edge of the stretcher, as shown in the photo below. Looking down on the joint from above, you'll see that the shoulder is also beveled at the front surface of the rear leg. This angle, which I'll call the horizontal angle, could be measured by laying the bevel square against the outside of the stretcher. All of the tenon shoulders, with the exception of those on the front seat rail, are angled either horizontally or vertically. Only the shoulders on the tenons at the back of the side stretchers are angled in both directions.

To measure the compound angle of the tenon shoulder at the back of one side stretcher, first lay the bevel square on the top edge (top) and then along the side of the stretcher (bottom).

I find that at least four cradles are necessary for this chair, since several of the mortises can be cut using the same cradle. The joints between the side stretchers and side seat rails and the front legs, for example, are beveled in only one direction. The side seat rails are angled horizontally at 80° to the front legs, and both mortises can be cut with the same cradle (hold the right leg in the cradle in the opposite direction from the left leg). The side stretchers are angled horizontally at 78° to the front leg, and the mortises can both be cut using a second cradle. All of the mortises in the front legs should be cut while the legs are still square stock. After the entire chair has been satisfactorily test-fitted, the front legs' inside edges are tapered and their outside edges are beveled flush with the seat rails.

Because the back surface of the rear legs is concave, the bottom of the third and fourth cradles has to be convex. Remember that the cradle for the mortises housing the rear side-stretcher tenons must hold the back legs at a compound angle.

A cradle is unnecessary for cutting the mortises that house the back seat rail and back stretcher in the rear legs. The rail and stretcher are angled vertically but are at a right angle to the sides, so you can rough them out simply by tilting the drill-press table or the leg in the vise to 95°. Any slight error made in cutting these mortises will occur in the narrow ends of the mortise rather than in its long sides and will become evident during the chair's assembly. The offending surface, which will be end grain, can be shaved with a chisel to fit the tenon.

For this project, I decided to make the mortise that houses the rear tenon on the side stretcher, since the joint is angled both vertically and horizontally and is the most difficult to cut. Though the mortise is not set at a right angle to the forward face of the leg, it is parallel to the leg's outside edge and can be laid out with a square and a marking gauge.

I placed the leg in its cradle and roughed out the mortise using a ¼-in. spoon bit. I selected a spoon bit for several reasons. Because the surface to be mortised is set at an angle, a bit with a scribe will not always be able to score a complete circle and might cause tearout. A bit with a lead, however, might break through the other side before the necessary depth has been cut. Also, because the spoon bit cuts with pressure, rather than being pulled through by a threaded lead, it cuts very fast. It can also change the angle of the hole it is drilling, a welcome feature when you're roughing out angled mortises by hand. The virtues of the spoon bit may explain why, when I'm repairing antique, joined chairs of this type, I have often noticed the unmistakable evidence of a spoon bit's round nose at the bottom of a mortise.

To begin the mortise, I drilled a row of 1-in.-deep holes that did not quite intersect with one another. (If they had, the spoon bit would have wandered into the adjacent hole.) I checked the bit's angle by holding a square next to it. By looking alternately head-on and along the front edge of the bench, I made sure the bit was vertical to the benchtop and entering the mortise at the desired angle.

Drilling the row of holes removed most of the wood in the mortise, and I cut the remainder loose with a ⅜-in. mortise chisel. Again, when shaping the sides of the mortise you can use the square to make sure the chisel stays perpendicular to the benchtop.

After the mortise was cut, I laid out the tenon on the stretcher. While the shoulders of most of the chair's tenons are cut to at least one angle so they sit flush with the surface of the adjoining leg, the tenons themselves are always cut parallel to the seat rails or stretchers. Thus their thickness can be laid out with a marking gauge set to ⅜ in. I laid out the shoulder and the top haunch with a bevel square. The horizontal angle is 102°, the supplementary angle for the front shoulders, which are beveled at 78°. I then continued the shoulder down the outside of the stretcher, again using the bevel square set to 102° for the vertical angle.

I shaped the tenon with a dovetail saw, cutting right down to the line on the shoulder but leaving the tenon slightly oversize. This gave me extra wood to pare down when fitting the tenon to the mortise.

It's worth noting that the chair's maker used an interesting technique to facilitate cutting the stretcher tenons and to strengthen the joinery on these thinner members. The tenons he cut have a shoulder only on the outside, while the inside is flush with the edge of the mortise. Because the stretchers are thinner than the rails, this design allows the mortises to be placed closer to the

center of each leg than they would have been had a shoulder been cut on the inside edge. The seat-rail tenons have an additional ⅛-in. inside shoulder and are further strengthened by glue blocks applied in all four corners, which support the slip seat. (The rear glue blocks present end-grain surfaces to the insides of the seat rails, so they have been reinforced with screws. Since the grain in the front glue blocks runs vertically, no screws are required.) The back seat rail is 1⅛ in. thick, so that its tenons can be centered without weakening the leg.

Except for the rear seat-rail tenons, the tops of the tenons joining the seat frame and stretchers to the legs are also offset by a shallow haunch. Without this, the mortises' upper corners would be exposed when the seat rails were molded or the stretchers' upper surfaces rounded. The bottoms of the tenons are flush with the bottoms of the mortises. Glued to the upper surface of the rear seat rail is the molded shoe, into which the splat is tenoned. The rear seat-rail tenons run the full height of the rail, and the ends of the shoe that butt the stiles function as a haunch.

The mortise-and-tenons joining the center stretcher to the side stretchers and the stiles to the crest rail are also constructed differently. The maker's choice of a two-shouldered mortise-and-tenon joint between the center and side stretchers is unusual. On most Federal-period chairs I have examined, the center stretcher is secured to the side stretchers with sliding dovetails cut in from the bottom, so that the joint is visible only from underneath.

Because this angled mortise is parallel to the outside edge of the leg, it can be laid out with a square and a marking gauge (top left). With the cradled leg held in the front vise of the bench, keep the bit and brace aligned with a try square while roughing out the mortise (above). Clean up the rough mortise with a ⅜-in. mortise chisel (bottom left).

Lay out the compound 102° angle on the top and side of the stretcher (top). Cut the tenon with a dovetail saw, leaving it slightly oversize for now so you can later fit it (bottom).

HEPPLEWHITE CHAIR

Scale: ⅛ in. = 1 in.

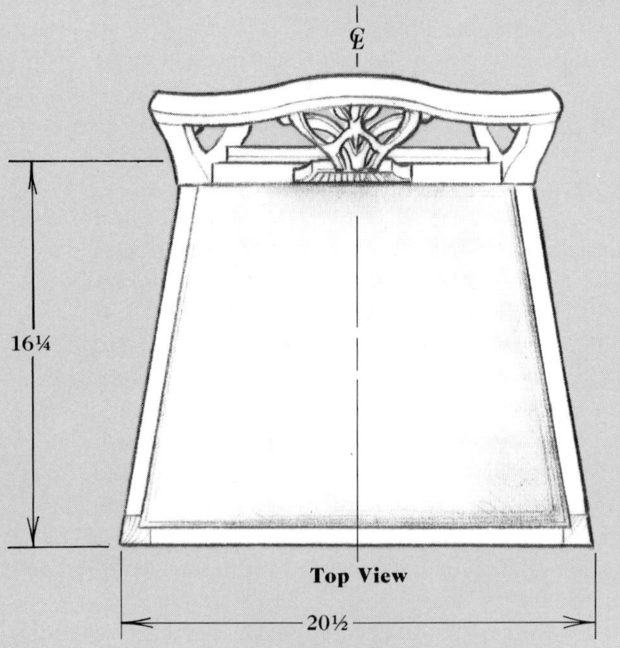

℄
16¼
Top View
20½

SLIP SEAT

Scale: ⅛ in. = 1 in.

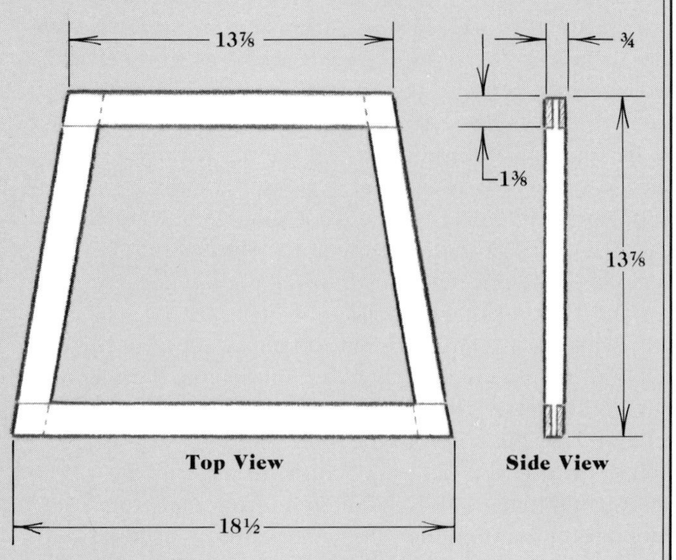

13⅞
¾
1⅜
13⅞
Top View
Side View
18½

Note: *Dimensions of slip seat are approximate. Cut and fit after chair is assembled.*

Note: *Back stiles are hand-shaped, with back side radiused and front side double-reeded on both edges.*

Vertical bevels achieved by tenon shoulders are shown in front and side views. Horizontal bevels achieved through angled mortises are shown in top views and sections on opposite page.

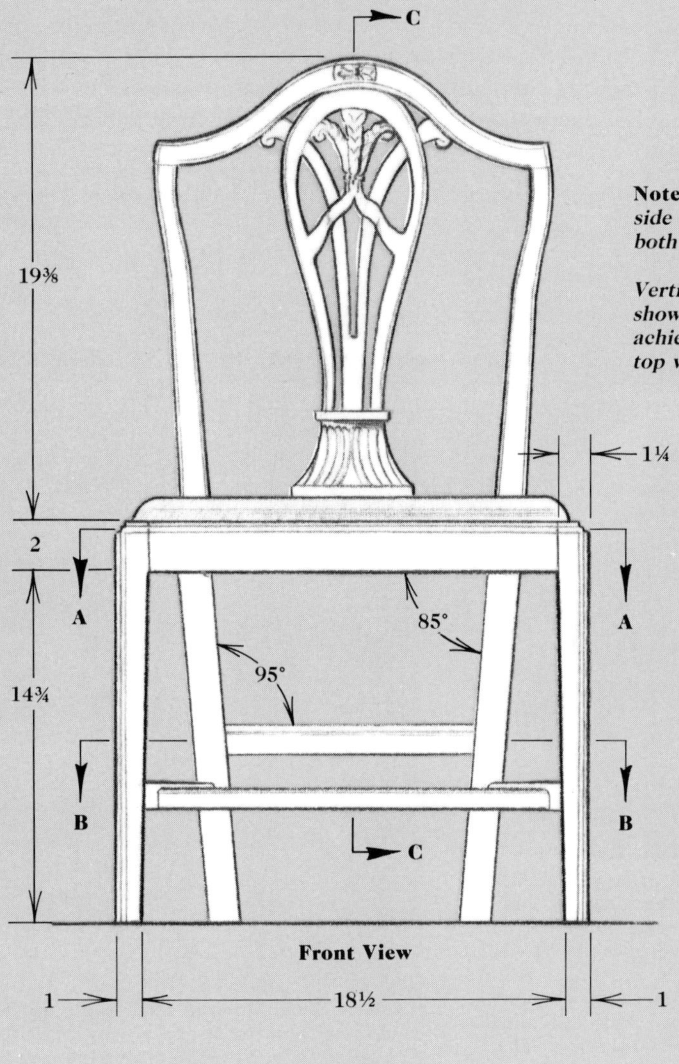

C
19⅜
1¼
2
A
A
85°
95°
14¾
B
B
C
Front View
1
18½
1

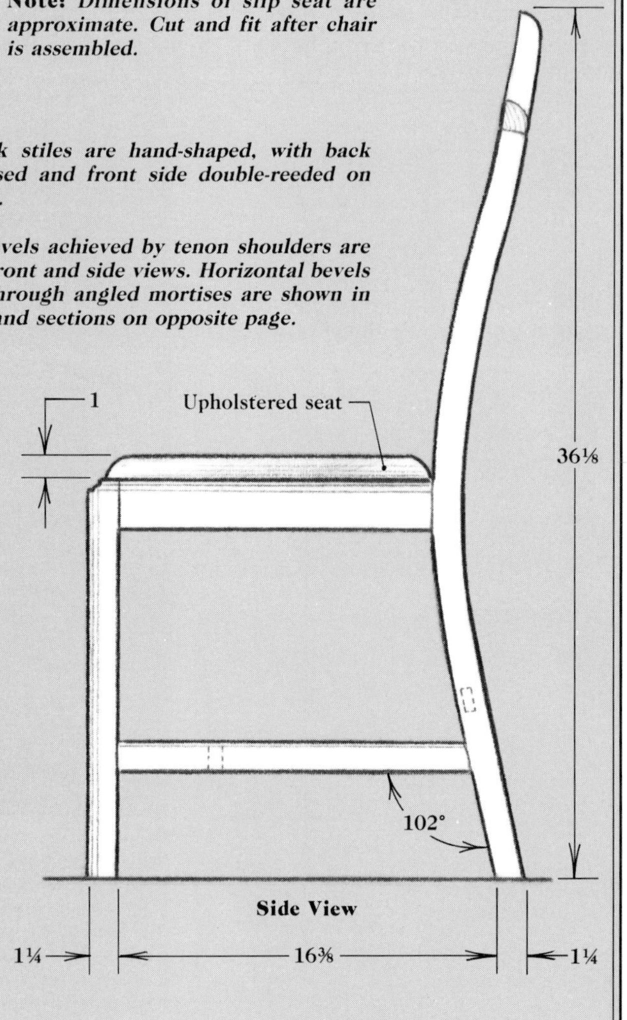

1
Upholstered seat
36⅛
102°
Side View
1¼
16⅜
1¼

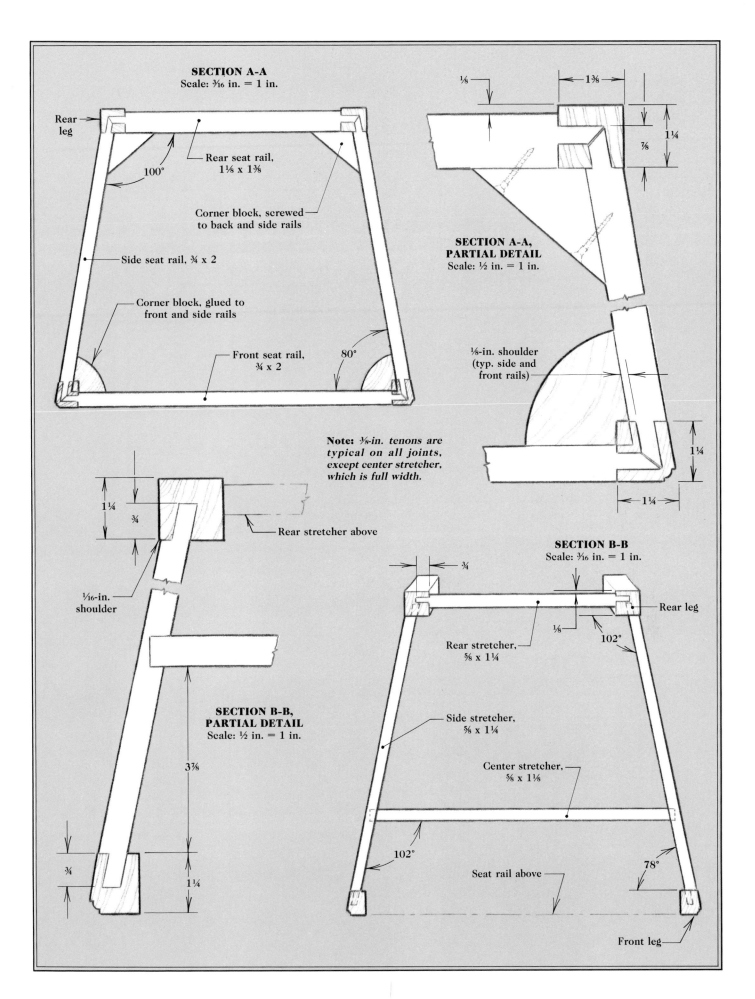

SECTION A-A
Scale: ³⁄₁₆ in. = 1 in.

Rear leg

100°

Rear seat rail, 1⅛ x 1⅜

Corner block, screwed to back and side rails

Side seat rail, ¾ x 2

Corner block, glued to front and side rails

Front seat rail, ¾ x 2

80°

SECTION A-A, PARTIAL DETAIL
Scale: ½ in. = 1 in.

⅛

1⅜

1¼

⅞

⅛-in. shoulder (typ. side and front rails)

1¼

1¼

Note: *⅜-in. tenons are typical on all joints, except center stretcher, which is full width.*

1¼

¾

Rear stretcher above

1⁄₁₆-in. shoulder

SECTION B-B, PARTIAL DETAIL
Scale: ½ in. = 1 in.

3⅞

¾

1¼

SECTION B-B
Scale: ³⁄₁₆ in. = 1 in.

¾

Rear leg

Rear stretcher, ⅝ x 1¼

⅛

102°

Side stretcher, ⅝ x 1¼

Center stretcher, ⅝ x 1⅛

102°

Seat rail above

78°

Front leg

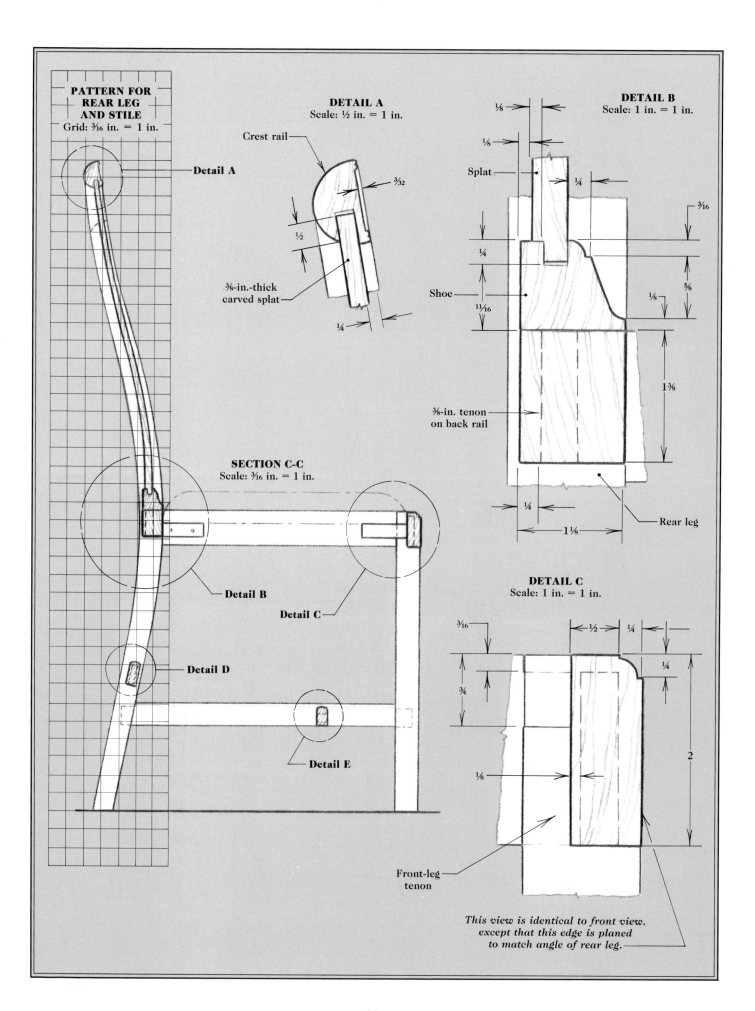

PATTERN FOR REAR LEG AND STILE
Grid: ³⁄₁₆ in. = 1 in.

Detail A

DETAIL A
Scale: ½ in. = 1 in.

Crest rail

³⁄₃₂

½

¼

⅜-in.-thick carved splat

DETAIL B
Scale: 1 in. = 1 in.

⅛

⅛

Splat

¼

³⁄₁₆

¼

Shoe

⅛

⁵⁄₈

11⁄16

1⅜

⅜-in. tenon on back rail

¼

1⅛

Rear leg

SECTION C-C
Scale: ³⁄₁₆ in. = 1 in.

Detail B

Detail C

DETAIL C
Scale: 1 in. = 1 in.

Detail D

³⁄₁₆

½

¼

¾

¼

Detail E

⅛

2

Front-leg tenon

This view is identical to front view, except that this edge is planed to match angle of rear leg.

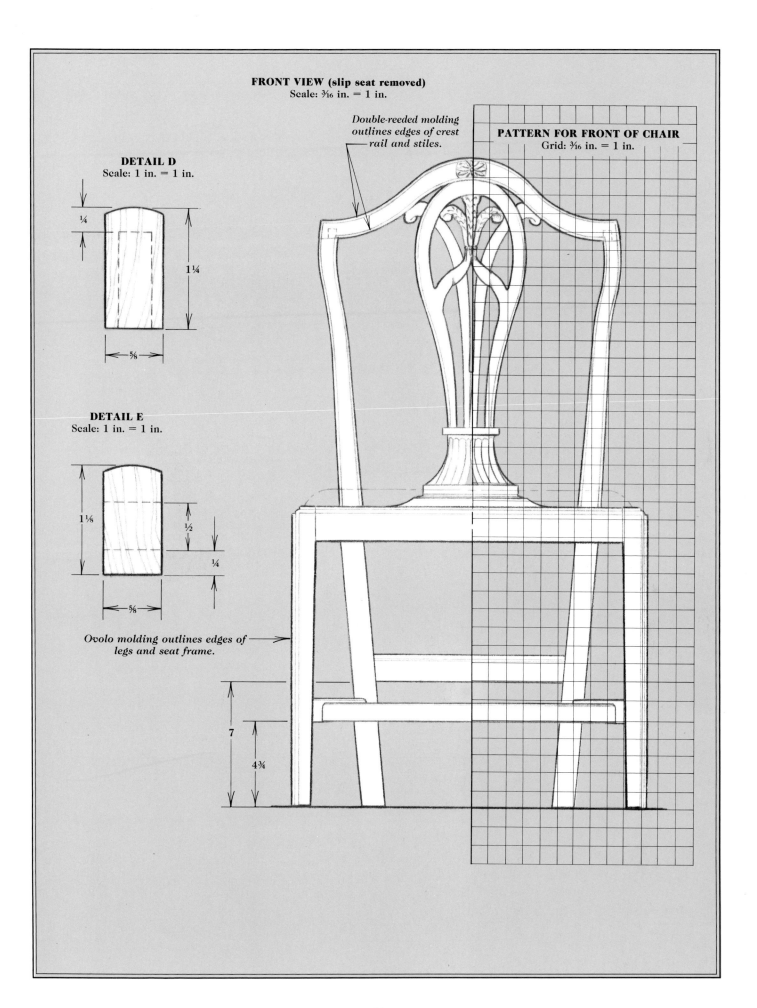

FRONT VIEW (slip seat removed)
Scale: ¾₁₆ in. = 1 in.

*Double-reeded molding
outlines edges of crest
rail and stiles.*

PATTERN FOR FRONT OF CHAIR
Grid: ¾₁₆ in. = 1 in.

DETAIL D
Scale: 1 in. = 1 in.

¼

1¼

⅝

DETAIL E
Scale: 1 in. = 1 in.

1⅛

½

¼

⅝

*Ovolo molding outlines edges of
legs and seat frame.*

7

4¾

This gateleg table is a Federal interpretation of a design for collapsible table space that originated in the first half of the 18th century. (Project: Wooden hinge, p. 94.)

Gateleg Table

Chapter 10

T hink of all the things we do at a table—eat, prepare food, write and work, for example— and you'll realize how important this piece of furniture is in our daily lives. Yet even though we regularly need to use a broad, flat surface, we often begrudge the amount of space a large tabletop takes up in a room.

This book presents plans for several tables that resolve this problem in different ways. The answer in the case of this particular table is drop leaves. The table's fixed top has a leaf hinged on either side. When a surface larger than the 16½-in.-wide by 42-in.-long fixed top is needed, one or both of the 12-in.-wide leaves can be raised to increase the working area of the folded table nearly two- or threefold. When the leaves are lowered, the table can be placed out of the way against a wall.

To support the raised leaves, a hinged gateleg swings out at a right angle from the skirt on both sides of the table. The table's two fixed legs, positioned diagonally across from one another, meanwhile support the fixed top.

This design for collapsible table space originated in the first half of the 18th century, and similarly constructed gateleg tables exist in both the Queen Anne and Chippendale styles. In the former, these tables have cabriole legs and pad feet, while in the latter they have square, molded legs or cabriole-type legs with ball-and-claw feet. On this Federal interpretation of the gateleg form, the tapered leg associates it with the Hepplewhite style. Had the piece been made in the Sheraton style, it would have had turned legs that might have been reeded.

For a long time this was our kitchen table. It is such a plain piece that it was probably originally intended for this purpose. The table's top, leaves, four legs and two fixed end rails are made of hard maple, while the hinged side rails and the inside nailers are white pine. The choice of white pine as a secondary wood leads me to suspect that the table was made in northern New England.

If you choose to make this table, first decide how and where it will be used. If it is intended for the kitchen, you might want to stay fairly close to the original design and choice of wood. You could, of course, substitute cherry for maple if you want a more pronounced figure. And if you want to paint or stain the table, you might try using birch, since this has almost no noticeable figure. Pine is easier to work with and is often more readily available in wider widths than cherry or birch, yet it is softer and more easily dented and scratched.

If the table is intended for a more formal setting, you might want to make it in mahogany or walnut, though, of course, curly maple or wavy birch is nice in any room in the house. Veneer works well on the fixed end rails if you make the top in a darker wood such as mahogany, and you could also inlay banding on the bottom edge of the skirt or the ankles. If you really want to make your table in high-style Hepplewhite, look at the card table on p. 10 for some ideas on formal decoration.

If you need to seat no more than six people, use the dimensions given in the drawings. A 48-in.-sq., opened top will seat eight, although, of course, it requires a large room. For a smaller kitchen, you can decrease the open top to as little as 36 in. sq., which will comfortably seat four. Because the full width of the fixed top on the original table is 17¼ in., including the ⅜-in. molded edges of the two rule joints, it will not be difficult to find the necessary stock in mahogany, but locating native woods of that width will require some searching. Depending on the wood and the table size you choose, you may have to begin the project by gluing up the top.

Before leaving aside the question of which wood to use for the table, I want to share one final observation. After about 170 years of use, the wooden hinges on the side rails of the original table had worn enough to allow the legs to chuck back and forth. Therefore a couple of years ago, Carol and I decided that since everyday use endangered the table, it should be retired upstairs, where we now use it to eat supper at while watching the evening news. Based on this experience, I would recommend using hardwood instead of pine for the side rails. If you do use pine, however, the problem of a worn joint will probably not occur in your lifetime.

Whether or not you glue up the top, the wood will have to be surfaced. The top of the original table is ¾ in. thick. Were it any thicker, it would violate the feeling of delicacy that was so important to Federal-period furnituremakers. While it is, of course, possible to take a 1-in.-thick board down to ¾ in. with a hand plane, this is heavy, tedious work. I would suggest that you take your stock to a lumberyard that does custom milling if you don't have a thickness planer. Have them thickness-plane the top to slightly over ¾ in., then you can hand-plane away the milling marks.

After the leaves have been surfaced, they should be molded on one edge to a special shape called a rule joint. This joint was first created in the early 18th century and has been standard for drop-leaf tables ever since. The reason it is so long-lived is simply that it works well. Its principal function is to hide the table's hinges, but it also serves a hygienic purpose. Because this table is used for both eating at and preparing food on, a great deal of material inevitably works its way into the joints between the leaves. When the leaves on the gateleg are lowered, the rule joints are sufficiently exposed to be cleaned with a sponge.

On the original table, the rule joint was shaped with a pair of special molding planes called table-leaf planes. (I have included a picture of my planes in the chapter on the Pembroke table on p. 156). If you cannot find a set of table-leaf planes, make your rule joint with a router.

Before cutting the actual rule joint, I suggest you make a trial joint on scrapwood. Then I recommend molding the edges of the leaves before cutting the leaves to final width—that way, if you make a mistake, you may still have enough room to rejoint the edge and try again.

Begin the rule joint by shaping the convex curve of the joint on both sides of the fixed top. Next shape the concave curve of the inside edge of the two leaves. When this is done, lay the leaves and fixed top down, right side up, and mesh the two rule joints to test their fit. When the fit is correct, secure the joints permanently in position with four table-leaf hinges. The mounting of this special hinge is discussed in detail in the Pembroke-table chapter.

After completing the rule joint and mounting the table-leaf hinges, make the wooden hinges in the side rails that allow the gatelegs to swing out. You'll find full instructions for making these hinges in the project section of this chapter on p. 94.

A wooden hinge in both side rails allows one segment of the rails to swing out and the attached gatelegs to support the raised leaves of the table.

When the wooden hinges are finished, make and assemble the parts of the base. Begin by shaping the legs. The two inside surfaces of the lower legs are tapered, while the upper ends are square, as shown in the drawing on p. 98. This design allows the outside surfaces of the legs to be parallel to the skirt and also makes the legs appear thinner than they really are. Lay out the tapers with a pencil and a straightedge and plane to the line with a smoothing plane. While shaping the legs, remember to chamfer the inside corner where the tapers meet. This will add a subtle but pleasing detail to the overall look of the table.

Next cut the mortise-and-tenon joints on the side and end rails and the legs. The two fixed legs are joined on one side to the fixed end rail and on the other side to the fixed portion of the side rail. The two gatelegs are joined to the movable portion of the side rail. Therefore each fixed leg has two mortises, while each gateleg has only one. I would begin by cutting the mortise-and-tenons for the fixed legs and then cut those for the gatelegs. Although you will, of course, need to test-fit these parts, I would suggest doing any assembly at this point dry, waiting to glue the parts until everything has been cut and fit. On the original table, each joint was also secured with two wooden whittled pins that pierced the mortise-and-tenons. You might want to add similar pins, since they ensure against glue failure.

With the joints for the legs completed, you can turn your attention to dovetailing the inside nailers to the free end of each end rail. These inside boards can be cut to finished length after the dovetails have been fit. Note that the cut-off length of these boards is not crucial.

When all the joints are complete, assemble the wooden hinge in the side rail and slide in the metal pin, mushroomed end up, to hold the hinge in position. (Instructions for making the metal pin are included with those for the wooden hinge in the project section.)

The result of all this joinery has been to create two three-sided frames. Each frame has a leg attached to both ends of the side rail. When these two three-sided frames are nested, they form the base of the table. All that remains to complete the base is to combine the two frames. Do this by smearing glue on the back surface of the fixed portion of the side rail and clamping the parts into position to dry. On the original table, these glue joints were further secured with wrought-iron clench nails. These nails are very soft and were drawn out by a nailor (a special type of blacksmith) to a needle point. When a clench nail is driven through a board and into a heavy metal hammer, it will clench, or turn back on itself, much like a fishhook. When correctly clenched, only the nail head and the apex of the curve in the hook are visible. The way a nail is clenched nowadays is a very different matter. It is simply driven through a board and the exposed end banged down, a crude facsimile of what was once a very neat, permanent method of finishing off and securing a nail. If you know a blacksmith who is willing to make wrought nails out of mild steel, you can clench them properly yourself. If you prefer a simpler approach, I suggest securing the two glued faces on the base by driving some wood screws through them.

To attach the top to the base, wrought-iron T-headed finish nails, also once made by nailors, were used on the original. Nails were driven through the top into each of the fixed legs and into the skirt near the dovetail joints. When this nail is set, all that is visible is a thin sliver of metal. Since these nails are no longer made, however, and it may be difficult to find a blacksmith willing to produce them for you, I would suggest an alternative method for joining the top and base. This method requires only standard wood screws and is invisible from the top. On the inside surfaces of the rails, use an in-cannel gouge to cut away four screw pockets like those shown in the drawing on p. 98. At each of these places, drill a hole (slightly larger than the screw's diameter) at a steep angle from the bottom of the cut to the top edge of the rail. Slide a screw in this hole until it bites into the tabletop. As you work, watch for the telltale dimple that indicates the screw is about to come through the upper surface. If necessary, back out the screw and grind away the point.

On the table I made for our kitchen, I fastened two thin blocks to the underside of each leaf to straddle the gateleg when it is open. These blocks ensure that the gateleg is always positioned to best support the leaf. The blocks can be secured with glue, or you might use brads. One word of warning about using your table: Never lift a leaf any higher than necessary to open the gateleg. Doing so would put strain on the hinges and might cause a section of the rule joint to break out.

Once the construction is complete, the table is ready for finishing. Because the original table was a purely functional piece of furniture put to hard use, it was painted with a thin red wash, which antique collectors often call "old red stain." This finish was perfectly suited to the table's purpose, as it was resistant to almost anything the table's owners could place or spill on it. The wash, a thin paint with little body, was largely absorbed into the wood immediately upon application. This meant that hot pans from the fireplace would not blister it, nor would alcohol or other harsh household solutions dissolve it. Furthermore, it would not readily scrub off.

The thin paint in this red wash consisted of an iron-oxide pigment suspended in an oil base. It probably also contained some white lead, since that was a standard ingredient of paint at the time, but because this table was an inexpensive piece, the cabinetmaker probably skimped on the lead. The resulting mixture was a wash with about the same body as a wiping stain. I make a similar wash with a commercial milk paint, thinning it more than the instructions suggest. I then brush it on like an oil wiping stain. Over this I apply a light coat of linseed oil, thinned with turpentine, which gives a mat sheen to the very flat milk paint.

If you do not want to finish your table with a colored wash, I suggest a matte varnish, which washes easily and is durable. If you make your table in mahogany, walnut, curly maple or some other exotic wood and you wish to put it to more formal use, you might consider a shellac finish. In time, this finish will develop its own patina and create a very handsome effect.

Wooden hinge

From the time this particular style of gateleg table was introduced, the wooden hinge became the standard for such tables. Although the concept of the hinge remained unchanged, the workmanship from table to table was as individual as a signature, and each Federal-period craftsman seemed to prefer his own design, size and number of knuckles, method of undercutting, and so forth.

To lay out the knuckles of the hinge on the side rail, begin with stock that is 31⅞ in. long by 1¼ in. thick by 6 in. wide. First measure 9½ in. from the shoulder of the 1½-in. tenon that secures the gateleg. Using a square, scribe a vertical line at this point. Next draw an additional parallel line on either side of the first line, 1⅜ in. from it. Extend these three lines on both ends of the board around the other side.

These three lines should next be crisscrossed at right angles by a series of four lines that delineate the knuckles. The distance between each of these new lines is 1³⁄₁₆ in., with the top and bottom lines equidistant from the top and bottom edges of the board.

Before separating the two sections of the side rail, mark the waste squares of the knuckles with an *X* to prevent

After determining the placement of the hinge, lay out the knuckles on both sides of the board and mark the waste areas.

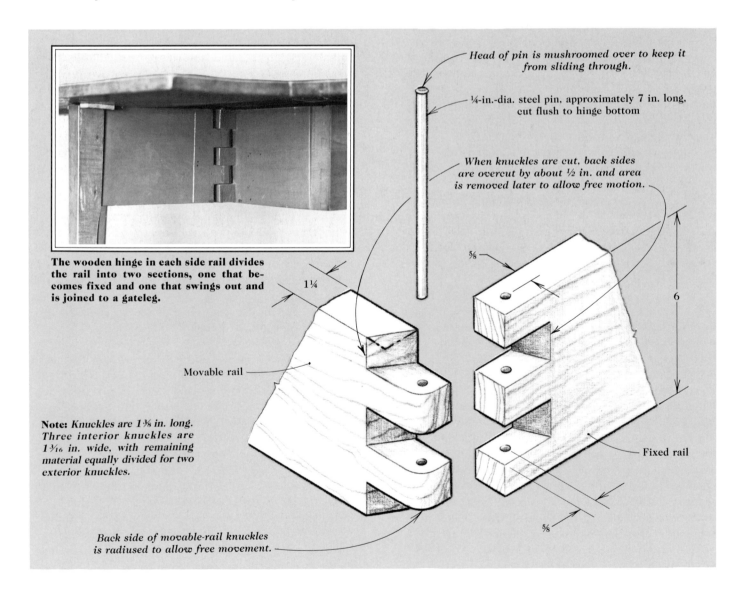

The wooden hinge in each side rail divides the rail into two sections, one that becomes fixed and one that swings out and is joined to a gateleg.

Note: Knuckles are 1⅜ in. long. Three interior knuckles are 1³⁄₁₆ in. wide, with remaining material equally divided for two exterior knuckles.

Head of pin is mushroomed over to keep it from sliding through.

¼-in.-dia. steel pin, approximately 7 in. long, cut flush to hinge bottom

When knuckles are cut, back sides are overcut by about ½ in. and area is removed later to allow free motion.

Movable rail

Back side of movable-rail knuckles is radiused to allow free movement.

Fixed rail

1¼

⅝

6

⅝

Separate the knuckles with a sawcut that's about ½ in. deeper on the back of the board than on the front (above). Cut away the inner waste areas with a coping saw, and use a backsaw to cut off the outside waste areas on the movable section of the hinge (right).

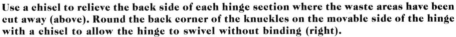

Use a chisel to relieve the back side of each hinge section where the waste areas have been cut away (above). Round the back corner of the knuckles on the movable side of the hinge with a chisel to allow the hinge to swivel without binding (right).

later confusion. (The fixed section will have three knuckles, and the movable section with the gateleg will have two.) Then cut along the center vertical line with a crosscut saw to separate the two sections of the skirt. Place each of the sections in a vise, with the knuckles up and the layout lines facing you, and continue the horizontal layout lines on the end grain and down the back side. With a backsaw, cut along the lines that divide the knuckles. On both sections of the rail, be sure to make your cuts on the waste side of the line. This will create a tighter fit and give more leeway for adjusting the mesh of the knuckles. To make it easier later to relieve the back side below each waste section, lift the saw handle while cutting the knuckle and extend the kerf down on the rear side to undercut the wood approximately ½ in. below the front line.

Use a coping saw to remove the inner waste areas between the knuckles, and the backsaw to cut away the two end pieces of waste. Test-fit the two parts of the hinge and shave any tight areas with a chisel. If the knuckles are too tight, they may bind when the wood swells with seasonal moisture changes. You should be able to see a fine halo of daylight around each part of the joint.

Take the piece out of the vise and turn it over to work on the back side. Where the waste has been removed, relieve the backs for a distance of about ½ in. with a chisel. Next place the movable gateleg section of the hinge in the vise, with its two knuckles up and the back surface facing you, and round the back corner of both knuckles with a chisel. You may have to fine-tune these cuts after the joint is assembled, but it is easier to remove most of the corner now.

While drilling a ¼-in. pivot hole through the center of the knuckles on the fixed section of the hinge, use a square to help keep the bit vertical.

Once you have ground a rounded end on a ¼-in.-dia., soft-steel pin, peen the other end with a hammer to mushroom the head.

After the knuckles have been shaped, mount the fixed section of the hinge horizontally in the vise. Locate the center of the topmost, outside knuckle by marking an X from corner to corner on the knuckle's top edge. Pierce the center of this knuckle with a ¼-in. drill. If you work with a brace and bit or an electric hand drill, use a square to ensure that the bit stays vertical. Drill through the first knuckle and then center the bit on the middle knuckle. Drill only about halfway through this knuckle.

Flip the board over and remount it in the vise. Then find and drill the center of the other outside knuckle in the same way as the first. Once the bit has drilled completely through this knuckle, center it on the middle knuckle and drill until the bit breaks through the hole drilled halfway through from the other side. Reassemble the fixed and movable sides of the hinge and place both pieces together in the vise, making sure they are properly aligned. Place the bit in the hole you have already drilled in the top knuckle. This hole should hold the bit in line while you continue to bore through the remaining two knuckles on the fixed side. You should be able to drill completely through the hinge without turning the rail over.

To hold the hinge in position, a metal pin must be friction-fit in the holes. To make this pin, first grind or file a rounded tip on one end of a ¼-in. soft-steel rod that is about 7½ in. long. Next place the rod in a vise with the unshaped end protruding above the jaws. Peen this end of the pin with a hammer by striking the edges with glancing blows, working around the entire edge so that it is evenly mushroomed. Since the holes in the knuckles will change diameter seasonally and will eventually wear, this mushroomed end will prevent the pin from falling out of the joint.

Assemble the joint for the final time. Insert the pin from the top side and drive it in with a hammer. The rounded tip will prevent it from hanging up as it passes through the row of holes in the knuckles. When the pin is completely inserted, use a hacksaw to cut the end of the pin flush with the lower edge of the rail.

With the hinge assembled, the knuckles should clear each other. If they do not, use a chisel to adjust the fit. Once the joint swings freely, lay the side rail flat on the surface of the workbench and hold the fixed section firmly down with one hand. Use your free hand to raise the gateleg section. You will be able to feel if the rounded back sides of the knuckles rub against the benchtop. The rubbing should mark the high spots so that they can be easily found and shaved with a chisel.

GATELEG TABLE

Scale: ³⁄₃₂ in. = 1 in.

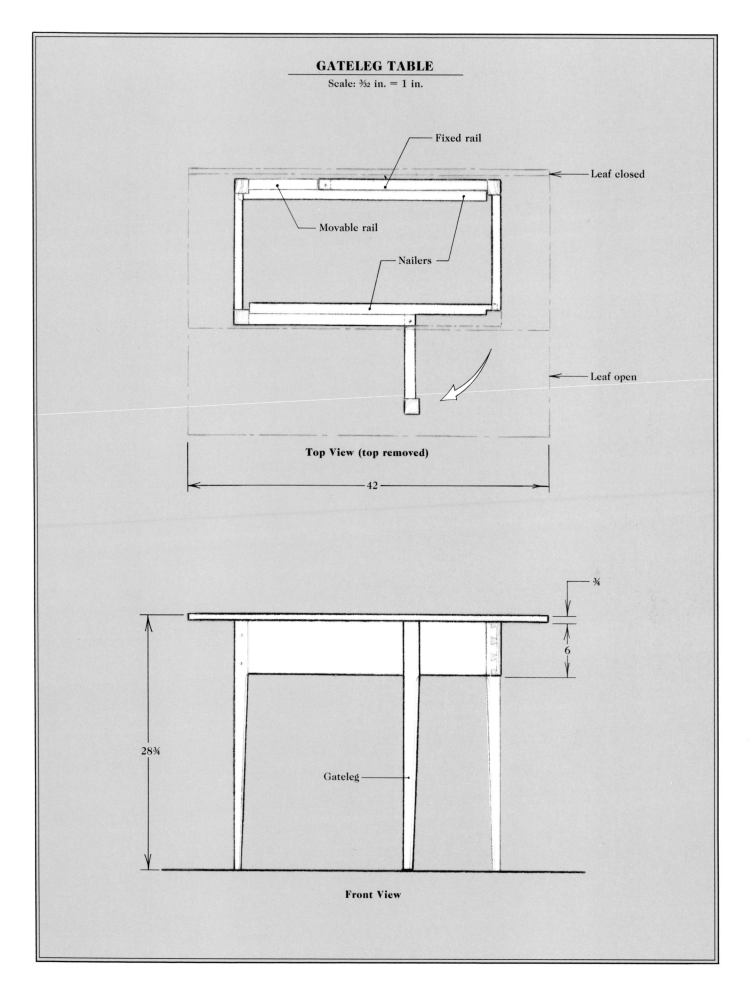

Fixed rail

Leaf closed

Movable rail

Nailers

Leaf open

Top View (top removed)

42

¾

6

28¾

Gateleg

Front View

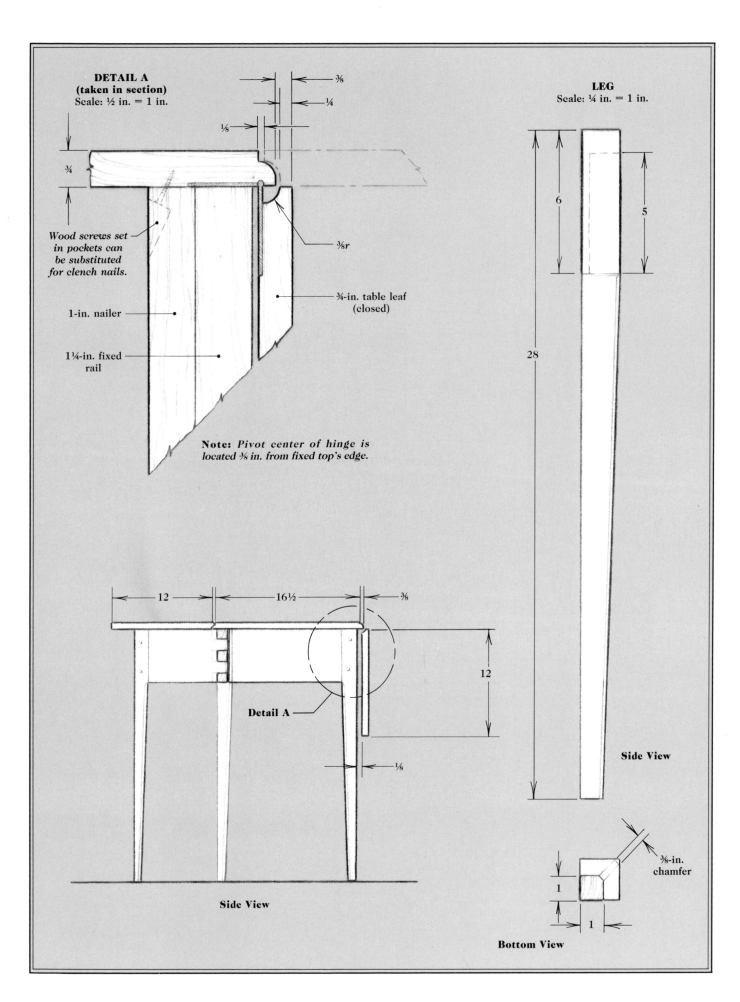

DETAIL A
(taken in section)
Scale: ½ in. = 1 in.

⅜

¼

⅛

¾

Wood screws set
in pockets can
be substituted
for clench nails.

⅜r

1-in. nailer

1¼-in. fixed
rail

¾-in. table leaf
(closed)

Note: *Pivot center of hinge is
located ⅜ in. from fixed top's edge.*

12

16½

⅜

12

Detail A

⅛

Side View

LEG
Scale: ¼ in. = 1 in.

6

5

28

Side View

⅜-in.
chamfer

1

1

Bottom View

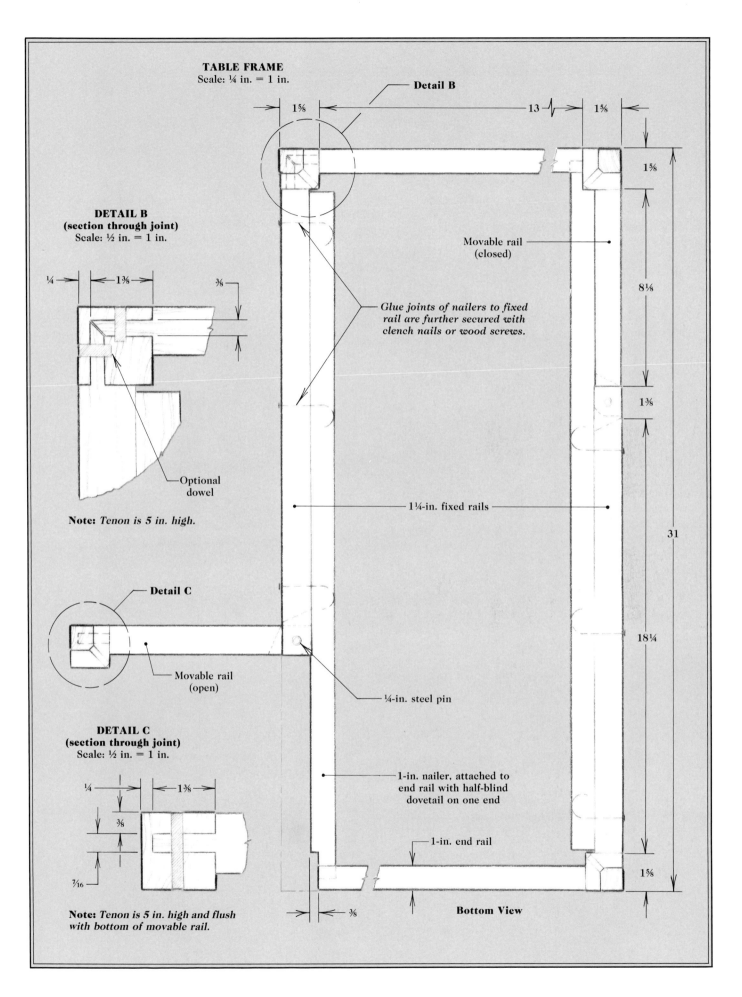

TABLE FRAME
Scale: ¼ in. = 1 in.

Detail B

1⅝   13   1⅝

1⅝

Movable rail
(closed)

8⅛

DETAIL B
(section through joint)
Scale: ½ in. = 1 in.

¼   1⅜   ⅜

1⅜

31

Glue joints of nailers to fixed
rail are further secured with
clench nails or wood screws.

Optional
dowel

Note: *Tenon is 5 in. high.*

1¼-in. fixed rails

Detail C

18¼

Movable rail
(open)

¼-in. steel pin

DETAIL C
(section through joint)
Scale: ½ in. = 1 in.

¼   1⅜

⅜

1-in. nailer, attached to
end rail with half-blind
dovetail on one end

1-in. end rail

7/16

1⅝

⅜

Bottom View

Note: *Tenon is 5 in. high and flush
with bottom of movable rail.*

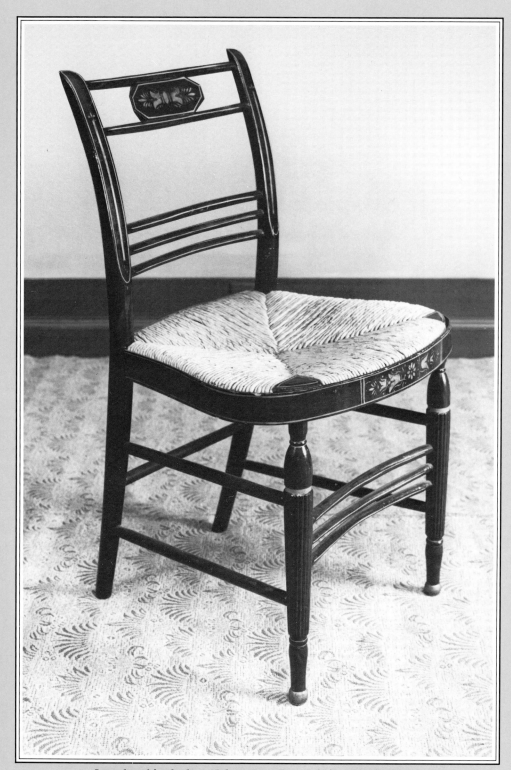

Introduced in the late 18th century, Fancy chairs quickly gained enormous popularity, and Fancy and Windsor chair shops became some of the laboratories in which the principles of mass-producing furniture were developed and tested. (Project: Reeding with a plane, p. 103.)

Fancy Chair

Chapter 11

This chair is known today, as it was in the Federal period, as a Fancy chair. Most of the pieces presented in this book represent Federal interpretations of forms of furniture that were well known before the period. This is not so with the Fancy chair, however, which was introduced in the late 18th century.

The Fancy chair embodies the Federal concept of delicacy without fragility. It weighs only about 8 lb., yet is capable of supporting 200 lb. It is not only lightweight, strong and portable but also comfortable and good-looking. Nearly two centuries after it was built, the chair shown here (as well as the others from the set of ten Fancies we have in our dining room) still retains these qualities, which is partly why I selected it for the book.

The manufacture of both Fancy chairs and Windsor chairs represented an important milestone in the history of furnituremaking. Though introduced later than Windsors, Fancies gained popularity over Windsors with Federal-period Americans. In time, Fancy chairmakers largely absorbed the production of Windsor chairs and began to offer both types of chairs. The Federal-period shops in which these chairs were made became laboratories in which the mass-production principles of interchangeable parts, subcontracting and the assembly line were applied and tested. In these laboratories and in the Windsor and Fancy chairs themselves are the roots of our modern furniture industry. In fact, Lambert Hitchcock, the man generally credited with creating the first furniture factory in the early 19th century in Riverton, Connecticut, was, as a boy, apprenticed to and trained by a Fancy chairmaker. The ubiquitous Hitchcock chair is really nothing more than a late Federal-period interpretation of the Fancy.

Another reason I wanted to include a Fancy chair in this book is that it presents an historical perspective on our current attitude toward wood that may seem unusual to modern-day woodworkers. We tend now to devote considerable attention in woodworking to choosing just the right wood for a given project. An elaborate figure is considered desirable and, as a result, is integral to most modern custom furniture. The Fancy chairmaker's attitude toward wood was quite different. For him, it was the finish, not the wood itself, that was of interest. In fact, the Fancy chair's painted and decorated finish was of such importance that it gave rise to the chair's name and, as you'll see in a moment, also determined its design.

When a Fancy chairmaker selected his wood, he was principally concerned with its workability and the smoothness of its surface. He was interested in figure and grain only insofar as they affected the wood's use as a foundation for the finish. For example, he would not choose oak for his chairs because its open grain would not paint well. This secondary interest in figure and grain is reflected in other pieces in this book as well, namely the sofa (p. 30), the Windsor chair (p. 118) and the display shelf (p. 126). Although modern woodworkers may consider it heresy to grant such relatively minor importance to the wood itself in a piece of furniture, this idea was not unusual in the past. Certainly some of the finest furniture ever made treated wood in this manner, and the maker of this chair was no less a woodworker than the craftsmen responsible for the card table (p. 10), the large tip-top table (p. 50) or the secretary (p. 58), all of which capitalize on elaborate figure.

The Fancy's painted finish not only dictated the selection of material, it also determined the chair's design. The chairmaker had to provide the decorative painter with as many flat surfaces as possible—a task that required some clever design work, since the chair is basically made of turned parts. This need for unmolded surfaces to decorate explains the Fancy's traditionally flattened stiles, the thin seat band and such features as the medallion suspended between the crest rails.

The Fancy chairs in our set are made almost entirely of soft maple. This wood turns easily and is smooth when finished. The front seat rail with two exposed and decorated triangular blocks is also soft maple, but the side and back seat rails, which are entirely hidden by the rush, are ash. The seat band is pine.

The stock for these Fancies was riven, which means the turning billets were split directly from the log. Since riving results in straight grain, the stiles, front stretchers and back stretcher and rails could be bent with almost no risk of breaking. That same straight grain ensured that the wood in the front legs would be strong enough to be turned to a ⅝-in.-thick neck just below the seat band. If you decide to make this chair and do not rive your wood, be careful to select stock that is perfectly straight.

The front legs on this chair are reeded around three-quarters of their circumference. (A detailed explanation of how to reed the legs follows on the facing page.) In the unreeded area, sockets are drilled with a spoon bit for the front and side stretchers. These stretchers as well as the crest rails and back rails are all turned and then steamed and bent to shape on a form. The tenons on all of the chair's rails and stretchers are rounded on the ends to better fit the holes cut by the spoon bit. Note that the spoon bit can drill to very nearly the full thickness of the legs without breaking through the wood, and that the chair is best constructed with the deepest possible sockets and the longest possible tenons.

Painted striping and stenciled designs decorate the Fancy chair's unmolded surfaces. The striping mimics the string inlay found on more formal Federal furniture, and the stenciled designs simulate ormolu, or cast-brass ornament.

The rear legs are joined to the crest and back rails, the back stretcher, the side stretchers, and the back and side seat rails. In the case of the latter two rails, the rear seat rail should be installed first. The side seat-rail socket can then be drilled and will intersect the rear rail.

The pine seat band is a ⅜-in.-thick, steam-bent strip applied after the seat is woven. When softened in a steambox, this strip can be bent right over the outline of the seat and held in place with a bar clamp until dry. The band, made of two separate pieces for the front of the seat and the section between the rear legs, is tacked in position with T-headed brads. The brad heads become nearly invisible under the five coats of finish. The medallion between the two crest rails is also held in place with brads, one inserted from above and the other from below.

The finish on this Fancy chair, called japanning, is built up of numerous layers of oil paint and varnish. The first layer of paint is a Chinese red, which is polished smooth with an abrasive such as 000 steel wool. A second coat of the same color is then applied, but no further buffing is required.

A layer of flat black is next laid over the red and is "false-grained" to present an abstract interpretation of an exotic, real wood, in this case mahogany. This technique was commonly used during the Federal period to decorate informal furniture, and ranged in execution from the abstract to the true trompe l'oeil. To false-grain this chair, apply the black paint to the red a small area at a time. If the black is applied to the entire chair at once, it may set up so that it cannot be grained. I used a rag soaked in turpentine and wrung as dry as possible to produce the graining. Instead of drawing the rag over the wood, I removed the black with strokes that were halfway between a pat and a slap. If you're unhappy with the result, more black can simply be laid over the exposed red and the graining process begun anew. Two pieces of advice may be helpful in producing successful graining: Be subtle—the effect is supposed to be subdued. Also, be random—real wood figure does not occur in a repeated pattern.

The painted decoration on this chair is a combination of striping and stenciled symmetrical designs. (The book by Blanchard in the bibliography explains how to do both of these techniques.) Striping simulates the string inlay used to decorate more formal Federal furniture, like the card table on p. 10. The stencils are used to simulate ormolu, the cast-brass decoration that appears on late Federal-period furniture and was popularized by French cabinetmakers who came to America fleeing the French Revolution and Reign of Terror.

Once the striping and stenciling are dry, two coats of clear varnish are laid over the entire chair. This produces a finish that is five layers thick and extremely durable.

The rush seat on the Fancy chair was painted as well. The original seats on our dining-room set of chairs, once painted light blue-gray, have been replaced with similarly painted seats. Those who want to make this chair will find information on sources for rush in the suppliers list at the back of the book, and instructions for weaving a rush seat in a pamphlet in the bibliography.

Reeding with a plane

During the Federal period, Fancy chairs were inexpensive pieces of furniture, and the ornament on these chairs was usually produced with relatively easy and moderately priced methods. The reeding on the front legs of this particular Fancy, for example, was done with a reeding plane, called a center-bead plane, and was less difficult and less costly than reeding carved by hand. Because the plane can track only along a straight line, this method of reeding cannot be used on a vase-shaped turning like the arm post of the sofa (p. 30). The slight taper of the legs on this chair does cause the reeds to lean as they progress around the legs, but this angled reeding is not noticeable once the chair is assembled.

If you do not have a ⅜-in. center-bead plane, the reeding can also be made with a Stanley #55 or #45 or with a multi-plane. Whatever plane you use, the edges of the cutter must produce a V-groove rather than a flat-bottomed cut, called a quirk. If the cutter makes a quirk, the reeds will be undercut and damaged. If your plane does not have such a cutter, regrind a ⅜-in. cutter blade to the shape shown below.

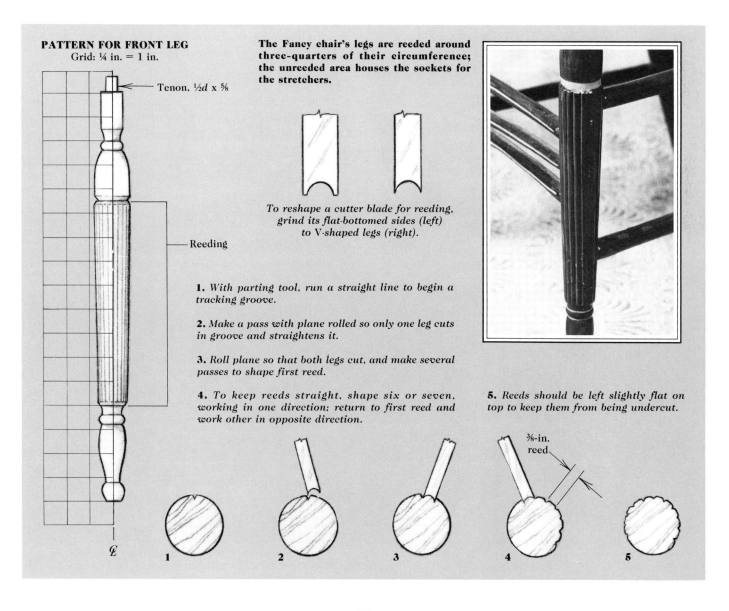

PATTERN FOR FRONT LEG
Grid: ¼ in. = 1 in.

Tenon, ½d x ⅝

Reeding

C₵

The Fancy chair's legs are reeded around three-quarters of their circumference; the unreeded area houses the sockets for the stretchers.

To reshape a cutter blade for reeding, grind its flat-bottomed sides (left) to V-shaped legs (right).

1. With parting tool, run a straight line to begin a tracking groove.

2. Make a pass with plane rolled so only one leg cuts in groove and straightens it.

3. Roll plane so that both legs cut, and make several passes to shape first reed.

4. To keep reeds straight, shape six or seven, working in one direction; return to first reed and work other in opposite direction.

5. Reeds should be left slightly flat on top to keep them from being undercut.

⅜-in. reed

1   2   3   4   5

After turning one of the front legs to the shape shown on the previous page, shut off the lathe and pull the plug to prevent an accidental start-up. Remove the turning and align the tool rest perfectly on the centerline between the tail and drive centers of the lathe, as described in the project section of the sofa chapter on p. 33. Then swing the rest out of the way, remount the turning and push the tool rest tightly against the area to be reeded. Trace a line using the rest as a straightedge. Swing the rest away from the turning and rotate the turning so that the line is on top. Run this line out with a *V*-shaped parting tool. Use the groove to guide one side of the center-bead's cutter, whose first pass will make the groove perfectly straight. This groove can then be used as a tracking groove to begin the reeding.

I find it easiest to do the reeding from behind the lathe, reaching over the leg to work. Draw the plane back so that one leg of the cutter is in the *V*-groove you just cut. Make the first pass, rolling the plane slightly so that only the one leg in the groove is cutting. This pass will deepen and straighten the groove. Then roll the plane so that both sides of the cutter are making contact with the leg and make another pass, which will produce a second beveled groove and define the first reed. If necessary, make another pass to complete the cuts. Do not develop the reed so it is a full half-round, however; it should be slightly flat on top, or you will run into problems in cutting the next reed.

After the first reed is completed, return the plane to the starting point of the reeding and place it so that the leg of the cutter that will do the tracking rides in the nearest of the two grooves just made. This will cause the plane to track parallel to the first reed while cutting the second. Make another pass or two to develop the second reed. Move the plane so that again one leg of the cutter rides in the nearest groove and the other leg rides on the unreeded surface. Cut the third reed in the same manner as the first two. As the number of reeds increases, they will begin to slant due to the leg's slight taper. You can minimize this slant by working six or seven reeds in one direction, then returning to the first reed and working the remaining reeds in the opposite direction. Use a small parting tool to do any cleanup needed at the top or bottom of the reeds.

Reed only about three-fourths of the circumference of the leg. The total number of reeds is unimportant, though of course the more consistent the reeding on the four legs of the chair, the better it will look. In our set of Fancies, there are as few as 13 reeds on a leg and as many as 15. The unreeded area on each front leg will be positioned diagonally backward so that it faces the opposite rear leg.

Using the tool rest as a guide, draw a straight line to mark the first reed.

Move the rest out of the way and cut a groove along the pencil line with a parting tool.

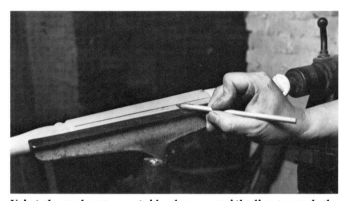

The plane will track in the groove to shape the first reed. Make the first cut with the plane guided by one leg.

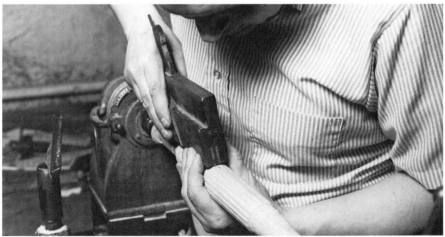

To minimize the slant of the reeding caused by the leg's taper, work half of the reeds in one direction around the circumference of the leg, then return to the first reed and finish reeding in the opposite direction.

FANCY CHAIR

Scale: ⅛ in. = 1 in.

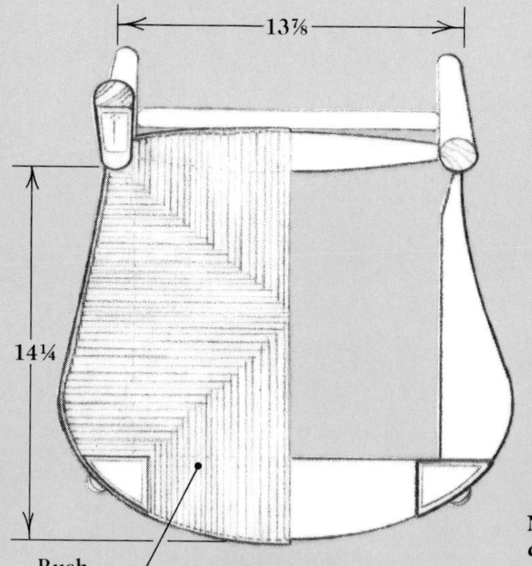

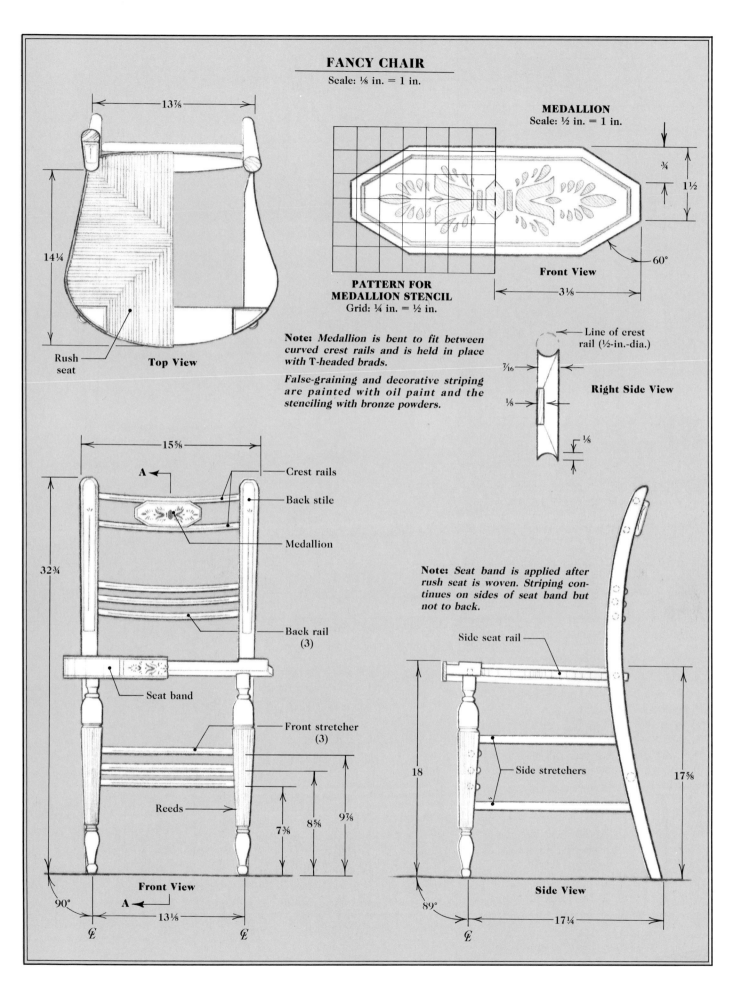

13⅞
14¼
Rush seat

Top View

MEDALLION

Scale: ½ in. = 1 in.

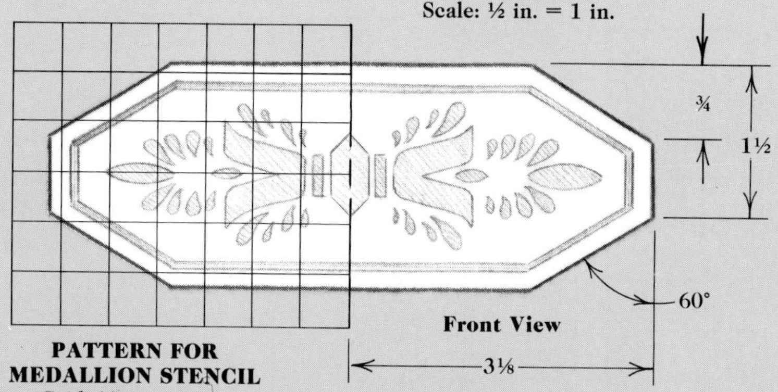

¾
1½
60°
3⅛

PATTERN FOR MEDALLION STENCIL

Grid: ¼ in. = ½ in.

Front View

Note: ***Medallion is bent to fit between curved crest rails and is held in place with T-headed brads.***

False-graining and decorative striping are painted with oil paint and the stenciling with bronze powders.

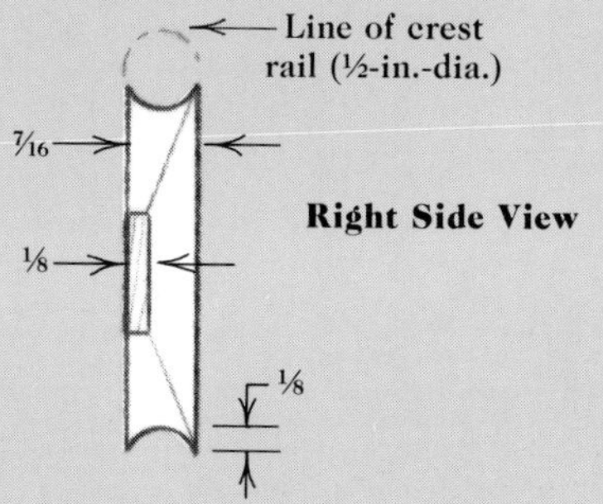

Line of crest rail (½-in.-dia.)
7/16
⅛
⅛

Right Side View

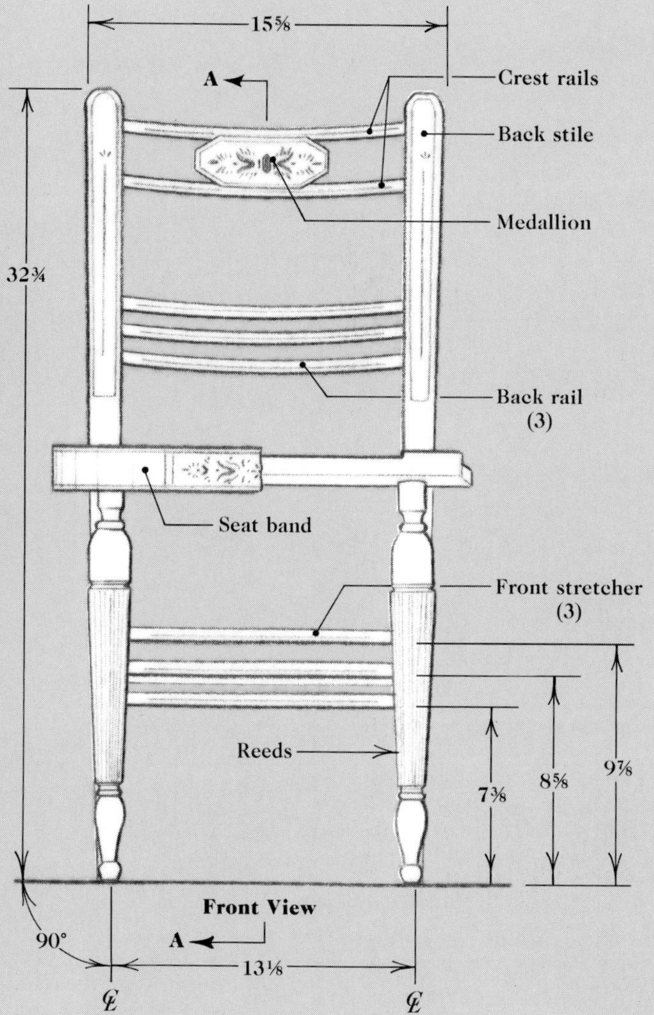

15⅝
A
Crest rails
Back stile
Medallion
32¾
Back rail (3)
Seat band
Front stretcher (3)
Reeds
7⅜
8⅝
9⅞
90°
A
13⅛
℄
℄

Front View

Note: ***Seat band is applied after rush seat is woven. Striping continues on sides of seat band but not to back.***

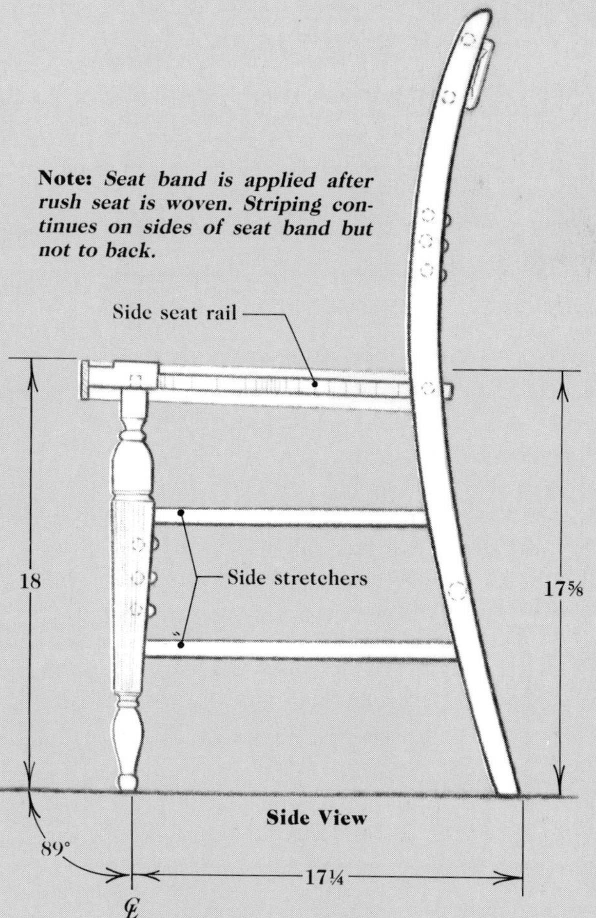

Side seat rail
18
Side stretchers
17⅝
89°
17¼
℄

Side View

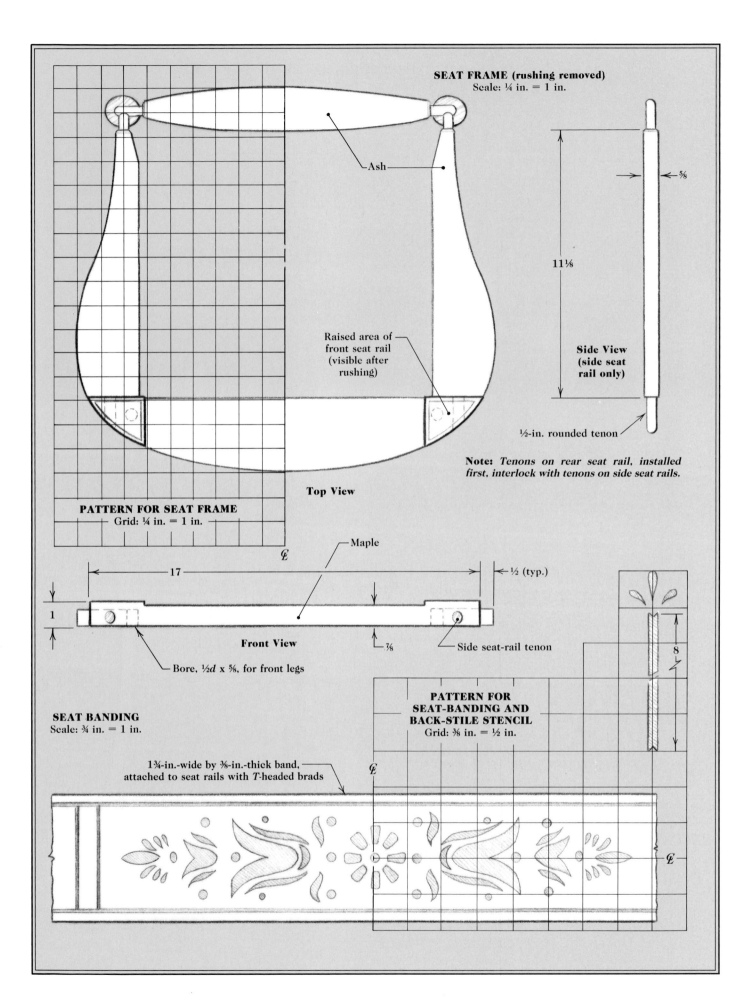

SEAT FRAME (rushing removed)
Scale: ¼ in. = 1 in.

Ash

Raised area of
front seat rail
(visible after
rushing)

Top View

PATTERN FOR SEAT FRAME
Grid: ¼ in. = 1 in.

⅝

11⅛

**Side View
(side seat
rail only)**

½-in. rounded tenon

Note: *Tenons on rear seat rail, installed
first, interlock with tenons on side seat rails.*

Maple

17

½ (typ.)

1

⅞

Front View

Side seat-rail tenon

Bore, ½d x ⅝, for front legs

SEAT BANDING
Scale: ¾ in. = 1 in.

**PATTERN FOR
SEAT-BANDING AND
BACK-STILE STENCIL**
Grid: ⅜ in. = ½ in.

8

1¾-in.-wide by ⅜-in.-thick band,
attached to seat rails with *T*-headed brads

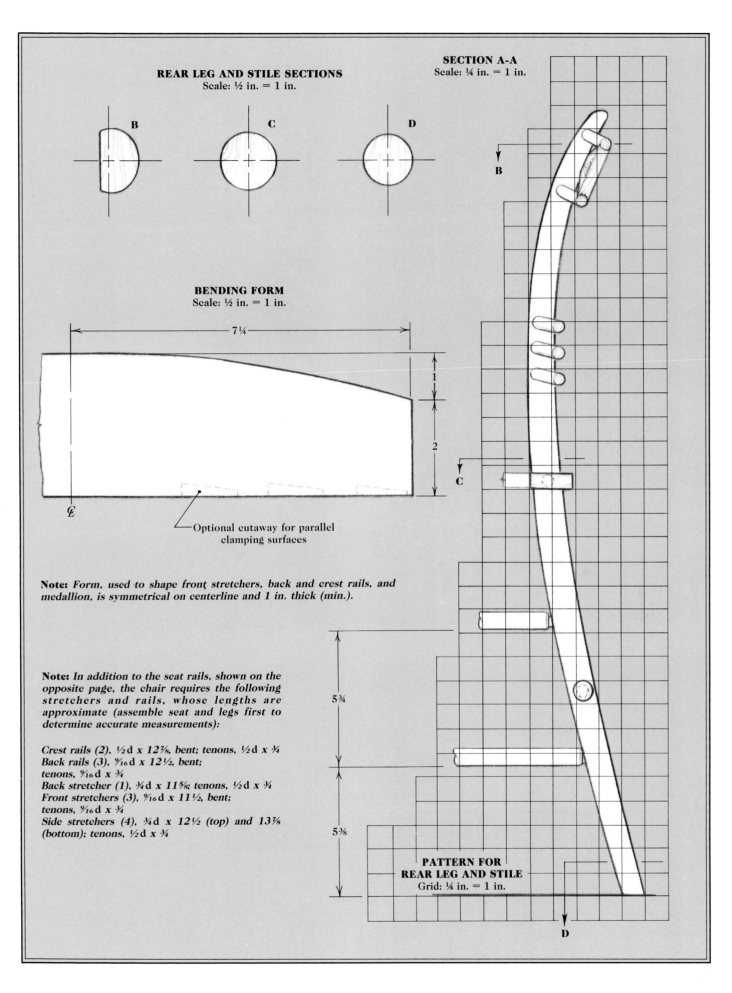

REAR LEG AND STILE SECTIONS
Scale: ½ in. = 1 in.

B   C   D

SECTION A-A
Scale: ¼ in. = 1 in.

B

C

BENDING FORM
Scale: ½ in. = 1 in.

7¼

1

2

C̸L

Optional cutaway for parallel
clamping surfaces

Note: *Form, used to shape front stretchers, back and crest rails, and medallion, is symmetrical on centerline and 1 in. thick (min.).*

Note: *In addition to the seat rails, shown on the opposite page, the chair requires the following stretchers and rails, whose lengths are approximate (assemble seat and legs first to determine accurate measurements):*

Crest rails (2), ½d x 12⅞, bent; tenons, ½d x ¾
Back rails (3), ⁹⁄₁₆d x 12½, bent; tenons, ⁹⁄₁₆d x ¾
Back stretcher (1), ¾d x 11⅝; tenons, ½d x ¾
Front stretchers (3), ⁹⁄₁₆d x 11½, bent; tenons, ⁹⁄₁₆d x ¾
Side stretchers (4), ¾d x 12½ (top) and 13⅞ (bottom); tenons, ½d x ¾

5¾

5⅜

PATTERN FOR
REAR LEG AND STILE
Grid: ¼ in. = 1 in.

D

In Federal homes, where the only source of heat was the fire-place, bellows were an essential tool for quickly building a fire and keeping it ablaze. (Project: Front-board decoration, p. 111.)

Bellows

Chapter 12

Before the development of the woodstove in the late 18th century, fireplaces were the only source of heat in a house. In New England, where the temperature in winter regularly falls well below zero, the ability to keep a fire blazing or to quickly build a new one meant the difference between relative comfort and extreme discomfort for the Federal-period family. At night when everyone retired, fires were banked with ashes heaped over the live coals. The next morning, before the household could start its daily routine, the ashes were shoveled away to expose the still-glowing coals, and kindling was placed on these coals. If one waited for the fires to catch by themselves, it meant dressing in a subfreezing room. It also meant eating a very cold breakfast, since all cooking was done in the kitchen fireplace, whose fire was also banked during the night.

The device that ensured the quick rekindling of a fire was the bellows. This essential fireplace tool is basically a leather lung, which is expanded to fill with air and compressed to expel the air and fan an incipient fire. Like most Federal homes, our house has a fireplace in all the major rooms. We don't rely on these fireplaces as our primary heat source, but we do enjoy using them. Therefore we find it handy to hang a pair of bellows next to each.

The several bellows we own reflect the function and character of the rooms in which they are kept. Those made of turned and carved mahogany are hung in the most formal rooms, while the pairs with painted decoration are kept in the bedchambers. The one chosen for this chapter is kept in the dining room and hangs from a brass knob screwed into the backband around the fireplace architrave. The knob is nearly as old as the house, and its presence indicates that this is where the Lord family hung the bellows they used in this room. When the fireplace was bricked up and a stove installed in the mid-19th century, no one bothered to remove the knob.

Since the awkward shape of a pair of bellows doesn't allow them to stand by themselves, they are usually hung when not in use. Generally, bellows are suspended by either a strap attached to or a hole bored through one of the handles, and, when they are hung, only one side is normally visible. Since the backboard houses the air valve that makes the bellows work and must be face down for the mechanism to function, this side is unseen when the bellows are in use. The front board is therefore the one that is usually seen and most often embellished.

The maker of the bellows shown here ornamented the front board with a combination of turning and carving, and for that reason used mahogany for the front. For the back, however, he switched to a very even-grained, native hardwood, which might be poplar, tulipwood or soft maple—I can't positively identify it through the finish.

Faceplate turning was a common decoration on Federal-period bellows, even though colorful, painted ornament was more prevalent. Since period cabinetmakers were fond of geometric shapes but were usually unable to incorporate concentric circles in their furniture designs, the turned rings on a set of bellows were seen as a nice contrapuntal detail in a room full of essentially linear and curvilinear furniture.

While the variety of ornament possible with painted decoration was limited only by the artist's imagination, turning imposed certain distinct constraints. Turned decorations, for example, could be no more than an interesting series of concave or convex rings of various widths, which could not be deeply cut since the board itself was generally rather thin (the board used on these bellows is only $5/8$ in. thick). Yet even though the turned rings on these bellows are shallow, they appear much deeper in the shadows of candlelight.

I am particularly fond of these bellows because their maker went several steps beyond simple turning in their ornamentation. He added texture by carving several of the rings, and depth by attaching in the center of the front board a separately turned and carved boss. This boss is composed of an outer ring and a raised and carved center. The presence of the boss creates a difference of almost an inch between the top of this projection and the lowest point in the rings—quite an accomplishment on a ⅝-in.-thick board. As a result of this design, the bellows change character under different lighting conditions. On a bright, sunny day, the shallow, turned rings cast almost no shadows and are reduced to concentric lines. When this happens, the textured carving alone supplies visual interest. With the room lit by the softer, oblique light of candles, the carving loses much of its impact and the play of shadows among the convex and concave rings seizes the viewer's eye.

So much thought went into creating the front board that it is not surprising that the maker added some detail to the backboard. This side is also decorated with turnings, done in conjunction with cutting the hole for the valve. (If you decide to make these bellows and likewise cut the valve hole on the lathe, you will want to sandwich some thin shims between the wood and the lathe faceplate, perhaps a couple of washers or a plywood shim slid over the attachment screws. This way, your tool will not come in contact with the metal lathe faceplate when it pierces the board.) While the backboard was spinning, the maker cut the center valve hole with a skew chisel, producing an opening with sides that curve inward and which measures 2¼ in. in diameter at the front of the board and 1¾ in. at the back. He also turned a series of four shallow, evenly spaced rings on the back. These rings, though seldom seen, are quiet evidence of dedication to his craft.

Making a pair of bellows presents some construction details not encountered elsewhere in this book, the most obvious being the faceplate turning, which will be further discussed in the project section, and the leather work. The leather work is not difficult, but you may nonetheless want to find a competent leather worker to do the job. The main leather component of the bellows is the leather bag that joins the front board and backboard, and the most complicated leather element is the woven hinge. From the drawings on pp. 113-115, you should be able to construct these and the other leather parts.

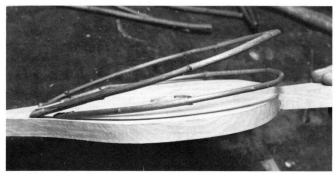

The ribs of the bellows, cut from green shoots, keep the leather bag from collapsing when the bellows are not inflated.

Another element of construction unique to the bellows is the valve. Located on the inside surface of the backboard, this thin, wooden flap tacked to a leather hinge covers the air hole in the center of the backboard. When the handles are pulled apart, the valve opens and allows air to be drawn into the bellows; when the handles are compressed, it closes to force the air out the nozzle. (A loose, 1-in.-wide leather strap attached to the inside of the backboard prevents the valve from opening too far and becoming hung up on the front board.) As air is drawn into the bellows, gravity holds the valve loosely against the backboard. When the two handles are forced together, the increased air pressure in the bellows seals the valve. Because the valve seals only if it is first held closed by gravity, the bellows must be used with the decorated front board face-up.

Finally, the bent ribs inside the bellows warrant note. The function of these two ribs is to prevent the bellows' leather bag from collapsing into a shapeless form when not filled with air. The ribs are made from green switches about 26 in. long and roughly 3/16 in. in diameter. The switches should be straight and vary little in diameter from end to end. If you are gathering shoots in the fall and winter when they are leafless, flex them to see if they are alive. If they are, they will be supple, whereas dead shoots will snap.

I cut the shoots I used from a lilac bush in our backyard. Out of curiosity, I also tried forsythia and wild cherry switches, which worked equally well. I suspect that any deciduous sapling or any bush that puts out suckers will also work, which means that this raw material should be readily available in urban areas too.

To make these ribs, first cut the shoots to 26-in. lengths and trim any small branches, although you can leave the bark on. Locate the position for the four holes on the inside of the backboard, as shown in the drawing on p. 114. Since the ends of the switches should fit tightly in these holes, drill test holes in a piece of scrap to determine the right diameter before drilling the actual holes. If need be, shave a tight end on a switch rather than settling for an oversize hole and loose fit.

Insert one end of a switch into the upper hole on one side, bend the switch over and press it flat against the backboard. Test the switch for strength by bending it to the rough shape of the bellows. If it doesn't break, mark on the switch the position of the second upper hole, add ⅝ in. to this measurement and cut the switch to length. Secure the first end in place with an upholstery tack, and again bend the switch around the perimeter of the bellows. Then insert the second end into its hole, press the switch flat against the backboard and tack this end in place.

Repeat the process to make the second rib, fitting the ends of this switch into the lower pair of holes. When finished, the second rib should separate from the first and lie in a higher plane, as in the photo at left. Don't worry if the switches don't perfectly retain the desired shape. They are very flexible and the leather bag, when attached, will push them back where they belong.

The cast-brass nozzle, which directs the stream of air from the bellows, can be purchased from the supply sources listed in the back of the book for reproduction-furniture hardware. (To attach the nozzle, you need only shave the end of the bellows until it fits.) The tacks, which secure the leather bag to the front board and backboard, are brass-headed upholstery tacks and can be obtained from any upholstery supply house. Most upholstery shops have these tacks on hand as well and will usually sell them in small amounts. Be sure to ask for tacks with solid-brass heads, since plated tacks would quickly wear through to the base metal. (The tacks sold at most hardware stores are brass-plated.)

This pair of bellows was finished with shellac, but any clear finish could be used. If you make your bellows out of a native hardwood with little figure, they could be given a colored wash that complements the room for which they are intended. I make such a wash out of diluted milk paint and use just one coat. Another coat of linseed oil, thinned with turpentine, can be added if you wish a bit more sheen than the flat milk paint provides. A coat of wax will seal the oil.

Since bellows are usually hung near a fireplace, you need to remember that the heat from the fireplace will eventually dry out the leather. Giving the leather on your bellows a yearly wiping with neat's-foot oil or clear shoe polish will keep it supple and prevent cracking.

Front-board decoration

To begin the front board, thickness-plane and surface a board that is 10 in. wide by 17 in. long by ⅝ in. thick. While the board is a rectangle, locate and mark its center. Then cut off the corners so that the board will be better balanced and less inclined to vibrate while being turned.

Center the lathe faceplate over the center mark on the board and drive in the screws to secure the faceplate to the board. I ground the tips of the three screws to shorten them so they wouldn't come in contact with the lathe tools. Since this eliminated the screws' self-tapping ability, however, I first made pilot holes with a brad awl.

On my lathe the headstock and tailstock are elevated, so I can turn inboard a piece of wood the size of the bellows. But whether you turn yours inboard or outboard, first lay out each of the rings with a pair of dividers. I made the deepest cuts first—the second from the center and the third from the outside. By establishing these deep cuts, you create reference points that make the other cuts easier.

After completing the rings on the front board, turn the boss. Since the boss is too small for three screws to be used in the faceplate, I attached it with a single screw in the center.

Once the bellows' front board and boss have been turned, hold them down on the bench to do the carving. The stylized motif used on the widest ring on the front

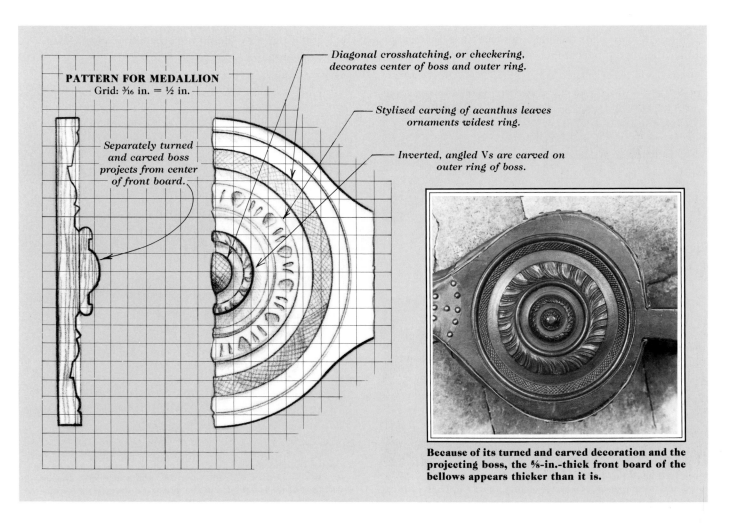

PATTERN FOR MEDALLION
Grid: ³⁄₁₆ in. = ½ in.

Separately turned and carved boss projects from center of front board.

Diagonal crosshatching, or checkering, decorates center of boss and outer ring.

Stylized carving of acanthus leaves ornaments widest ring.

Inverted, angled Vs are carved on outer ring of boss.

Because of its turned and carved decoration and the projecting boss, the ⅝-in.-thick front board of the bellows appears thicker than it is.

board is typically found on furniture made late in the Federal period after about 1810. It probably evolved from a depiction of the acanthus leaf, a classical motif used on the capitals of Corinthian columns. Early Federal-period carvers made accurate copies of the Greco-Roman stylization of the acanthus leaf. Over time, the leaf was gradually abstracted and reduced to a pattern of gouge strokes and veining. Thus, this became more of a textural motif than a shape and could be applied to any surface, even a ring.

To produce this motif, start with the gouge work, for which I used a No. 8 sweep, ¾-in. gouge. Each depression should be made with a single stroke, and the resulting shape should resemble a curved teardrop. Try to make the gouge strokes uniform and evenly spaced. Your first attempts may be very tentative, but after making several cuts, your hand will become surer. There will be variations in the carving, as this is the nature of work done by hand, but discrepancies will be hidden by the visual complexity of the carving.

Veining joins the gouge cuts. Two heavy strokes, carved with a V-shaped parting tool, fill the spaces between the gouge strokes. A pair of finer lines is cut into the depressions themselves.

The texture on the outer ring is called checkering, a pattern that results from diagonal crosshatching. These lines are also cut with the parting tool. Start by making all the cuts in one direction. They should be at about a 45° angle to the rings above and below and should have a slight arc. It is easy for the angle of these lines to increase and for the cuts to become more vertical. If you find this

happening, don't make a sudden change in the angle of the next cut; instead, gradually work the line back out to the desired angle. In carving these lines, try to keep the depth of the cuts and the distance between them uniform. When the first series of lines is finished, cut those running in the opposite direction, again keeping in mind the uniformity of the cuts. Each new line will now result in a series of small diamonds, or checkers. When the piece is completed, shadows will fall in the lines, and the finish on the checkers will reflect glistening spots of light.

The boss has three turned rings, which are also ornamented with carving. Because the boss is so small, in order to be carved it needs to be held in the wooden jaw of a handscrew, with the handscrew clamped in a vise. Also because of the boss' size, the detail in the carving is even less clear than that on the front board. The center dome of the boss is also checkered, although on the original pair of bellows, wear and handling during the last 170 years have erased much of this pattern.

The boss' small inner ring is simply nicked vertically with a parting tool. As with the other carving, try to keep the spacing even on these cuts. The decoration on the outer ring is a series of inverted, angled Vs, also cut with the parting tool. Two passes of the tool cuts the legs of the V, and a single stroke cleans out the space between them.

When the carving on the front board and boss is complete, trace the pattern of the bellows onto the front board, glue the boss onto the center and cut the board to shape. The sawn edges will for the most part be covered by leather, but they should nonetheless be cleaned up with a spokeshave.

A stylized acanthus-leaf motif decorates one ring of the front board and is comprised of a series of gouge cuts (top) and veining (bottom), or pairs of fine lines.

To make the checkering on the outer ring, carve a series of diagonal cuts angled at 45° to the rings and uniformly spaced. A second set of diagonal cuts in the opposite direction overlaps the first to create the checkered pattern.

BELLOWS

Scale: ¼ in, = 1 in.

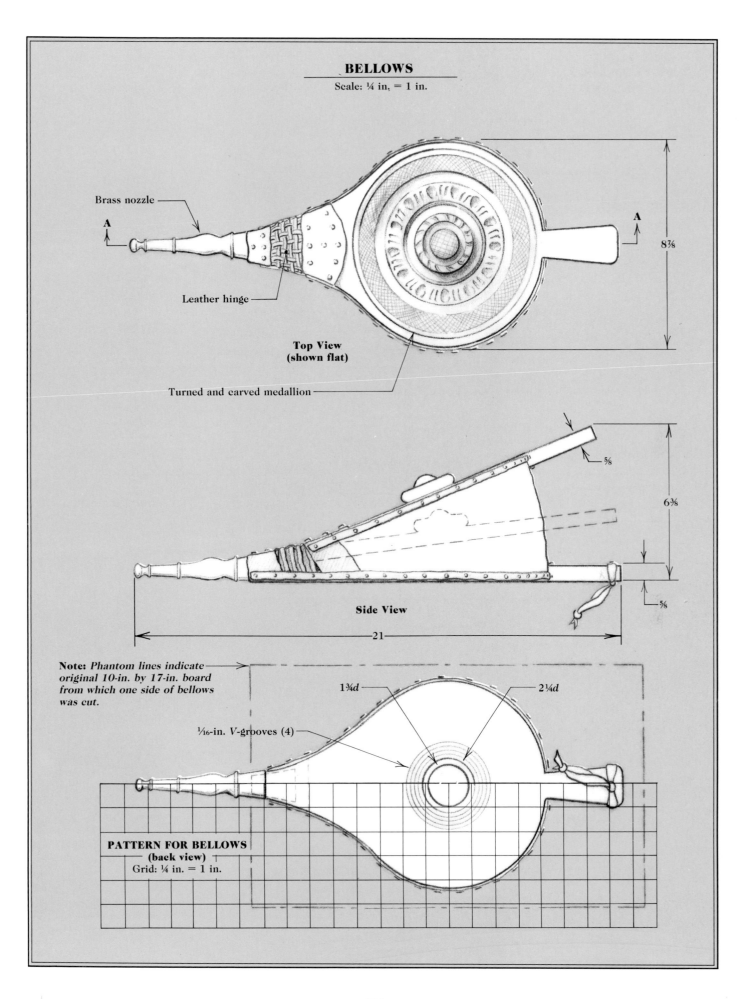

Brass nozzle

A

Leather hinge

A

8⅞

**Top View
(shown flat)**

Turned and carved medallion

⅝

6⅜

Side View

⅝

21

Note: *Phantom lines indicate
original 10-in. by 17-in. board
from which one side of bellows
was cut.*

1¾d

2¼d

1/16-in. *V-grooves* (4)

**PATTERN FOR BELLOWS
(back view)**
Grid: ¼ in. = 1 in.

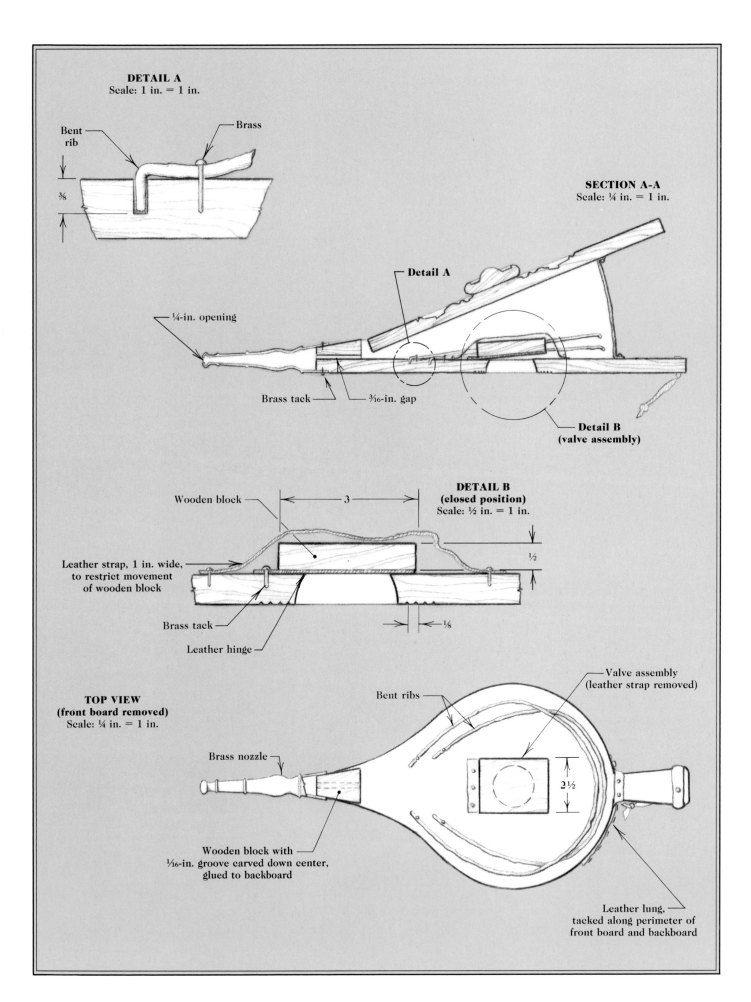

DETAIL A
Scale: 1 in. = 1 in.

Bent rib

Brass

$\frac{3}{8}$

SECTION A-A
Scale: ¼ in. = 1 in.

Detail A

¼-in. opening

Brass tack

³⁄₁₆-in. gap

Detail B
(valve assembly)

DETAIL B
(closed position)
Scale: ½ in. = 1 in.

Wooden block

3

½

Leather strap, 1 in. wide,
to restrict movement
of wooden block

Brass tack

Leather hinge

⅛

TOP VIEW
(front board removed)
Scale: ¼ in. = 1 in.

Valve assembly
(leather strap removed)

Bent ribs

Brass nozzle

2½

Wooden block with
¹⁄₁₆-in. groove carved down center,
glued to backboard

Leather lung,
tacked along perimeter of
front board and backboard

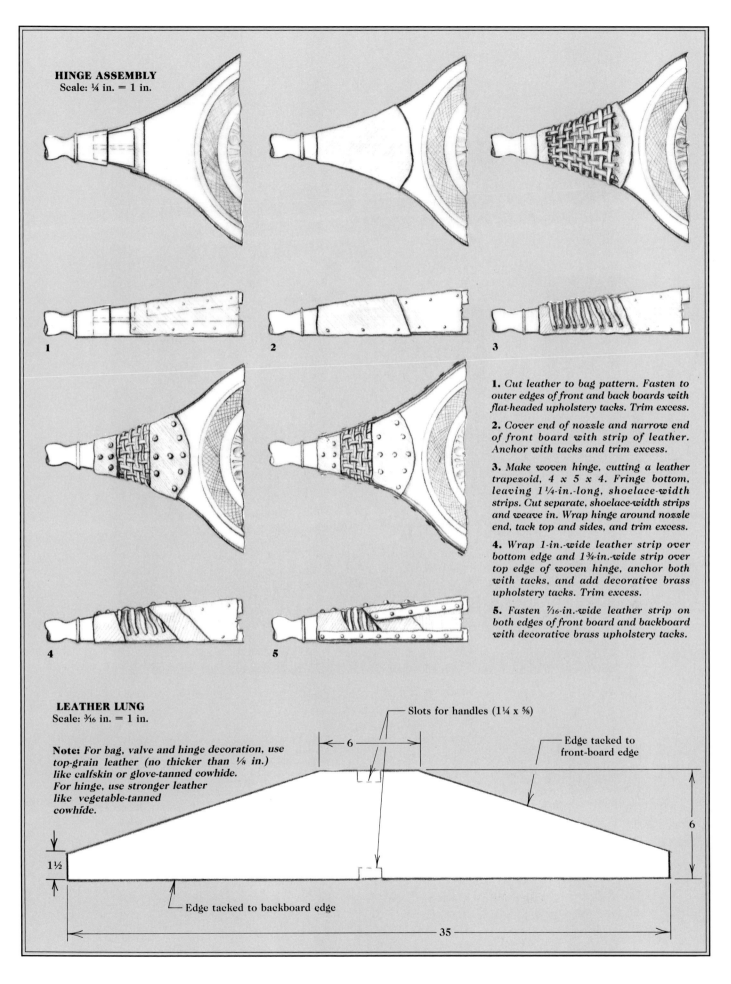

HINGE ASSEMBLY
Scale: ¼ in. = 1 in.

1

2

3

1. *Cut leather to bag pattern. Fasten to outer edges of front and back boards with flat-headed upholstery tacks. Trim excess.*

2. *Cover end of nozzle and narrow end of front board with strip of leather. Anchor with tacks and trim excess.*

3. *Make woven hinge, cutting a leather trapezoid, 4 x 5 x 4. Fringe bottom, leaving 1¼-in.-long, shoelace-width strips. Cut separate, shoelace-width strips and weave in. Wrap hinge around nozzle end, tack top and sides, and trim excess.*

4. *Wrap 1-in.-wide leather strip over bottom edge and 1¾-in.-wide strip over top edge of woven hinge, anchor both with tacks, and add decorative brass upholstery tacks. Trim excess.*

5. *Fasten ⁷⁄₁₆-in.-wide leather strip on both edges of front board and backboard with decorative brass upholstery tacks.*

4

5

LEATHER LUNG
Scale: ³⁄₁₆ in. = 1 in.

Note: *For bag, valve and hinge decoration, use top-grain leather (no thicker than ⅛ in.) like calfskin or glove-tanned cowhide. For hinge, use stronger leather like vegetable-tanned cowhide.*

Slots for handles (1¼ x ⅝)

6

Edge tacked to front-board edge

6

1½

Edge tacked to backboard edge

35

THE KITCHEN

The kitchen's main purpose during the Federal period, as it is today, was for food preparation. Meals were cooked in a fireplace, as the cast-iron cookstove was not then widely available. Because preparation, cooking and cleanup took so much time, the kitchen was a spot of nearly constant activity from morning to evening.

The cooking fireplace was usually the largest in the house. It was wider, higher and deeper than the other fireplaces to accommodate numerous cast-iron cooking vessels and to provide the cook easy access to them. The kitchen fireplace also contained an oven, which was a brick cavity built into either the side wall (called a cheek) or rear wall of the firebox.

We have restored the kitchen in our house to its original appearance but felt the room was too important to be modernized to function as a 20th-century kitchen. We use this room only for informal eating and socializing, although we do enjoy cooking in the fireplace and baking in the oven, especially for guests who appreciate the experience. A modern kitchen has been built in an adjacent chamber, and closing a door is all that's necessary to separate the two.

Our kitchen is long and narrow, about 18 ft. by 10 ft., and one wall is dominated by the large mouth of the fireplace. The opening, 51 in. high by 71 in. long, is set off by the color of the cheeks and jambs of the fireplace, painted red, as they originally were. Set into a whitewashed plaster wall, this fireplace creates a dramatic effect.

Although there is a lot of woodwork in the kitchen (six passage doors, two cased posts and wainscoting), the work is quite simple and is painted its original gray. The pine floorboards are unpainted, as they would have been during the Federal period, and I periodically clean them by scrubbing them with steel wool and a mixture of water and bleach. The custom of the day was to cover wooden floors with a thin sprinkling of fine sand, which, with traffic through the room, acted like a fine sandpaper, keeping the floors free of stains. Like sawdust on a barroom floor, the sand absorbed spills and could be swept up when dirty. When a fresh layer of sand was spread, housewives sometimes made patterns in it with a broom. This is perhaps the most ephemeral of early American decorative arts, lasting only until the first new footsteps across the floor.

Our kitchen is lighted by a single window with a northerly exposure. The window is such a natural place to locate the table that, when I was removing the paint from the wainscoting, I was not surprised to find a long depression about 29 in. above the floor. This mark had been worn by the edge of all the earlier kitchen tabletops that had been placed in the same spot.

The most enduring of all Federal furniture forms, the Windsor
chair has been continuously made since it was first introduced to
the Colonies in the mid-1700s. This Windsor design, known as a
rod-back, substitutes a square back for the traditional bent bow.
(Project: Shaping the seat, p. 122.)

Windsor Chair

Chapter 13

No other furniture form presented in this book is as universally recognized as the Windsor chair. Even if you did not know these chairs by name, chances are you are familiar with them. They are so widely reproduced that we see them everywhere. Yet their current popularity does not result from their being rediscovered. Since Windsors were first introduced to the Colonies during the mid-18th century, Americans have never stopped making them.

Not only has the Windsor form endured, a tremendous number of the original chairs have survived as well. The reason for this is that during the Federal period these chairs were made in larger quantities than almost any other type of furniture.

Windsors were both a product of and a contributor to the Industrial Revolution. The Federal period was ripe with a spirit of enterprise as Americans looked for new ways to make products more quickly, more efficiently and more cheaply. In Windsor-chair shops, the concepts of interchangeable parts and a division of labor among specialists were applied and tested. By using these new techniques, craftsmen could produce an average chair of the type shown in this chapter in only eight to ten man-hours. This enabled Windsor chairmakers to turn out their products at an unprecedented rate and to reduce their prices to a level nearly everyone could afford. In response, Federal-period Americans went on a Windsor-chair-buying binge, often purchasing sets in numbers that we might consider excessive. In the 1805 inventory of our eight-room house, for example, 40 chairs are listed, 18 of them Windsors.

The new speed of manufacture, which allowed a three-man chair shop to turn out nearly a thousand chairs a year, had an important consequence. Mass production freed Windsor chairmakers to experiment with design—if a new idea failed, only a day's effort was lost. This ability to daily modify the chair form yielded designs so successful that they have endured unchanged for almost 200 years.

The first Windsors introduced in America were large, commodious easy chairs, meant for comfortable sitting rather than for formal dining. During the Federal period, Windsors became smaller, portable, and inexpensive enough to be purchased in sets. As a result, Windsors became popular seats for working, relaxing, dining and innumerable other purposes.

During the Federal period, everyday furniture was usually painted. Paint provided a durable, washable surface and also satisfied people's desire for color in the home. Since Windsors were informal in nature, they too were painted. The usual choice of color was green, probably in imitation of the contemporary European fashion of having green chairs in the garden. Knowing that his work would be painted, the chairmaker had no reason to use figured wood, and therefore focused his attention on the more difficult and more challenging element of line. As a result, strong vertical and horizontal lines and sensuous curves move the viewer's eye through these chairs in a purposeful manner made possible by a uniform color.

The four Windsors shown in this chapter are more than good examples of this chair form. They are achievements in the element of line. Each is complex, and none allows itself to be seen entirely unless the viewer stands too far back to grasp detail. Upon close inspection, however, one will find a logical visual flow through each chair, which results from the maker's understanding of how line produces visual movement. One of the chairmaker's most important concerns was to restrain the design of the chair's individual parts so that no one element dominated and disrupted the chair's overall visual impact.

By becoming very conscious of my own interaction with these chairs, I gradually discovered that making a successful Windsor is akin to designing a good magazine advertisement. In both cases, the viewer's visual involvement generally lasts only a few seconds. In the case of the successful Windsor, this involvement occurs

The continuous-arm Windsor chair was introduced around 1800.

On the sack-back chair, the arm rail is higher than on other Windsors.

The oval-back Windsor was often made without the tailpiece and bracing spindles.

between the time one decides to sit and does so. Because we don't usually look carefully at a chair before occupying it and we can't really do so once settled in it, the chair's design must subconsciously connect with us before we sit and cause us to take a longer look.

Windsors do this by drawing the eye and hand to the most logical place to grasp the chair—usually the top of the back. From here, some strong line must pull the eye back down to the seat. That motion, plus the visual complexity of the seat, prolongs the viewer's involvement. The chairmaker has succeeded when the person ready to sit down says, "That's a nice-looking chair."

The continuous-arm chair, like that shown in the photo at top left, is usually considered the purest expression of American Windsor design. It was the first type of Windsor made in America that did not have a direct English antecedent, and it was the last style introduced before the Sheraton influence produced the square-back Windsor. The origins of the continuous-arm style are uncertain. It was probably developed in New York City and seems to be the Windsor interpretation of the upholstered French bergère chair, whose armrests are an extension of the curve of its rounded back.

The double bend of the arm on this chair eliminates the joints that occur on all other Windsor armchairs. This projection into two planes allows the continuous arm to move the eye more smoothly and farther without interruption than any other style of Windsor.

The sack-back Windsor chair is a contemporary of the continuous-arm. It too uses the element of line, but does so differently. The major difference between this chair and most other Windsors is the height of the arm rail in relation to the upper surface of the seat. In the case of the example shown at top center, the arm rail is almost 2 in.

higher than usual. With the arm rail thus raised, the maker shortened the upper section of the long spindles, eliminating the visual uplift typical of Windsors. The flattened curve in the center of the bow, the arm rail, the seat and the center stretcher divide the chair into three sections and suggest width rather than uplift. A long curve along the front edge of the seat produces a smooth, gentle sweep to the pommel, or peak of the seat, and contributes to a circular visual flow that begins and ends at the top of the bow. The use of line in this chair contrasts markedly with that in the continuous-arm. The overall movement is smooth and circular, as compared with the graceful dance of S-shaped curves in the continuous-arm.

The chair shown at top right is now commonly called a bow-back, a hoop-back or a loop-back. Its maker would have called it an oval-back, the term I prefer since the other names are often applied to sack-backs as well.

This chair is the most exuberant Windsor shown in this chapter. Its oval back seizes the eye in typical Windsor fashion, drawing it up to the apex of the bow with the spindles. As the eye ascends, it encounters two angled, bracing spindles that intersect with the top and add interest to a back otherwise made of severe, nearly parallel verticals. When the eye travels down the curved outline of the back, there is nothing to slow its free-fall descent until it reaches the seat. There it finds, cut into the side of the seat, a dynamic, S-shaped cyma curve. The bold, vigorous curve is not repeated on the seat's front edge, since to do so would have been overstatement and would have also eliminated support for the sitter's thighs. The maker instead heavily relieved the seat's upper and lower surfaces and drew out the front to a knife edge. This thin front edge acts as a visual brake to slow the eye as it concludes its turbulent ride.

For me, the chair shown on p. 118 is probably the most important piece in this book. If not for it, I would never have begun working wood or written this book. Carol and I were married during my junior year in college. I was a French major and planned to go on to earn my doctorate. At the time I didn't know a thing about woodworking.

We had very little money to furnish our apartment. As a result, I often unwillingly accompanied Carol to yard sales, and it was at one in Sutton, Massachusetts, that I found this chair. For the first time in my life, I became visually involved with a piece of furniture. There was something about this wooden chair that was different from any other I had ever seen. I knew I had to own it, even though its $10 price tag was then one-quarter of our monthly rent.

I would sit up at night, looking at this chair after Carol had gone to bed. I quickly discovered that it took on a different character under different types of illumination, which I have since learned is a feature of most Federal furniture. Trying to find out what this chair was, I spent hours pouring over books at the library and at last found pictures of Windsors. I wanted to own more of them but quickly discovered that old Windsors generally sold for far more that I had paid for this one. The only chairs I could afford were those that were badly damaged.

I taught myself to make repairs on the broken Windsors I was able to buy. I replaced a back here, a leg there and even some of the parts in between. Making an entire chair became a personal challenge. I became so involved with these chairs that I don't know how I made it through my senior year. Many days I didn't even bother to attend class, working instead on my chairs in my parents' barn. By graduation I had rented a garage and had contracted with the Early American Society to make an initial run of 50 chairs. The PhD in French was completely forgotten. I was in business as a Windsor chairmaker.

Perhaps with the exception of my marriage, nothing else has had such a profound effect on my life as has this chair. It is next to me while I write, and I can feel that it still has that old magic. The name Stickney is penciled on the bottom of the seat. Comparing this rather unique hand with the signatures on a stack of receipts in the collection of the Beverly Historical Society in Beverly, Massachusetts, leaves no doubt that this chair was made by Samuel Stickney, a Beverly cabinetmaker in the late 18th and early 19th centuries. This is the only piece of his work that has been identified, which is regrettable because he was an insightful designer. I once made 18 chairs for the rotunda of Monticello, Thomas Jefferson's home in Charlottesville, Virginia. I based those chairs on the design of this one.

Stickney did not develop the chair's form. It is a rod-back Windsor, introduced about 1800. Its square back consists of two stiles and a crest rail, instead of a bent bow, showing the influence of Sheraton mahogany chairs. Had this chair been made in an urban shop by a formally trained Windsor maker, it would have had bamboo-like rings turned on the spindles, legs and stretchers (influence from America's growing involvement in the China trade) and would have displayed a diminished interest in the element of line in favor of painted and carved ornament.

Stickney, however, took the urban chair and stripped it of ornament in order to continue to work with his perhaps conservative preference for line. Without a curved back to pull the eye down to the chair's seat, he made the crest rail as thin as possible so that it appears too delicate to be used to lift the chair. One therefore instinctively reaches for the more substantial stiles. These two members are the strong lines, whose angles pull the eye to the shield-shaped seat with its bold, S-curved edges.

The chair has a pine seat; the rest is riven hickory, which is extremely strong and can be worked into very slender parts without the piece being weakened. The use of hickory makes possible the airy, delicate feeling of the chair, which, even with its solid-wood seat, weighs only 8 lb.

Stickney could finish this piece in no other color than black. To do so would have robbed it of the dramatic starkness that's so important to its effect. A natural finish would have been a disaster.

Like other Windsors, Fancies and ladder-back chairs, this rod-back is constructed with socketed joints. In contrast to joined chairs, like the Hepplewhite on p. 80, which have rectangular mortise-and-tenon joints, socketed chairs are assembled with turned or whittled tenons that fit into drilled holes. Drilling these holes at the correct angles is the most difficult task in making a Windsor, which is why a master chairmaker, called a chair framer, did only the assembly. Often the chair's turned parts were subcontracted to a turner and its other parts made by apprentices or journeymen.

I use spoon bits to drill the sockets, since their round cutting lip and lack of lead make it possible to correct an angle even after the socket has been started. To correct angles, you can set bevel squares and sight along them, as explained for roughing out the Hepplewhite chair's mortises on p. 83.

This chair uses both blind joints and through joints, all of which are glued. Blind joints connect the stretchers to the legs, the spindles to the seat and the crest rail to the stiles. The other joints are through joints, further secured with wedges. After the joints are assembled, the splits for these wedges can be made by driving a chisel into the exposed end of the tenons. This is simpler than cutting the splits with a saw and allows you to easily place them at a right angle to the grain of the part housing the socket.

Most Windsor chairs have bent parts in their back. In this rod-back it is the crest rail that's bent. This rail can be softened, or plasticized, in a steambox or in boiling water in a flat pan. I bend short parts in a press, a form with convex and concave faces, cut from a length of 2x6 stock slightly longer than the part being bent. A bar clamp is sufficient to pull both sides of the press together, bending the crest rail at the same time. If you leave the rail in the press until it dries, it will hold its shape.

When making a Windsor, I always assemble the undercarriage and then attach it to the seat. All four of the legs' through joints are wedged and the wedges shaved flush with the upper surface of the seat. I assemble the back of the chair last.

Shaping the seat

The one thing all Windsor chairs have in common is the solid-wood seat that acts as the anchor for the two separate systems of the chair's undercarriage and back. But not only does this 1¾-in.-thick slab have to hold the chair together, it also has to work with the element of line that is so important in the chair's design.

There is a logic about making the seat, which takes into account its contribution to the chair's design, construction and comfort. Windsor chairmakers found various ways to lighten the appearance of the seat, while leaving it still nearly full thickness at the joints. Their visual legerdemain also included chamfering or shaping the edges of the seat to pull them back out of sight and at the same time create lines to draw the viewer's eye to the seat.

Shaping the seat requires some tools that will be unfamiliar to many woodworkers. Some of these tools are even obsolete, but most are available in antique-tool shops or as reproductions, or they can be made by adapting other tools.

Begin by finding a piece of 1¾-in.-thick pine, 16 in. by 17 in. If need be, glue up two or more pieces, with the grain running along the 17-in. side. Next trace the seat pattern on the blank, making sure that the grain runs front to back. Then remove the waste, using either a bandsaw or a bowsaw. I prefer a 25-in.-long bowsaw (I don't own a bandsaw), and when using it, my speed is competitive with that of a bandsaw.

To shape the edge of the seat, place the blank in a vise. The front vise on my workbench works well for this, but you could also use a leg vise or even clamp the seat to the benchtop upside down. Start shaping the seat at the rear edge, which should be fashioned to a flat bevel rather than a rounded contour. This edge can be worked entirely with a spokeshave, and I find that a wooden-bodied shave produces far superior results to those obtained with a metal-bodied shave. If the shave is sharp, it will leave very gentle tracks, which I don't bother to sand.

The bevel on the two concave sides of the seat is steeper than that across the back. I therefore remove as much of the wood as I can in this section with a drawknife and then finish the surface with a spokeshave. The drawknife is a largely unappreciated tool but is a marvelous device for removing a lot of wood quickly with a surprising amount of control. Since many readers may be unfamiliar with this tool, I should mention that it is used correctly with its bevel up. Always pull it toward you in a smooth, complete stroke, being careful to cut, not hack. If you try to use the drawknife as a two-handled hatchet, it will never give you the results it's capable of. After the initial shaping with the drawknife, I use a small spokeshave to work and clean up the radius of the curve.

The seat's front edge is similar to the rear edge and can be shaped completely with a spokeshave. Since the front edge will need to be blended with the seat's upper surface, it should be shaped after this surface is saddled.

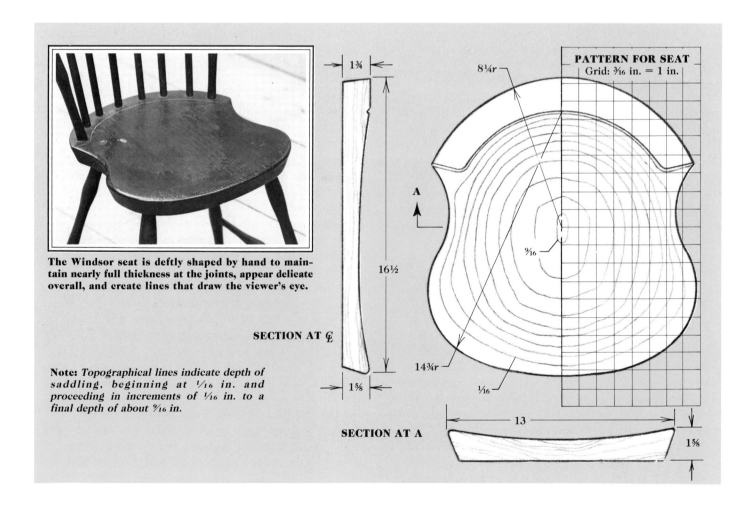

The Windsor seat is deftly shaped by hand to maintain nearly full thickness at the joints, appear delicate overall, and create lines that draw the viewer's eye.

SECTION AT ₵

Note: *Topographical lines indicate depth of saddling, beginning at ¹⁄₁₆ in. and proceeding in increments of ¹⁄₁₆ in. to a final depth of about ⁹⁄₁₆ in.*

1¾

16½

1⅝

8¼r

9⁄16

14¾r

¹⁄₁₆

A

PATTERN FOR SEAT
Grid: ³⁄₁₆ in. = 1 in.

13

1⅝

SECTION AT A

To prepare for saddling the seat, clamp the seat to the workbench, placing the clamps away from the area to be worked. Trace the line that separates the saddling from the flat area where the spindles will be joined to the back of the seat. In the photos, I'm working with white pine, which is very soft. For this reason, and also because this seat is not as deeply saddled as those on the other Windsor chairs shown in this chapter, I can use a scorp with a semicircular blade to remove most of the waste. (Scorps with a flat-bottomed, *U*-shaped blade do not work very well on a concave chair seat.) If you're working with a harder wood or making the saddle deeper, use a gutter adze to remove wood before working with the scorp.

The saddling is a single, shallow curve running from front to back on the seat. I stand in front of the seat to remove the wood from the back of the saddle area. Then, instead of unclamping and shifting the seat to remove the wood at the front, I sit on the bench and work from behind.

When you are satisfied with the shape of the saddling, you'll need to smooth the surface tool marks left by the scorp. I do this in two steps, first working with a small compass plane and then with a travisher. The compass plane I generally use in my own work is an antique, ebony plane. The one I take for giving workshops, however, is one I made by adapting a Japanese compass plane purchased from a tool catalog. It was originally designed to be pulled, Japanese-style, but because I prefer to push a plane, I trimmed the toe considerably. I also removed the

corners to prevent blisters and planed the sides to narrow the stock, or body. The sole was already rounded front to back, but I reshaped it to round it side to side as well. Then I reground the iron to match the sole's new shape.

To use the compass plane, hold it with both hands, being careful not to cover the mouth and make it choke. Use short strokes from the top to the bottom of the saddle. Lift the plane off the wood before it ascends the saddle's opposite slope to prevent tearout on that side. Work from both directions to smooth away the scorp marks.

To clean up the gentle furrows left by the compass plane, I use a travisher, a tool that looks like a bent spokeshave. This tool seems to have been developed and used exclusively by Windsor chairmakers. As far as I know, it is no longer produced and would have to be found on the antique-tool market or made.

Travishers do very fine cleanup, leaving a surface that needs little, if any, sanding. The tool is used like the compass plane. Stroke from the front and rear edges of the seat toward the center, being careful not to catch the tool in the grain in the far side of the saddling. If you don't have a travisher among your tools, you can clean up after the compass plane with fine sandpaper. Once the saddled area is smooth, use a spokeshave to round the upper front edge of the seat.

All that remains is to carve the groove around the saddling that defines the back of the seat. I do this carving freehand with a #11 veiner.

Use a drawknife to shape the concave sides of the seat.

Rough out the saddle with a scorp, working from top to bottom on the hollowed area.

You can stand in front of the seat to shape the back of the saddle and sit on the bench behind it to shape the front.

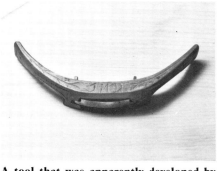

A tool that was apparently developed by Windsor chairmakers, the travisher is used for fine cleanup after the seat has been saddled and initially smoothed with a compass plane.

Round the upper front edge of the seat with a spokeshave.

ROD-BACK WINDSOR CHAIR

Scale: ⅛ in. = 1 in.

Note: *Spindles and stiles are 2⅝ in. on center at crest rail.*

Note: *Holes in seat for stiles and spindles are 2¹⁄₁₆ in. on center.*

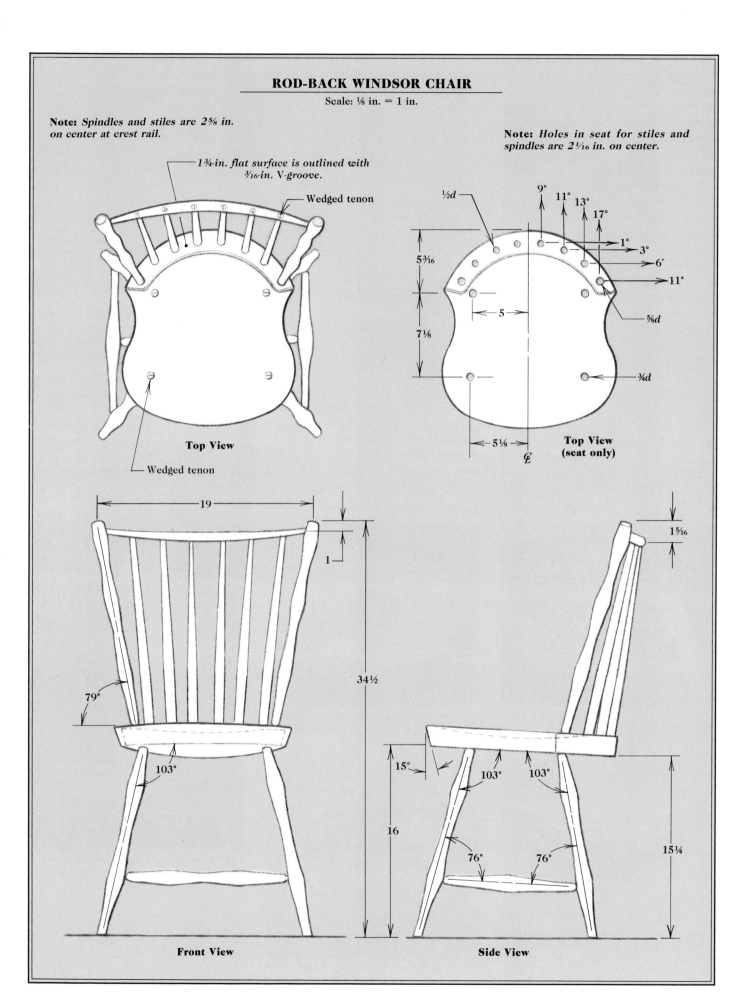

1¾-in. flat surface is outlined with ³⁄₁₆-in. V-groove.

Wedged tenon

Top View

Wedged tenon

½d

9°
11°
13°
17°
1°
3°
6°
11°

5³⁄₁₆

7⅛

5

⅝d

¾d

5⅛

₵L

Top View (seat only)

19

1

34½

79°

103°

16

1⁵⁄₁₆

15°

103°   103°

76°   76°

15¼

Front View

Side View

UPPER AND LOWER PARTS
Scale: ⅜ in. = 1 in.

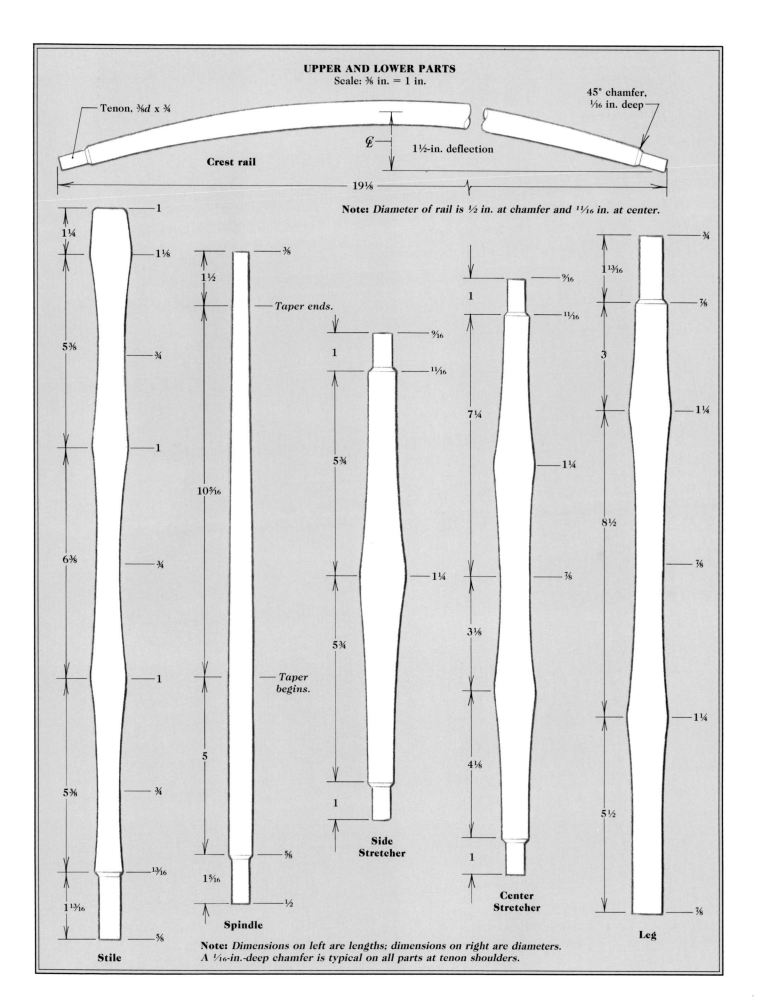

Tenon, ⅜d x ¾

Crest rail

45° chamfer, 1/16 in. deep

₵

1½-in. deflection

19⅛

Note: *Diameter of rail is ½ in. at chamfer and 11/16 in. at center.*

1

1¼

1⅛

5⅜

1

6⅜

¾

5⅜

¾

1

13/16

1 13/16

⅝

Stile

⅜

1½

Taper ends.

¾

1

10 5/16

1

Taper begins.

5

¾

1 5/16

⅝

½

Spindle

9/16

1

11/16

5¾

1¼

5¾

1

Side Stretcher

9/16

1

11/16

7¼

1¼

⅞

3⅛

4⅛

1

Center Stretcher

¾

1 13/16

⅞

3

1¼

8½

⅞

5½

1¼

⅞

Leg

Note: *Dimensions on left are lengths; dimensions on right are diameters.*
A 1/16-in.-deep chamfer is typical on all parts at tenon shoulders.

This informal pine display shelf has held mementoes and cherished objects for its various owners for almost two centuries.
(Project: Stop dadoes, p. 128.)

Display Shelf

Chapter 14

very household has a number of small objects that are cherished by their owners. Unfortunately, though, when these articles are displayed on various surfaces in a room, they are often lost among the larger furnishings.

The shelf shown here was made during the Federal period specifically to show off someone's small possessions, and it can be either hung on a wall or stood on a flat surface. My wife and I purchased it to house objects that are important to us, and I have included it in this book because you might want to make one for the special decorative belongings in your own home.

I remember when the piece was brought to me by an antique dealer. I held it up, studying the lobes on the sides of the shelf, which seem to droop, and thought, "It looks like it was placed too near the fire and began to melt." When I set the shelf on a table and stood back to examine it from the perspective the maker had intended, however, I realized that he was more sophisticated than I had first imagined, and so was his shelf.

From a distance, the lobes seem to cascade lightheartedly, a design that offered the maker an easy and natural way to establish the graduating shelves. The upward sweep at the top of each lobe makes the lobe appear to be smiling, and each time I study this piece, I find myself smiling too.

When the shelf is hanging on a wall, my eye does not go into free-fall after traveling to the bottom lobe. The lobe acts as a logical termination. Yet when the piece is placed on a table or bureau, the cut-out area below this projection creates the effect of feet by allowing light to pass underneath. This effect suggests that the shelf was probably meant to be stood on a flat surface rather than hung on a wall.

When I purchased this piece, it was painted black and had been crudely striped with gold radiator paint. Holding the shelf so that light could pass obliquely over it, I could

see decorative painting underneath the outer layer. I then decided to remove the black and gold paint, yet save the original surface. This I did by applying paint stripper with an artists' brush, one square inch at a time. The outer coat of paint immediately shriveled and lifted, and I could wipe it away without disturbing the original finish.

It took an entire Saturday morning, but the shelf survived, looking just as it must have before the black was applied—wear spots and all. Careful stripping had revealed a hand-painted blue peony with a yellow center on each of the four small upper lobes, and red-and-white carnations on the four lower lobes. A pair of green vines with shaded green leaves connects the four flowers on each end of the piece, and another green tendril undulates along the front edge of the top shelf. I also discovered that the painted decoration had been applied over a coat of orange shellac, which has darkened to a deep brown. The floral design is so integral to the shelf, the piece would appear naked in just natural wood. In the hope that you will want to add the flower-and-vine decoration when you make the display shelf, I have included the pattern.

The original shelf is made of pine. You could also use poplar, tulipwood, birch or soft maple, depending on what you have on hand. None of these woods has a pronounced figure, an important consideration since the wood is visible beneath the shellac finish and you don't want its figure to compete with the hand-painted foliage. On the other hand, if you are not going to embellish the piece, you might want to use a wood with an interesting figure—perhaps mahogany, walnut, cherry or curly maple.

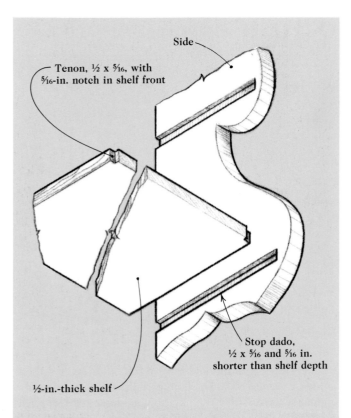

Tenon, ½ x ⁵⁄₁₆, with ⁵⁄₁₆-in. notch in shelf front

Side

Stop dado, ½ x ⁵⁄₁₆ and ⁵⁄₁₆ in. shorter than shelf depth

½-in.-thick shelf

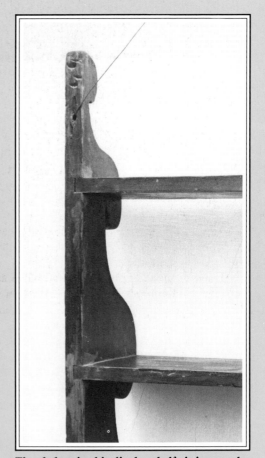

The shelves in this display shelf sit in stop dadoes cut into the sides and should fit snugly to prevent racking.

You can probably make this shelf in an afternoon. If the original is not sizable enough for your needs, you can enlarge it. I don't think the design would work on a smaller scale, however. Begin by cutting the sides out of ¾-in. stock with a coping saw or a bandsaw. Since the edges of the curves are very noticeable, clean them up with a spokeshave and chisel, then sand them lightly with 100- and 220-grit paper, keeping the edges sharp and well defined.

The shelves sit in stop dadoes cut in the sides. This construction, explained below, makes the whole piece sufficiently rigid, since the only load the shelves have to bear is vertical. If you are planning to hang the shelf, bore and countersink a screw hole in each side just below the top lobe.

Prepare the surface for painting by applying two coats of orange shellac, rubbing between coats with 000 steel wool. Don't stain the wood before sealing it; this would accentuate the figure of the wood and therefore detract from the floral design.

If you lack confidence in your ability to do the painted decoration but want to learn how, consult the books in the bibliography on decorative techniques, or take a continuing-education course in decorative painting. Even if you decide not to do the painting yourself, the instructor of such a course might agree to do it for you for a reasonable fee, or might suggest someone who would. I would recommend that the artist not stray far from the original pattern, but there is room for self-expression. The artist who did my shelf probably could not have painted it exactly the same way a second time.

Stop dadoes

Each shelf is housed in a ½-in.-wide by ⁵⁄₁₆-in.-deep stop dado cut in the sides. These dadoes are called stop dadoes because they do not run the complete depth of the sides. Therefore you cannot use a dado plane to make these joints. If you have chosen a soft, even-grained wood like pine, however, the dadoes can be cut with a mat knife and cleaned out with a chisel. Clamp one side of the display shelf to the benchtop with the inside surface facing up. Each shelf is to be square to and flush with the back edge of the side, so to lay out each dado, start at the back edge and mark two parallel lines with a pencil, ½ in. apart and as long as the depth of the shelf. Mark the blind, or stop, end of the dado ⁵⁄₁₆ in. short of the full shelf depth. (You'll need to cut a corresponding ⁵⁄₁₆-in.-deep notch in the front corners of the shelf itself to make the tenons that slide into the stop dadoes.)

Lay a square along each of the parallel lines and score the wood with a mat knife. (Be sure to put in a new blade, as a dull one won't make a clean cut across the grain.) You'll need to make several passes to cut deep enough to prevent the dado edges from tearing while the waste is being removed. Next score the stop end of the dado. Be careful—you'll be cutting along the grain and it is easy to slip and cut farther than you'd like. It's also possible to break off the end of the lobe across this section of short grain, so don't exert too much pressure here.

Use a long, ½-in.-wide firmer chisel to pare the waste out of the dado. With a long chisel you'll be able to get down into the corners where the dado stops and remove all slivers that might interfere with the fit of the shelf. Use the chisel with the bevel up—riding on its flat, bottom face, the tool will leave a smooth, uniform bottom on the dado, whereas if used bevel-down it may produce an uneven surface.

Test-fit each shelf in its dado. It should be tight, or the joint will not be rigid enough to prevent the piece from racking out of square. If the fit is too snug, though, pare fine shavings off the shoulders of the dado, testing after each cut.

When all is assembled, secure the shelves in their dadoes with *T*-headed brads, using two evenly spaced brads per lobe for the upper two shelves and three brads per lobe on the bottom shelf. To allow for seasonal movement of the wood, do not glue the shelves in place, or the sides may eventually crack. In any event, there's no point in trying to glue end grain to long grain—you'll never get a strong glue joint.

Make several passes with a sharp mat knife along the blade of a square to cut the two parallel lines for each dado. Then score the stop ends.

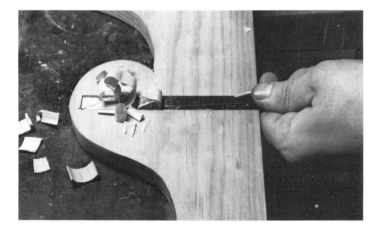

Clear the waste out of the dado with a long firmer chisel, used bevel side up (left). Be sure to remove all slivers from the inside corners so the shelf will fit properly (above).

DISPLAY SHELF
Scale: ³⁄₁₆ in. = 1 in.

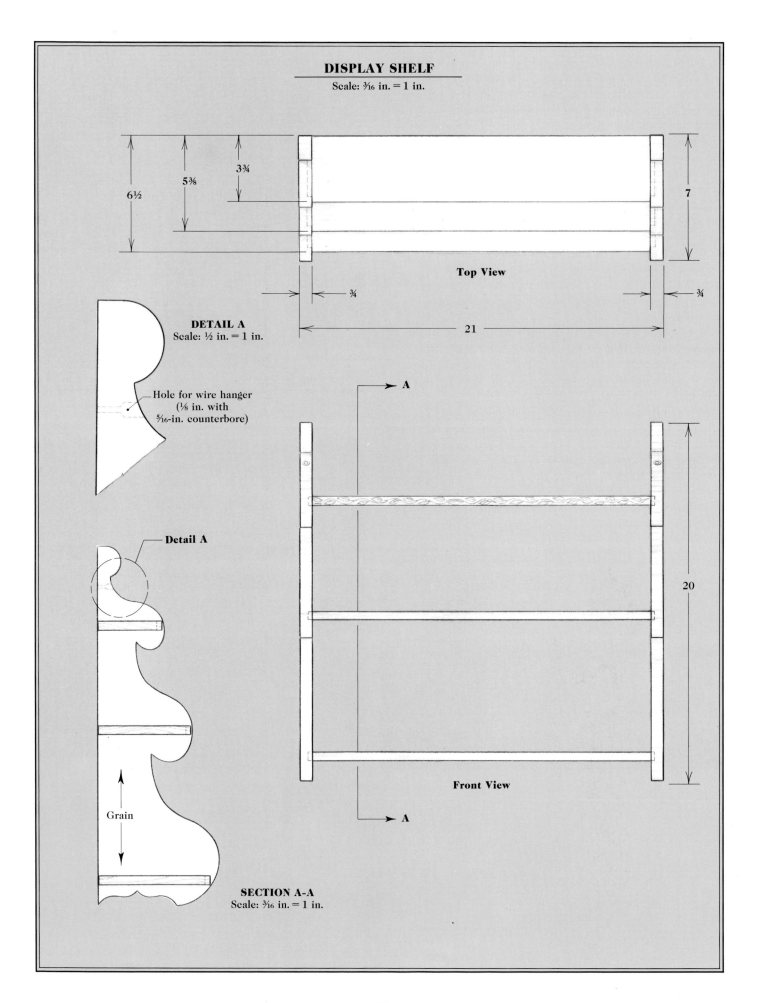

3¾

5⅜

6½

7

Top View

¾

¾

21

DETAIL A
Scale: ½ in. = 1 in.

Hole for wire hanger
(⅛ in. with
⁵⁄₁₆-in. counterbore)

A

Detail A

20

Front View

Grain

A

SECTION A-A
Scale: ³⁄₁₆ in. = 1 in.

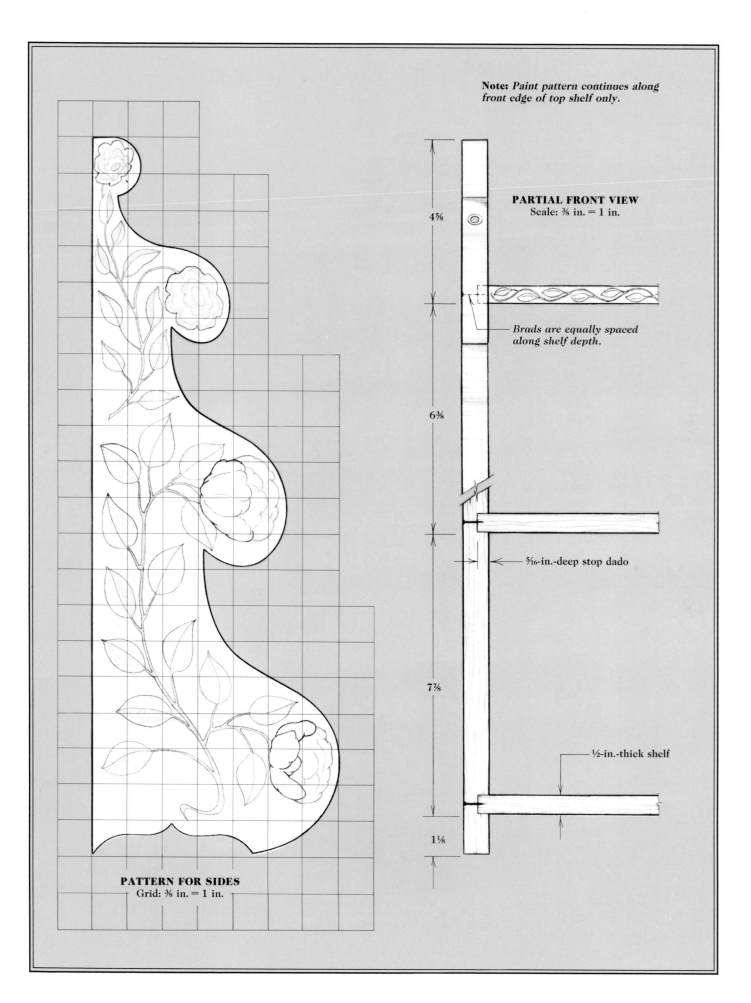

Note: *Paint pattern continues along front edge of top shelf only.*

PARTIAL FRONT VIEW
Scale: ⅜ in. = 1 in.

Brads are equally spaced along shelf depth.

4⅝

6⅜

7⅞

1⅛

← ⁵⁄₁₆-in.-deep stop dado

½-in.-thick shelf

PATTERN FOR SIDES
Grid: ⅜ in. = 1 in.

This informal oak box stored the candles that would illuminate a
Federal-period home at night. (Project: Sliding lid, p. 134.)

Candle Box

Chapter 15

One of the things I've discovered while living in a Federal-period house is that both the house and the furniture take on another character by candlelight. Period cabinetmakers and joiners knew that after sundown their work would be seen under these conditions, and designed and built with this in mind. I derive a great deal of pleasure from watching shadows flicker in deep moldings, across textured surfaces and behind curved outlines.

To experience this enjoyment, Carol and I burn a lot of candles, and that is why we own this box, created specifically to store them. Candles are laid inside the box lengthwise, the lid closed and the box hung up. When a fresh candle is needed, the lid can be slid upward and the candle drawn out. This is the only time we interact with this piece; the rest of the time it's just another interesting object. We hang our candle box in the kitchen on one of the cased posts typically found in a Federal braced-frame house. Visitors do not sit in our kitchen long before they reach up to touch the box and say, "That's a nice box. What's it for?"

The original box is made of riven oak, meaning that the stock was split from the log rather than sawn. This suggests that the box might be English or Continental, since the use of riven oak was more common in Europe than in America. The box could also be American, however, made by an immigrant who retained old-world preferences. (The back of the box is branded "L.D.," which could be the initials of the maker, an owner, or just someone with a hot branding iron.) By riving the wood, the maker obtained quartered boards, which are dimensionally more stable than flat-sawn boards. With oak, this grain orientation also produces a pronounced fleck on the wood's surface.

This box can be completed in an afternoon and made of any wood you choose. The lid and backboard are ⅜ in. thick, while the sides, top and bottom are all ½ in. thick.

The box is dovetailed together, and since the direction of pull is downward, the tails are cut on the sides and the pins cut on the top and bottom. The sides and bottom are wider than the top so that the lid can slide unencumbered in its grooves; the full width of the bottom prevents it from falling out.

The rear edge of the top is recessed ⅜ in., the thickness of the backboard. This allows the backboard to be inset. The backboard rests on the bottom of the box and is held in place with *T*-headed brads. These are driven through the rear edges of the sides into the backboard, and through its rear upper edge into the top.

The shape of the top of the backboard is familiar to anyone who has ever spent time in old cemeteries, as it is common on Federal-period gravestones. It was also a popular Georgian/Federal molding profile called an astragal and cove, and was widely used on chair rails and the edges of interior window sills and stair treads.

The profile of the top of the backboard easily lends itself to self-expression, should you decide not to use the astragal and cove. I recommend the survey books in the bibliography for ideas for alternative molding profiles.

The sliding lid is a simple raised panel. All four edges are beveled on the front surface. The bevels on the sides of the lid allow it to slide easily in the grooves; the top and bottom edges are beveled for visual effect. A semicircular fingerhold is cut near the upper edge.

The original box appears to have been finished with oil and wax, which turned it a pleasant deep brown. How you finish your box should be a function of the wood used. Mahogany, walnut and other heavily figured woods demand clear finishes. Pine, bass, poplar or tulipwood can be painted, false-grained or even stenciled. You might decorate the box with your own designs or with country or folk motifs. The possibilities for painted decoration are infinite, and I would recommend for reference the books on decorating techniques listed in the bibliography.

Adjust the plow plane to make a ¼-in.-wide groove, ¼ in. deep and ³⁄₁₆ in. from the inside front edges of the candle-box sides. In an antique American set of graduated irons, the No. 2 iron is ¼ in. wide.

Lay out the bevels on the front and edges of the panel using a marking gauge (center). Bevel the ends of the panel first (bottom). To prevent chipping, clamp a waste block against the corner you are planing toward. Use a smoothing plane to remove most of the wood and finish with a block plane on the end grain.

Sliding lid

Before making the lid, you should cut the pieces for the box it will fit into and groove the sides to take the sliding panel. Since the two sides, the bottom and the top of the candle box are the same thickness, they can all be cut from the same board. Cut the bottom, but before cutting the sides to length, run a groove ¼ in. wide by ¼ in. deep, ³⁄₁₆ in. from the inside front edge of the board to take the lid. I used an adjustable plow plane, made of boxwood and produced in a Connecticut tool factory about the time of the Civil War. New plow planes, however, are still available through many tool catalogs in this country.

Modern planes have all the same features as mine, except that my set of irons is graduated in sixteenths of an inch, while those made in Europe and Japan are often graduated in millimeters. A graduated set of irons allows the user to select any of eight possible widths. The plow plane has a fence attached to the body by two threaded arms. The distance between the fence and the sole of the plane is adjusted with four locking nuts. Depth of cut is set by turning a thumbscrew in the top of the body, which advances or retracts the adjustable sole located in front of the cutter. These three features allow the user to make grooves of various widths and depths, at various distances from the edge of the board. On this candle box, the ¼-in.-wide by ¼-in.-deep grooves require the No. 2 iron.

Set the plane and grip the stock lengthwise between the benchdogs, inside face up. Set the edge of the plane's fence on the edge of the board. As you push the plow, hold the fence tightly against the work—do not let it wander, or the groove will not be straight. Each pass will take out a shaving that looks like a corkscrew curl. When the groove is the desired depth, the adjustable sole will prevent the plane from cutting any deeper.

To make the sliding lid, you will need a marking gauge, a smoothing plane and a block plane. Begin by squaring a 5½-in. by 13⅝-in. board. Set the marking gauge to ¹¹⁄₁₆ in. and run a line parallel to all four edges on the outside face of the board. Reset the marking gauge to ³⁄₁₆ in. and run another line on all four edges. These two lines mark the highest and lowest points of the bevels. You need to be able to see the lines, but be sure that you make them as light as possible. (The lines in the photos were darkened so they would be visible.) If they're too deep, you won't be able to plane them away and still maintain the correct bevel on the edges of the board.

Start working the bevel across the end grain at the top or bottom of the panel. Clamp the lid between the benchdogs so that one end of the board overhangs the bench. To avoid chipping the corner, make sure there is a strip of waste on the far side, flush with the surface and the end of the panel, as shown at left. You should plane the two ends before planing the sides. If you plane the bevel on the sides first, the waste block will protect only the corner and cannot prevent tearout along the miter. Remove most of the wood with the smoothing plane. When the bevel gets close to the lines on the surface and end, switch to the block plane; the low angle of its iron will ensure a cleaner cut on the end grain.

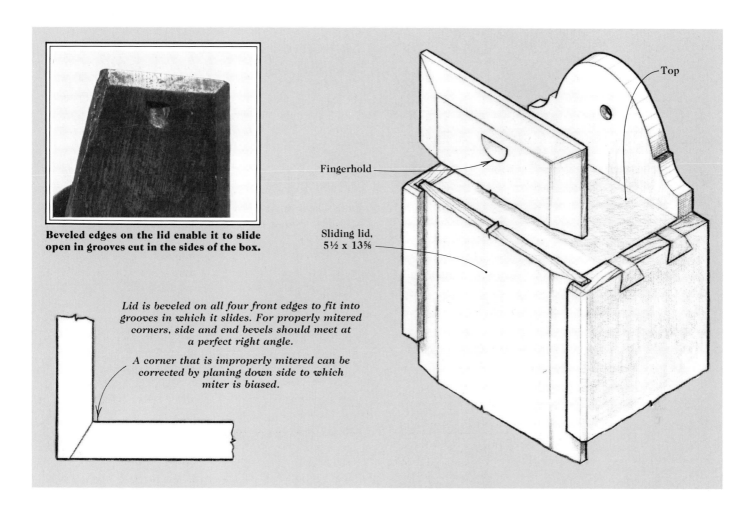

Beveled edges on the lid enable it to slide
open in grooves cut in the sides of the box.

*Lid is beveled on all four front edges to fit into
grooves in which it slides. For properly mitered
corners, side and end bevels should meet at
a perfect right angle.*

*A corner that is improperly mitered can be
corrected by planing down side to which
miter is biased.*

Fingerhold

Top

Sliding lid,
5½ x 13⅝

When the bevel meets both scribed lines at each end,
set the board along its length between the dogs and create
the bevel on each side edge of the lid. This can be done
completely with the smoothing plane since you'll be
working on edge grain. The miters at the two corners will
develop as you complete each side bevel. It's imperative
that the miters work out correctly because they are very
visible. If a miter does not come out perfectly, adjust it by
planing more wood from the side to which the miter is
biased, or too fully cut.

Test the lid in the grooves. It should slide easily. If it
doesn't, look to see where it's binding. If the lid is binding
in the bottom of a groove, the panel may be too wide. You
can correct this by planing a bit from each edge to slightly
reduce the panel's width. If the beveled surface is binding,
the bevel angle may be too steep and can be decreased
with a block plane. Either of these adjustments might also
mean correcting the miters so that they once again meet
at the corners.

Once you're satisfied that the lid fits properly, make the
fingerhold in the upper end of the panel. With a ⅞-in.
chisel, score a line about 1 in. below and parallel to the
bevel on the top edge of the lid and centered across its
width. Hold the chisel perfectly vertical, with the chisel
bevel facing the bottom of the panel, and strike the handle
sharply with a mallet to make a 3/16-in.-deep line ⅞ in.
long. Sketch a semicircle under this line and excavate a
sloping fingerhold with a ¾-in. gouge.

Use a ¾-in. gouge to excavate a semicircular fingerhold that
slopes downward to meet a 3/16-in.-deep chiseled line.

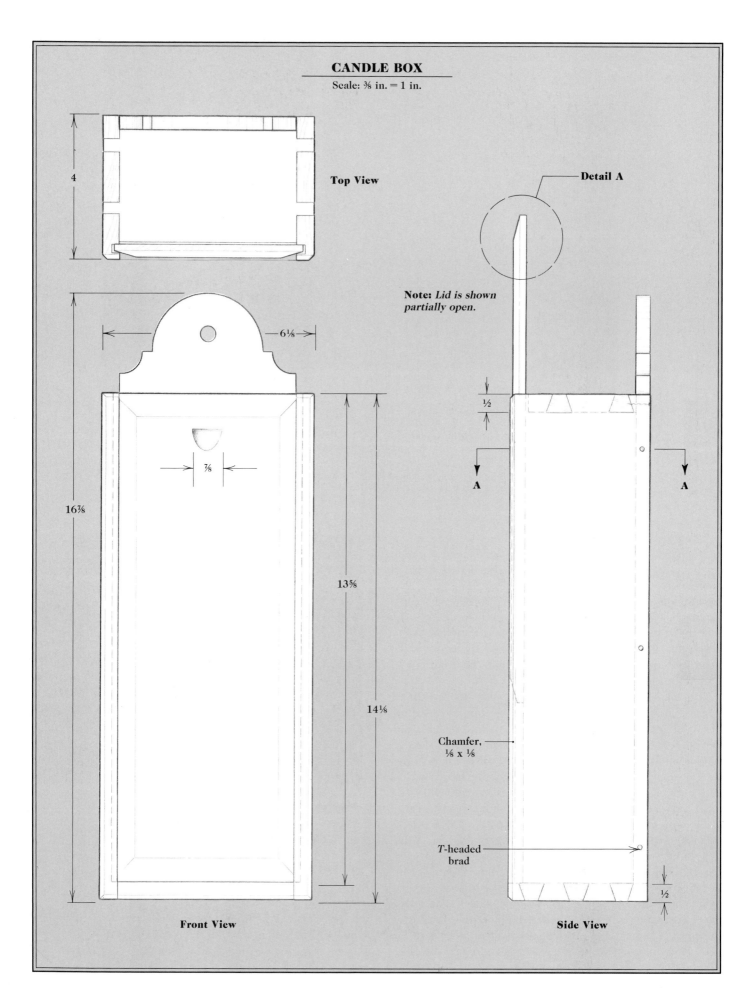

CANDLE BOX

Scale: ⅜ in. = 1 in.

Top View

Detail A

Note: *Lid is shown partially open.*

4

6⅛

⅞

16⅞

13⅝

14⅛

½

A

A

Chamfer,
⅛ x ⅛

T-headed
brad

½

Front View

Side View

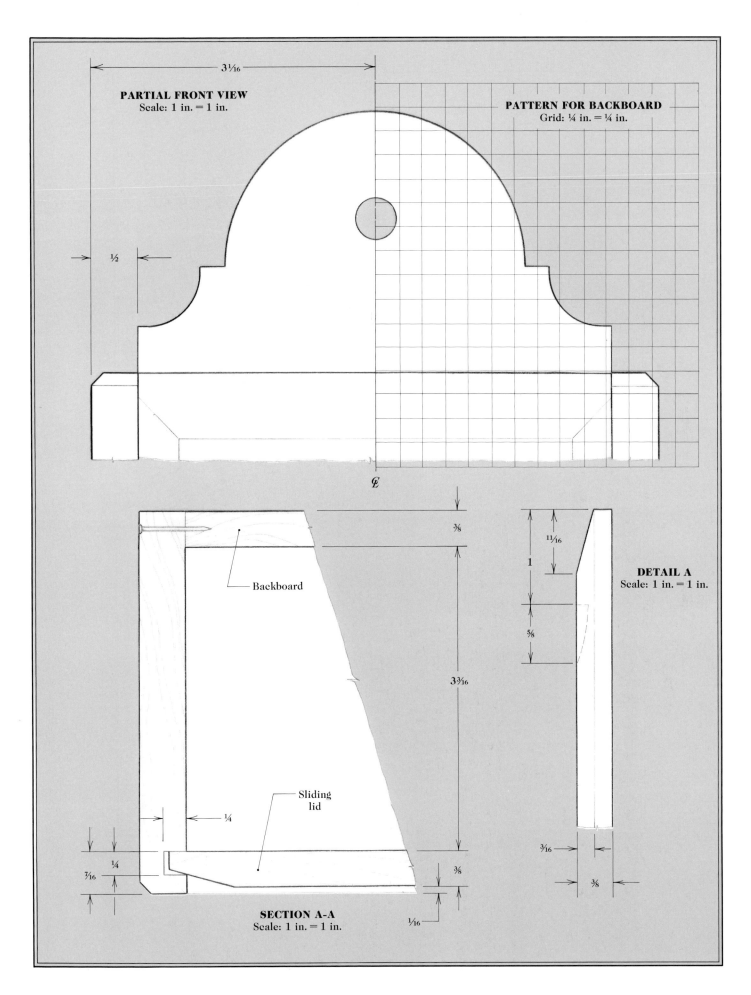

PARTIAL FRONT VIEW
Scale: 1 in. = 1 in.

3¹⁄₁₆

½

PATTERN FOR BACKBOARD
Grid: ¼ in. = ¼ in.

₵

Backboard

Sliding
lid

¼

¼

⁷⁄₁₆

SECTION A-A
Scale: 1 in. = 1 in.

³⁄₈

3³⁄₁₆

³⁄₈

¹⁄₁₆

DETAIL A
Scale: 1 in. = 1 in.

¹¹⁄₁₆

1

⁵⁄₈

³⁄₁₆

³⁄₈

This stand-up desk, which its maker would have called a desk on frame, was designed for use in a commercial establishment. (Project: Simulated four-way miter joints, p. 141.)

Desk on Frame

Chapter 16

Of all the furniture illustrated in this book, only Windsor chairs are more widely recognized than this piece. It is generally referred to as a schoolmaster's desk, but this term is really a misnomer. The maker would have called it a desk on frame. Originally designed for use in a commercial establishment, this stand-up desk reflects the fact that it is more efficient to handle many business affairs while standing rather than scouting up a chair and a free writing surface for every brief clerical task. With divided compartments and a deep well to provide storage for account books and papers, the desk's interior space was perfectly designed for the piece's function.

I originally purchased this desk for use in my shop at Strawbery Banke, a house museum in Portsmouth, where my business was located for four years. When I left Strawbery Banke, my wife commandeered the piece for her kitchen and uses it while attending to the many routine clerical tasks necessary to managing a household. The divided cubbyholes in the back of the well neatly house paperwork and writing paraphernalia, while the well itself holds larger items. It's also a handy spot for stashing normal household clutter when we are surprised by unexpected visitors.

This desk on frame is quite large, measuring 50¾ in. high and just over 39¼ in. wide. Since we live in a big house, we have the space that this piece requires. If your space is limited and you want to make this desk, you may want to scale down your copy. If you do, I recommend decreasing the width rather than the depth and height. Making the desk narrower may mean eliminating one of the interior compartments.

On the original desk, both pine and maple were used as primary woods, reflecting the piece's utilitarian purpose. Like many informal Federal-period pieces, this desk was painted. The heavy-bodied, light mustard-yellow paint that the maker selected served, among other functions, to unify the desk's various woods. Yet the paint's function was not only aesthetic; this finish was also the only one available in the period that was able to stand up to hard use. Since your desk will probably not be subjected to the extensive wear of the original, a clear finish could be used if you like, which also means that the piece could be made of a single species of wood.

Maple was used for the desk's base, or frame, since that part of the piece would be subjected to the most wear. Pine was used for all the other parts. Cherry, birch, maple or even walnut would be appropriate if you want to use only one primary wood for the piece. If you want to work with two primary woods, pine, poplar or tulipwood would be equally acceptable for the desk itself, but I would not recommend these woods for the frame, as they are not as strong as the base requires. I would also avoid oak and ash, since their grain is too coarse for a writing surface, and mahogany is too formal for such a simple piece. Before selecting a wood, think about how you want to finish the desk and where you want to place it. The upper section has broad surfaces that would be ideal for false graining and perhaps some ornamental striping.

The construction of the base is straightforward. The four simple, square legs are held together by a skirt and a box stretcher, whose joints are standard mortise-and-tenons, which are further secured with pins. Over the years these pins have raised above the surface of the legs, but I wouldn't think of shaving them flush. They are part of the desk's character and act as points of interest on the surface much as brass hardware, inlay or carving would. Although the maker certainly didn't intend for the pins to show in this way, they serve as a reminder that wood furniture is an organic, changing entity.

The only joint that is not mortise-and-tenoned occurs over the large, lower drawer. This piece of the skirt is fitted into a lap joint cut into the top of both front legs and held in place by nails driven through it into the end grain of the legs. This method of construction is sufficiently sturdy here, since the base's function is simply to bear the weight of the desk box.

A bead molding is run on the bottom edge of the skirt, and the same shape is repeated on the top edges of the box stretcher. These are simple but necessary details. Without some ornament, the desk could easily read as a simple, clunky box.

The drawer in the base is designed differently from the other drawers shown in this book. It does not sit flush with the front of the base, nor is it beaded like the drawers on the secretary (p. 58) or those on the chest of drawers (p. 170). Instead, this drawer projects slightly over the frame, and the molding used on the edges of the drawer front is called a thumbnail (look at the thumbnail molding in the drawing on p. 145 and you'll understand its name). This molding detail is unusual on Federal furniture and is a survival feature dating from the previous period.

If you choose to make this desk, a bead molding could easily be used on the drawer front without upsetting its design. But if you elect to copy the thumbnail molding on the original, run the rabbet around the back, top and side edges of the drawer front first. This rabbet creates a thin lip, on the outer edge of which the molding is cut. With this exception, the drawer is constructed in traditional fashion: the back of the drawer is joined to the sides with through dovetails, the sides are joined to the front with half-blind dovetails, and the bottom slides into grooves cut in the sides. The drawer runners are nailed to the inside of the skirt.

The desk box is of ⅞-in.-thick pine. If you make your desk out of hardwood, you may want to thickness-plane your stock to ¾ in. If you scale down your desk and make the box of hardwood, you can plane it as thin as ⅝ in.

The carcase of the desk box is joined with through dovetails. After making the joints and test-fitting them, disassemble the four sides and mark the dadoes for the horizontal tier of the divided compartments. There is no reason you have to use the same layout as that on the original. Make these compartments as small or as large as you like. You can cut the dadoes with a router or, if you're working with a softwood, with a mat knife and chisel, as explained in the chapter on the display shelf (p. 126).

The original desk uses a single ½-in.-thick horizontal board and ¼-in.-thick vertical dividers to create the two tiers of compartments. If you're using hardwood for these parts, they can be made even thinner. The horizontal piece has V-shaped grooves cut into it, top and bottom, and the corresponding edge on the vertical divider is beveled on both sides, duplicating the V shape. When both the upper and lower dividers are in place, the joints appear to be mitered. The visual effect of this construction is far more successful than square-sided dadoes would be, and a description of how to make these simulated four-way miter joints is provided on the facing page.

Before you begin making the top of the desk, note that both the fixed part of the top and the hinged lid slightly overhang the carcase and that their overhanging edges are rounded. Although this molded edge can be produced in a number of ways, I would use a nosing plane. If you don't have this particular plane, the rounding on this piece can be done with a bench plane or a router. The edge of the fixed top to which the lid is hinged is cut at a 98° angle and can be beveled either with a plane or by tilting the blade of a tablesaw.

Once the carcase of the desk box is completed and the top and bottom cut to shape, the bottom is simply nailed to the carcase. (The stop dadoes, which are cut into the bottom to hold the lower dividers in place, should, of course, be fitted before the bottom is nailed on.) Ordinarily one would not nail the bottom onto a box, as the load would pull the nails loose. Nailing works here, however, because the bottom of the box actually sits on top of the lower frame's skirt, which bears the weight of the desk. The fixed part of the top is also nailed in place, since it too has no load to bear.

Next make the desk's small interior drawers and lid. The drawers are just small versions of the other drawers shown in this book, with the corners dovetailed and the bottom slid into grooves cut in the drawer sides. The lid has three edges that are rounded; the fourth is cut at a 98° angle and butts against the fixed top.

There are two wide battens attached to the underside of the lid, whose purpose is to prevent the wide lid from warping. Both are beaded on their long edges and chamfered across their width. They are attached with wrought clench nails on the original desk but could just as easily be secured with screws.

If I were making this desk, I would probably also add a thin strip of wood to the outside bottom edge of the lid to keep papers and pencils from sliding off. This strip could simply be tacked in place with brads, or a groove could be routed and the strip glued in place.

On the original desk, the lid is hinged to the top with hand-wrought table-leaf hinges, which are attached with wrought clench nails. The cabinetmaker undoubtedly had these hinges on hand and thought them adequate for such a utilitarian piece. Other hinges, like butt hinges for example, could be used instead. If you don't want the hinges to lay flat like the originals, mount them so that their leaves are hidden by the joint of the lid and top. The knuckles will protrude, but not enough to be a problem. Foliated brass hinges could also be used and would be both decorative and functional.

The last step in completing the desk's construction is making the cove molding that forms a lip on the top of the frame and holds the desk box in place. It's useful to wait until both parts of the desk are finished before applying this molding, so that it can be fitted to the carcase and accommodate any variations from the plans in the piece's final dimensions. The molding is mitered at the corners and held in place with T-headed finish nails. The molding profile is simple and appropriate for such a plain piece of furniture.

Before finishing the piece, give some thought to its hardware. This desk has wooden pulls on the front drawer, but these are not original. They probably replaced brass mushroom knobs similar in shape but larger than those on the small interior drawers. This desk is so generic in design that almost any type of Federal reproduction hardware would be appropriate. Wooden pulls like those on this desk could, of course, be made, but they would look best if the entire piece were painted or false-grained in a simple pattern. If you have used a hardwood such as walnut or cherry for the desk, I would recommend brass hardware. A simple version of the Chippendale bat's-wing drawer pulls would be in keeping with the thumbnail molding on the drawer. Alternatively, Hepplewhite oval pulls or Sheraton rosettes would do well, too. If you decide to use brass pulls, place escutcheons on both the lower drawer and the desk even if you don't fit the piece with locks. All of the hardware mentioned above can be obtained from reproduction-hardware suppliers listed in the appendices at the back of the book.

Simulated four-way miter joints

The small compartments inside this desk are commonly called pigeonholes, probably because they resemble the coops in which racing pigeons are raised. The desk's pigeonholes are handy because they allow various papers to be stored separately, and as a result they are still a common feature on modern desks.

Even if you change the number and size of the pigeonholes when making this desk, you will still want to use the same construction techniques used on the original piece. The ends of the pigeonhole dividers that are fitted into the top, bottom and sides of the desk carcase are housed in stop dadoes, a joint that is neat and well concealed. If you are working with hand tools, I would cut these stop dadoes in the way shown in the project section of the display-shelf chapter (p. 128). Where the vertical pigeonhole dividers intersect the horizontal shelf, however, the joint is visible, and the maker therefore used something more interesting to look at than a dado: a simulated four-way miter.

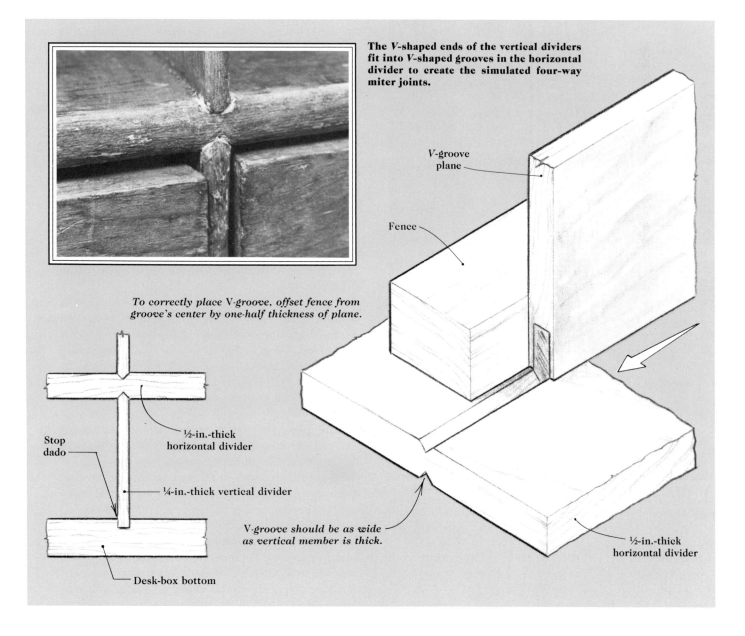

The *V*-shaped ends of the vertical dividers fit into *V*-shaped grooves in the horizontal divider to create the simulated four-way miter joints.

V-groove plane

Fence

To correctly place V-groove, offset fence from groove's center by one-half thickness of plane.

Stop dado

½-in.-thick horizontal divider

¼-in.-thick vertical divider

V-groove should be as wide as vertical member is thick.

Desk-box bottom

½-in.-thick horizontal divider

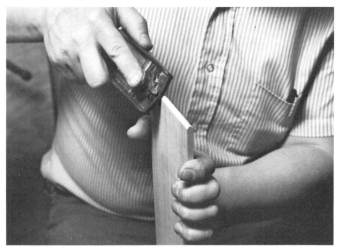

Use a low-angle block plane to shape one end of each vertical divider into a 90° *V*.

A special *V*-groove plane (center) is needed to cut the grooves in the horizontal divider. Before cutting the *V*-groove, set up a fence, positioned to allow for the groove's full width, and place a piece of scrap behind the divider to prevent tearout (bottom).

A real four-way miter joint is used to connect the applied muntins on the doors of the secretary (p. 58). On that piece, each muntin piece terminates on one end in a 90° *V* shape, and at two points in the center of each door four muntins intersect, creating four-way miters. This joint produces a visual continuity of the muntins' narrow moldings, which would be impossible with a butt joint. In the pigeonholes on this desk, the vertical and horizontal dividers are also very narrow but, unlike the secretary's muntins, are very deep. As a result, these joints need to be made differently.

While the secretary's four-way miter joints are made of muntins that all end in the same shape, the desk's joints are composed of two separate contours: *V*-shaped ends on the vertical dividers and *V*-shaped grooves on the long, horizontal divider. To begin this joint, locate the center of the bottom edge of the vertical divider and mark it. With a miter square, lay out the 90° *V*. A low-angle block plane, once called a miter plane, is ideal for fashioning the *V*-shaped ends of the vertical dividers. Do so on all of the vertical dividers, both above and below the horizontal divider. Remember to shape only one end of the verticals; the other fits into a stop dado and is left square. I would suggest waiting until after the miters have been fit to cut the vertical dividers to final length. This will ensure a tight fit at the top.

To make the grooves in the horizontal divider, another specialty plane called a *V*-groove plane is required. Simple *V*-groove planes like the one I'm using in the photos at left are commonly available from most old-tool dealers. Before cutting the *V*-grooves, set up a fence for the plane using a straight-edged piece of scrap and a clamp. The fence should be at least 1 in. thick to provide a good bearing surface for the flat side of the plane. Also, the fence should not be placed tightly against the mark, because the center of the *V* is offset from the side of the plane. Hold the point of the plane's sole on the centerline and place the fence tightly against the plane before clamping it in place.

It is also necessary to clamp a strip of waste behind the far edge of the work so that any tearout will occur in the waste, not on the edge of the divider. If your plane has a depth stop, it can be preset to stop the cutting action. If it doesn't have this device, you'll have to periodically test the fit with the *V*-shaped end of the vertical divider. When you're satisfied with the fit of the divider, the *V*-groove is done.

Once one side of the horizontal divider has been grooved, turn the divider over and make the *V*-grooves on the opposite side. For the four-way miter to work visually, the *V*-grooves on both sides must line up. Be careful not to overcut the grooves and weaken the horizontal piece or cut it in two.

The horizontal divider is inserted into its stop dado while the dovetailed sides of the desk carcase are being assembled. The lower vertical dividers are set in when the bottom of the desk box is attached, and the upper verticals are put in place before the top is nailed on.

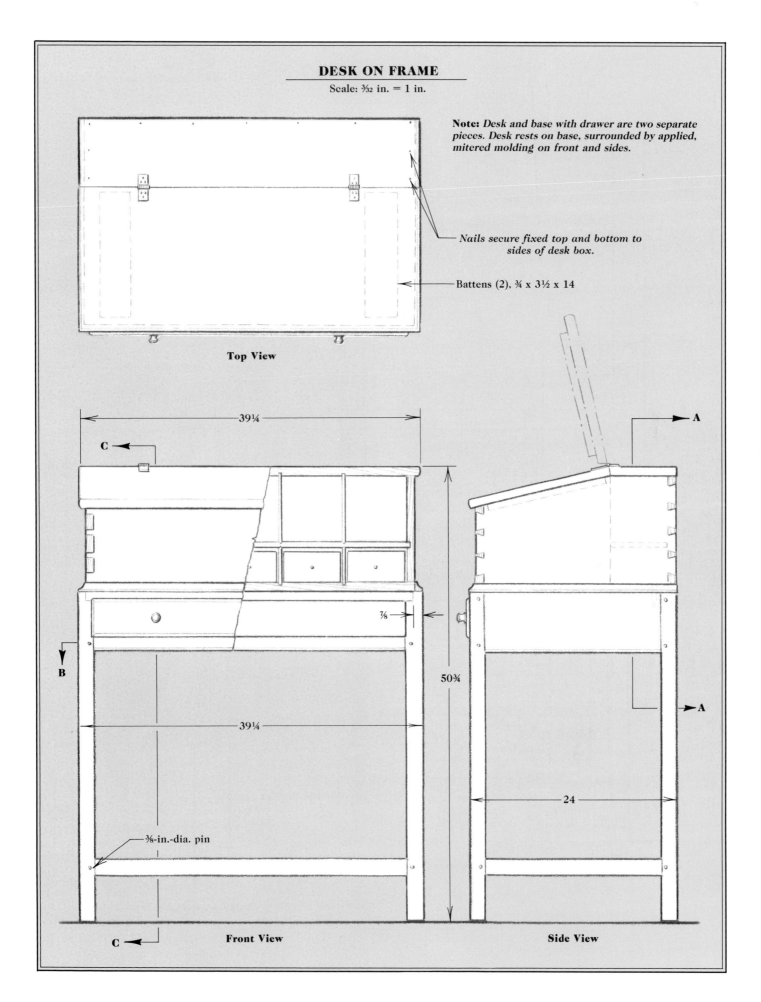

DESK ON FRAME
Scale: $^3/_{32}$ in. = 1 in.

Note: *Desk and base with drawer are two separate pieces. Desk rests on base, surrounded by applied, mitered molding on front and sides.*

Nails secure fixed top and bottom to sides of desk box.

Battens (2), ¾ x 3½ x 14

Top View

39¼

C

A

B

⅞

50¾

39¼

⅜-in.-dia. pin

24

A

C

Front View

Side View

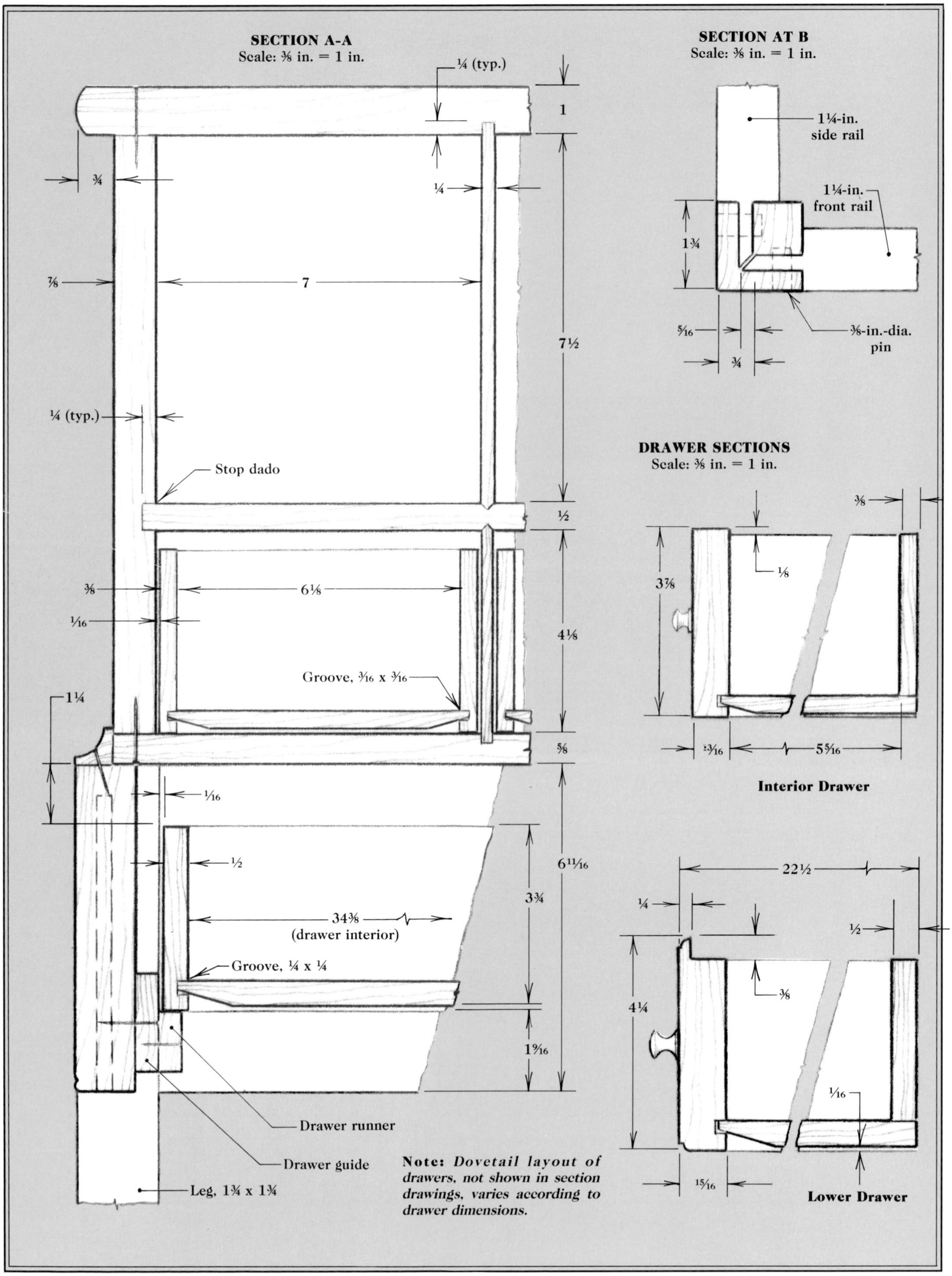
SECTION A-A
Scale: ⅜ in. = 1 in.
¼ (typ.)
1
¾
¼
⅞
7
7½
¼ (typ.)
Stop dado
½
⅜
6⅛
1⁄16
4⅛
Groove, 3⁄16 x 3⁄16
1¼
⅝
1⁄16
½
6 11⁄16
3¾
34⅜
(drawer interior)
Groove, ¼ x ¼
1 9⁄16
Drawer runner
Drawer guide
Leg, 1¾ x 1¾
Note: Dovetail layout of drawers, not shown in section drawings, varies according to drawer dimensions.
SECTION AT B
Scale: ⅜ in. = 1 in.
1¼-in.
side rail
1¼-in.
front rail
1¾
5⁄16
¾
⅜-in.-dia.
pin
DRAWER SECTIONS
Scale: ⅜ in. = 1 in.
⅜
⅛
3⅞
13⁄16
5 5⁄16
Interior Drawer
22½
¼
½
⅜
4¼
1⁄16
15⁄16
Lower Drawer

SECTION C-C
Scale: 3/16 in. = 1 in.

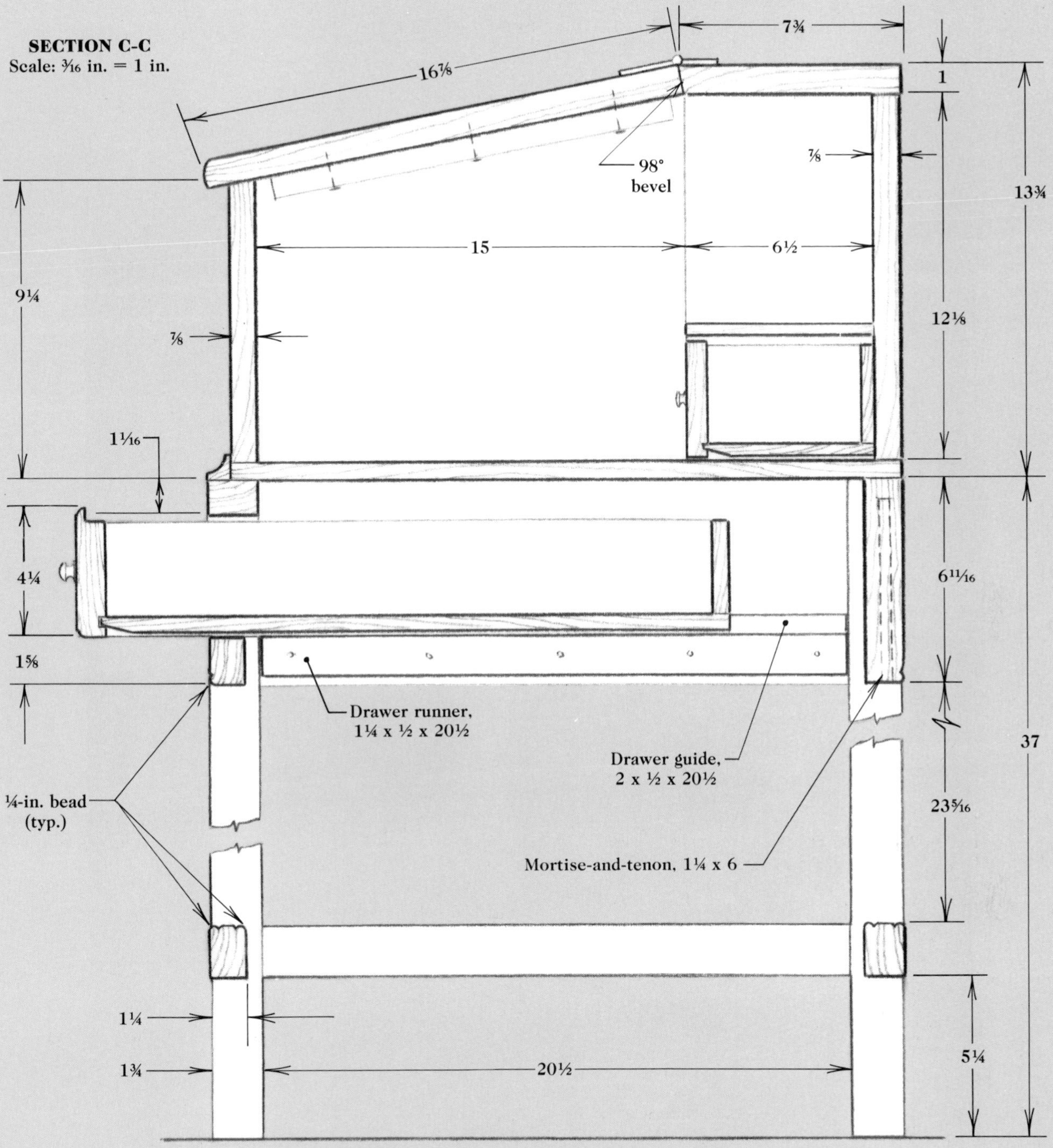

16⅞
7¾
1
⅞
98° bevel
13¾
9¼
15
6½
12⅛
⅞
1 1/16
4¼
6 11/16
1⅝
Drawer runner, 1¼ x ½ x 20½
Drawer guide, 2 x ½ x 20½
37
¼-in. bead (typ.)
23 5/16
Mortise-and-tenon, 1¼ x 6
1¼
1¾
20½
5¼

PATTERN FOR MOLDING PROFILES
Grid: ¼ in. = ¼ in.

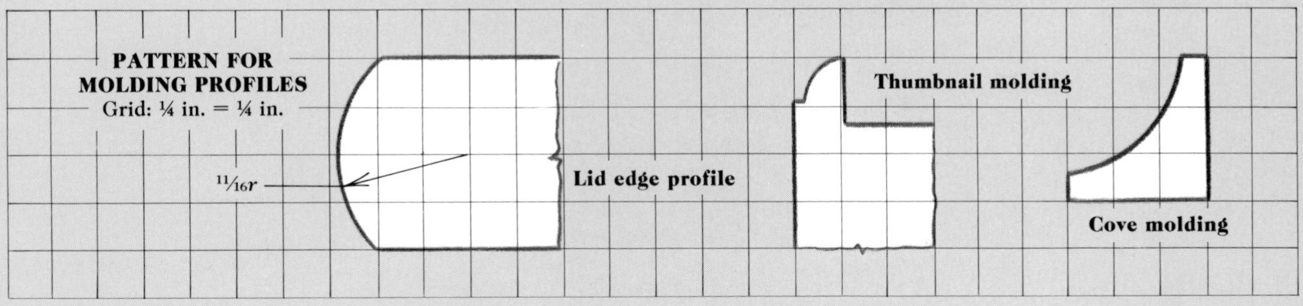

11/16r
Lid edge profile
Thumbnail molding
Cove molding

THE
BEDROOM

The parents of the families that have lived in our house have always used the east bedchamber as their bedroom, just as we do. The room has a southerly exposure, and the sunlight that streams in makes it a wonderful room to wake up in.

The original bedroom was a cheery room with its woodwork painted Prussian blue. Several years ago when I was insulating the attic, I found about a square foot of the bedroom's original wallpaper under the attic floorboards. Recently we found an example of the pattern's full repeat in the collection of the Society for the Preservation of New England Antiquities, and we can now have the original paper reproduced. This paper was probably an American version of the neoclassical French papers popular during the Federal period. The background color is a light blue, and each repeat consists of a central urn, topped by a cupid and surrounded by tendrils with perched birds. The urn is placed above a bar draped with swags and tassels.

We painted the room's woodwork the original color and, to maintain the blue-on-blue effect, used the background color of the original wallpaper on the plaster walls. Someday, after we have had the original paper reproduced, the room's basic decor will appear just as the original owners intended.

According to the 1805 inventory of the house, the bed in this room was one of the owners' most expensive possessions. Most of the value noted for the piece represented the bed furniture, that is, the pillows, sheets, blankets and bed curtains. The pattern on the bed curtains probably complemented that in the wallpaper and window curtains.

The various beds used in the room left dents in the floorboards. Each bed was placed near the front windows so that it and the bed furniture could be fully seen and appreciated by those passing by the bedroom door. Because the 20th century has brought a streetlight and automobile traffic to our front door, we have placed our bed against the room's rear wall.

Federal-period Americans saw the bedchamber as a room to be lived in. When I stripped the bedroom floor (which was not painted until the 20th century), I found patterns of wear in the raw pine boards that confirmed the room's regular use. In front of each window someone routinely sat in a Windsor chair. When that person rocked backward in the chair, the turned feet of the Windsor made crisp half-moon dents in the soft wooden floor. Another row of such dents occurs about 8 ft. from the mouth of the fireplace, the distance I have found most comfortable when sitting in front of a fire. From these patterns of wear I determined the location of some of the 18 Windsors listed in the 1805 inventory.

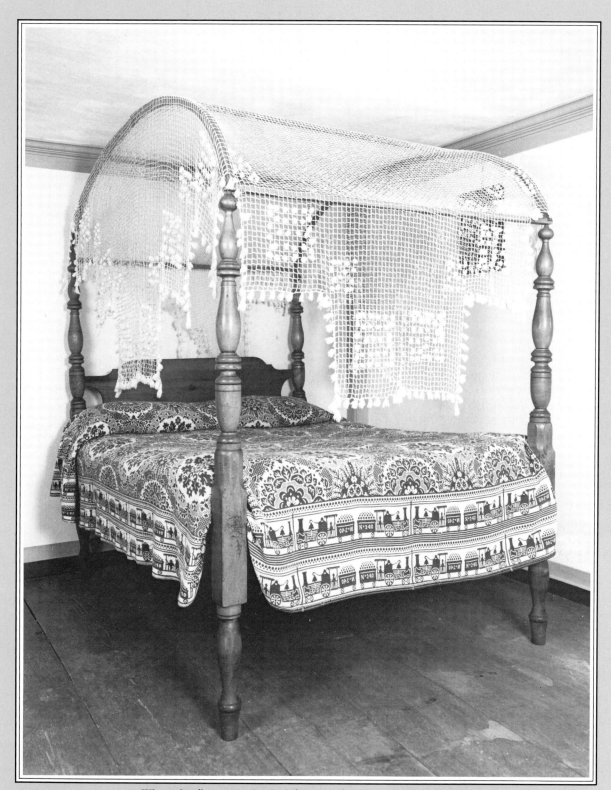

When the fires were banked for the night in a Federal-period home, the temperature indoors might drop well below freezing. To combat the cold, the full-length curtains originally hanging from this bed's canopy frame were drawn to form a tent that trapped heat inside. (Project: Roping the frame, p. 151.)

High-Post Bed
Chapter 17

I f you have ever slept in a house heated only by a fireplace or a woodstove, you will understand and appreciate the original purpose of the high-post bed. The tall posts, topped on this bed by a wooden arch called a canopy frame, were not intended to just look nice. Curtains covered the top and all four sides of the bed, creating, in effect, a tent. That tent trapped heat inside and protected the people huddled under the covers from room temperatures that often dipped well below freezing.

These curtains covered the bed so completely that there was little reason to make elaborate posts. It is therefore a tribute to the cabinetmaker who made this bed that he produced beautifully turned, if quite simple, posts.

Since central heating has eliminated the need for curtains that can be drawn shut against the night chill, at the same time hiding the bedposts, we can appreciate the bed in a way its original owner may not have. For us, a high-post bed may be more interesting as an architectural-size piece of furniture that works in three dimensions. Many modern beds are, by contrast, essentially broad, flat, two-dimensional sleeping surfaces, which share little with the high-post bed, except that they too take up much of the floor space in a bedroom. The high-post bed, however, occupies both an expanse of floor space and also considerable space above the mattress.

Making a bed is a rewarding project, yet it will require a great deal of advanced planning. Among the things to think about before beginning is that you will need access to a lathe with a 6-ft. bed (the posts are 5 ft. 1¼ in. long). You will also need to locate a source for enough 4-in.-thick hardwood for the bed's four 3¼-in.-dia. posts and four 3¼-in.-thick rails (with the exception of its poplar headboard, the original bed is made of birch). Native hardwoods this thick can be purchased from wholesale lumberyards, but it may take some fast talking to convince them to sell you only enough wood for one bed.

The stock I use for beds came from my family's farm. For many years I had admired a grove of cherry trees there, which had to come down when my father opened a new pasture. Among these trees were five that were at least 18 in. in diameter. I told the sawyer that I wanted the crown plank (the one with the pith in it) from each to be 4 in. thick. The wood on either side of the pith represents a radial cut and is very stable when sawn this way.

Your father may not have a grove of cherry trees he wants to cut down, but there may be a small sawmill somewhere close by. A mill will usually sell you a log and cut it to your specifications at enough of a premium to make up for the extra effort involved in dealing with a small-timer. If, however, there are surprises such as rot or wind shakes inside the log, the sawyer may remind you that you bought it. Take your losses with equanimity.

If you buy wood this way, paint the ends of the planks to prevent rapid drying and checking, and immediately rip the crown planks in a line that roughly follows the pith. The timber then needs to be stacked on skids and air-dried for several years.

Another thing to think about is the type of mattress you will use. The mattress on the original bed was supported by a woven rope web, which is discussed in detail on p. 151. I laid a sheet of ¾-in.-thick plywood over this rope web and a mattress over that. I use a horsehair mattress, which is quite hard (it's done wonders for my back problems). If you want something softer, try a futon or a dense foam mattress over the plywood. For a box spring and mattress, you'll have to suspend the box spring between the rails with angle brackets.

The original bed measures only 74¼ in. by 54¼ in. and was designed to hold a three-quarter-size mattress. This design is fine for people like myself who are only 5 ft. 8 in. tall, but you may want to expand your bed to take a standard, full-size mattress. You can do this by appropriately lengthening the rails, headboard and canopy frame. I would warn against making the bed wide enough and long enough for a queen-size or king-size mattress, though. Such proportions would make the bed look foolish.

Begin the bed by ripping the plank into stock for the bedposts and rails. Notice that the posts are 3¼ in. sq. in cross section, while the rails are 3¼ in. deep by a full 4 in. wide. Surface them to these dimensions. Then hand-plane the rails and chamfer all four edges to prevent bed covers from catching on any slivers or the arris. Plane the stock for the posts in the area of the mortises to keep milling marks from showing on your finished bed.

Turn the four posts to the shape shown in the drawing on p. 155. The original posts were never sanded, as the turner was skillful enough to turn a clean surface using only lathe tools. If you are not equally competent at the lathe, I recommend sanding the posts, but not while the lathe is turning. That would scratch the turning across the grain, something none of us would dream of doing on any other piece of wood, but which many of us do routinely with turnings. Even if you try to sand these scratches away, they will reappear when you apply the finish. For this reason, I suggest shutting off the lathe and, with the turning still mounted between centers, sanding lightly with 220-grit paper in the direction of the grain.

After the posts have been turned, the bed is ready to be joined with standard mortise-and-tenons. Unless you've done timber framing, you have probably never cut mortise-and-tenons this large, but they are done the same way as smaller joints. Lay them out with a square and a mortise gauge. I cut the ⅝-in. mortises with a mortise chisel. I would not make them any smaller than ⅝ in. and, if faced with a choice of larger chisel sizes, would opt to make them ¾ in.

Unlike most smaller joined pieces of furniture, beds occasionally have to be disassembled for the purpose of moving or redecorating. For this reason, no glue is used on the joints. To ensure the bed's correct reassembly, I suggest following what was standard practice in the Federal period: numbering the mortise-and-tenons. Chisel Roman numerals next to the mortises and on the ends of the rails near the tenons. Start with the right mortise on the left head post and advance clockwise around the bed in the traditional sequence.

The joints of the original bed are further secured with a rope web, woven through a series of 30 holes in the rails. Each side rail has nine holes and each end rail six holes. All of the holes are ⅝ in. in diameter and are relieved on the outside of the rail to keep the rope from chafing. They are evenly spaced along each rail and aligned with the holes on the opposite rail.

Although roping works well to tighten the bed frame, it interferes with fitting a box spring between the rails. You may therefore want instead to tighten the frame with bed bolts, which can be purchased from the reproduction-hardware dealers listed in the appendices.

Once the joinery for the rails is complete, you can cut the mortises for the headboard. On the original bed the headboard is ½ in. thick, but it could easily be ⅝ in. thick, which would allow you to use the same mortise

chisel throughout. I would avoid making it ¾ in. thick, however, since this begins to violate Federal-period cabinetmakers' tradition of delicate furniture.

There's no reason not to make the headboard of something more exotic than poplar, and almost any wood could be used. If you have enlarged the dimensions of the bed, expand your headboard from the middle of the pattern rather than from the ends.

With the headboard completed, turn your attention to the canopy frame. On the original bed this frame is a simple arch made of birch, but any hardwood would do and the frame's shape could just as well be serpentine. Eight pieces make up the frame: four arched segments and four cross struts. The arched segments are set up in pairs to make two full arches running the length of the bed. These segments meet in the middle with a butt joint and are secured on the underside with a leather hinge. Alternatively, a small metal hinge could be used. The entire canopy is assembled without glue to facilitate knockdown for moving.

To construct the canopy frame, first transfer the shape of the four arches from the drawing to your wood, nesting the patterns together to minimize waste. The arches are made from full-inch stock and can be cut out on a bandsaw or with a bowsaw. The sawn edges can be cleaned up with a spokeshave or a compass plane.

Next cut the four cross struts for the canopy, which are ¾ in. thick by 1⅛ in. wide. The two struts at the head and foot of the bed as well as the hinged arches are mounted on top of the posts with a metal pin. You can make these pins from 8d finish nails by cutting off the nail heads with a hacksaw. Drill a friction-tight hole in the top of the post (the lathe center marks the spot), and tap the nail in place, point up. You'll need to drill a somewhat larger hole through each end of the cross struts and through the lower end of each arched segment, so both the strut and arch can slide over the nails in the posts. When assembling the canopy, put the struts in place first and set the arches on top of them.

Before these pieces are assembled, however, the two center struts need to be joined with half-blind dovetails to the top surface of the arches. These struts are positioned to divide the arches into three equal sections. When in place, they do more than just support the cloth canopy. They also prevent lateral sway of the arches.

Once the bed is constructed, you'll want to think about finishing the piece. The original bed was finished with shellac, but because of the wear from the mattress and bedding, I would suggest something harder, like varnish or lacquer. If your bedroom has a country decor, you might want to use a red or blue milk-paint stain, mixed the way I described in the chapter on the gateleg table (p. 90).

If you want to make bed curtains, consult the book on textiles in the bibliography. You may prefer instead a simple, printed cotton canopy, or a crocheted fishnet canopy. You'll need to make your own cotton canopy, but fishnet canopies are available through a number of stores, which usually advertise in the antiques magazines listed in the sources of supply at the end of the book.

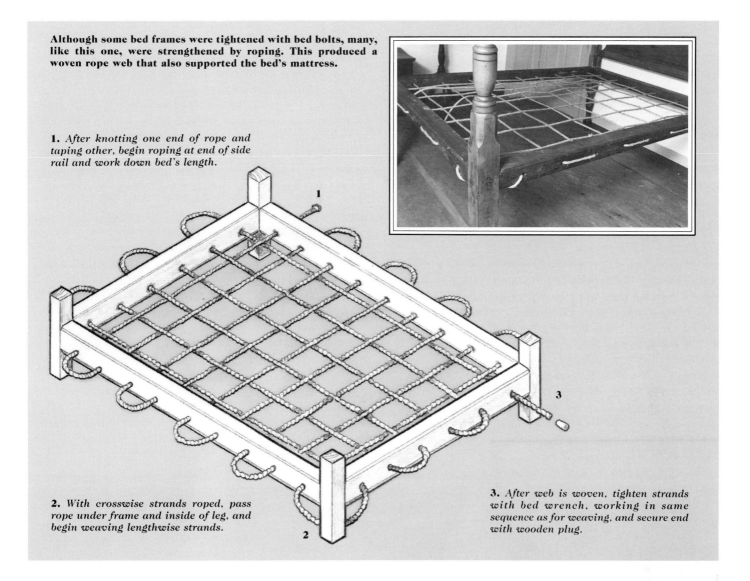

Although some bed frames were tightened with bed bolts, many, like this one, were strengthened by roping. This produced a woven rope web that also supported the bed's mattress.

1. *After knotting one end of rope and taping other, begin roping at end of side rail and work down bed's length.*

2. *With crosswise strands roped, pass rope under frame and inside of leg, and begin weaving lengthwise strands.*

3. *After web is woven, tighten strands with bed wrench, working in same sequence as for weaving, and secure end with wooden plug.*

Roping the frame

To rope a three-quarter-size bed, you'll need about 97 ft. of ⅜-in. hemp rope, and if you have expanded your bed to full-size, you'll need an extra 10 ft. of rope. Don't use nylon rope—it stretches. You'll also need two whittled and tapered, 9-in.-long hardwood pins, along with a hammer (I prefer a cobbler's hammer, but a carpenter's hammer will do) and a bed wrench. The wrench can be easily made from a turned dowel, 2 in. thick by 14 in. long. Cut a slot at least ⅝ in. wide in one end of the dowel, and pierce the other end with a 1-in. bit at a right angle to the center of the dowel. Insert a handle into this hole to complete the *T*-shaped tool.

To prepare the rope, whip one end by wrapping it with electrical or masking tape to keep it from fraying and mushrooming as you work. Tie a half-knot in the other end, which will anchor this end in the first hole.

Begin roping the frame in one corner, threading the whipped end of the rope from the outside through the first hole in the side rail. Pass the rope across the width of the bed and out through the corresponding hole in the opposite rail. Then pull the rope until the knot is tight against the first rail.

A simply constructed bed wrench is used to tighten the woven rope web.

Working on the side of the bed opposite the knot, pass the rope through the second hole in that rail and out the corresponding hole in the first side. Continue working back and forth in this way along the entire length of the bed, which will produce the foundation threads for the woven web. When you've pulled the rope through the last hole in the side rail, pass it under the rail, inside of the post and up to the outside of the end rail. Thread the rope into the first hole in the end rail, weave it alternately over and under the crosswise strands to the opposite rail and pass it out the opposite hole. Move to the next hole, just as you did on the side rails, and continue to weave the web. If you need to tie another piece of rope onto the first, use a square knot; this is strong but will untie easily if you need to disassemble the bed.

When the web is completed, it needs to be tightened. Start at the corner of the side rail opposite the knot and slip the wrench down over the short exposed length of the rope between the first two holes in the rail. Twist the wrench clockwise as tightly as you can. When I'm doing this by myself, I hold the wrench with one hand and my thigh, which leaves my other hand free to pick up a tapered pin. Press the point of the pin into the first hole and drive it with the hammer tight enough to keep the rope from slipping when the wrench is loosened.

Go to the opposite side of the bed and tighten the rope in the next hole in the same way, using the second pin to

anchor the rope. Then remove the first pin by pulling it straight back while you tap its side with the hammer as close as possible to the rail. The tapping will slowly loosen the pin. Avoid working the pin from side to side, as the tip may snap off in the hole.

Tighten the next strand of the foundation threads in the same way, using the first pin to hold the rope. Work in this leap-frog fashion down the entire length of the bed. The rope should be tight enough to vibrate when plucked like a guitar string. You may also see a noticeable bow in the heavy side rails. After I had finished roping this bed, the distance between the rails measured ½ in. less in the middle than at the ends.

Tighten the lengthwise strands in the same way, working across the width of the bed frame. When the last strand is tightened, lock it with the free pin. Then saw off the pin close to the rail so that it will not interfere with the bedding. To disassemble or retighten the bed, you can drive out this short pin from the inside. Don't cut the extra length of rope off—you'll need it the next time you have to rope the bed. Instead, pass it under the foot rail and weave it over the strands so that it doesn't hang down under the bed.

Although it's been removed for the photograph, we usually hang a dust ruffle from the rails, which is actually tacked to the sheet of plywood. The effect of this ruffle is to enlarge the bed's mass (and hide the rope).

The knotted end keeps the rope from pulling through the first hole and anchors the woven web.

Once the crosswise strands are threaded, pass the rope under the side rail, inside of the post and to the outside of the end rail to begin the lengthwise threads.

The bed wrench and tapered pins are used to tighten the webbing, working in the sequence in which it was woven (above). To keep from losing the tension on the rope, tighten and lock it in two consecutive holes in leap-frog fashion around the bed. With the rope thus secured, remove the tapered pin from the first hole by pulling straight backward and tapping the pin with a hammer near the rail.

After tightening the rope in the last hole, drive in the tapered pin with the hammer and saw off the end to make a plug.

HIGH-POST BED
Scale: ¹⁄₁₆ in. = 1 in.

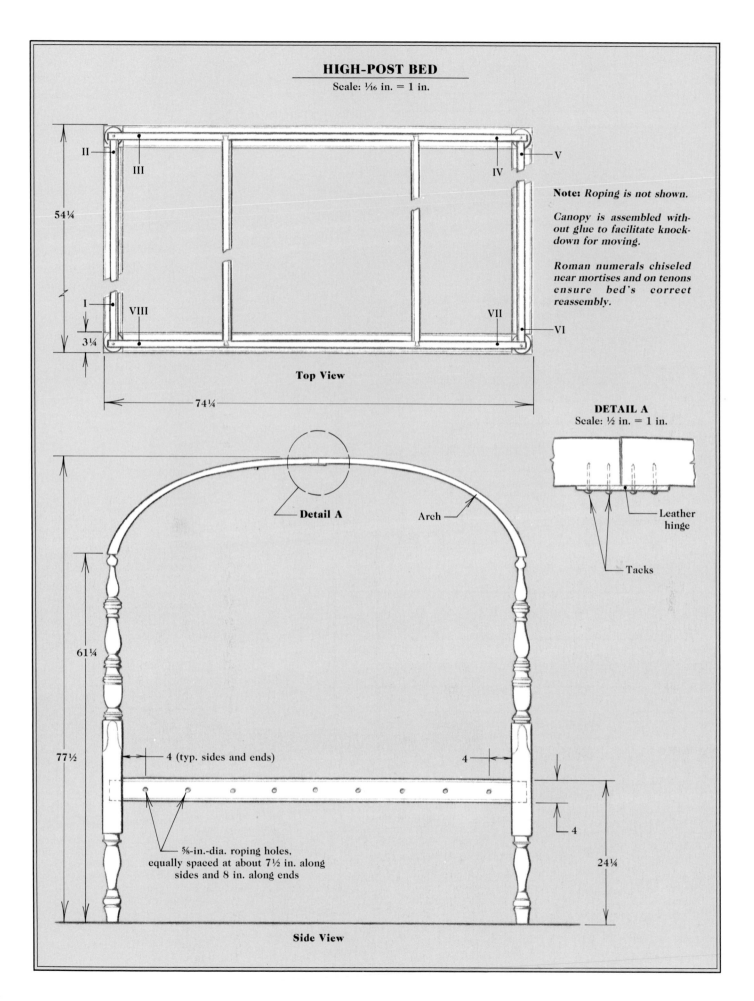

II

III

IV

V

54¼

Note: *Roping is not shown.*

Canopy is assembled without glue to facilitate knockdown for moving.

Roman numerals chiseled near mortises and on tenons ensure bed's correct reassembly.

I

VIII

VII

VI

3¼

Top View

74¼

DETAIL A
Scale: ½ in. = 1 in.

Leather hinge

Tacks

Detail A

Arch

61¼

4 (typ. sides and ends)

4

77½

4

24¼

⅝-in.-dia. roping holes, equally spaced at about 7½ in. along sides and 8 in. along ends

Side View

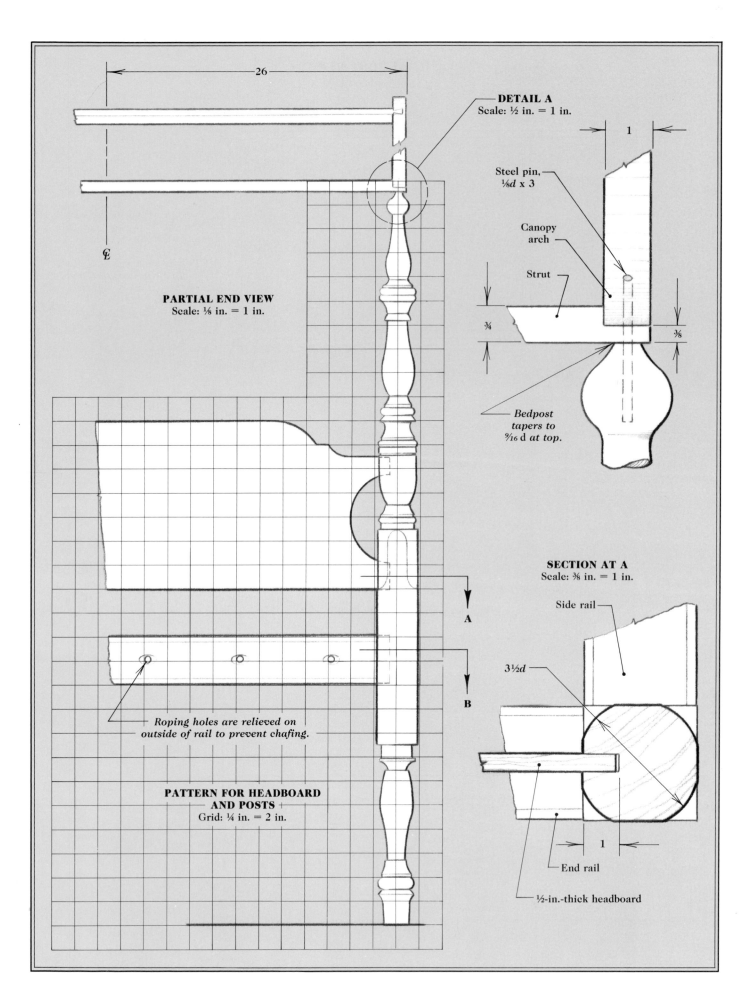

26

CL

DETAIL A
Scale: ½ in. = 1 in.

1

Steel pin,
⅛d x 3

Canopy
arch

Strut

¾

⅜

*Bedpost
tapers to
⁹⁄₁₆ d at top.*

PARTIAL END VIEW
Scale: ⅛ in. = 1 in.

A

B

*Roping holes are relieved on
outside of rail to prevent chafing.*

SECTION AT A
Scale: ⅜ in. = 1 in.

Side rail

3½d

1

**PATTERN FOR HEADBOARD
AND POSTS**
Grid: ¼ in. = 2 in.

End rail

½-in.-thick headboard

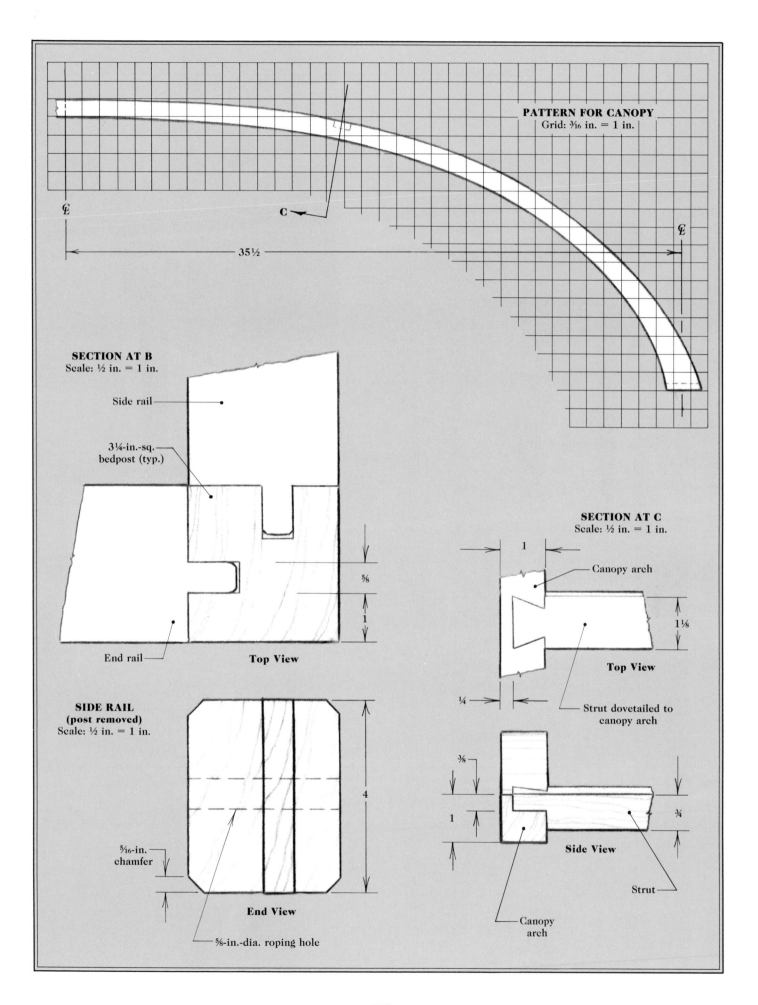

PATTERN FOR CANOPY
Grid: ³⁄₁₆ in. = 1 in.

CℒL

C

35½

SECTION AT B
Scale: ½ in. = 1 in.

Side rail

3¼-in.-sq.
bedpost (typ.)

⅝

1

End rail

Top View

SECTION AT C
Scale: ½ in. = 1 in.

1

Canopy arch

1⅛

Top View

¼

Strut dovetailed to
canopy arch

SIDE RAIL
(post removed)
Scale: ½ in. = 1 in.

4

⅜

¾

1

Side View

⁵⁄₁₆-in.
chamfer

End View

Strut

⅝-in.-dia. roping hole

Canopy
arch

— 155 —

With a wide, fixed top and narrow leaves, the Pembroke table
was originally designed as a portable table on which to have
breakfast or tea. Introduced during the Chippendale period, it
gained even greater popularity in the Federal period. (Project:
Rule joints, p. 158.)

Pembroke Table

Chapter 18

he table presented in this chapter is called a Pembroke. The feature that distinguishes a Pembroke from other small drop-leaf tables is the proportion of the wide top to the narrow leaves. Legend has it that the Earl of Pembroke was the first person to order a small, portable table of these proportions, and he is reported to have had no less a cabinetmaker than Thomas Chippendale make the piece for him. As a result, Pembroke's name was forever linked to this furniture form.

The only part of the story that can be accepted with certainty is that the Pembroke table was introduced during the Chippendale period and first made in that furniture style. The form reached its greatest popularity during the Federal period, when Pembrokes were made in great quantity. Consequently, a tremendous number of Federal examples of this form still survive in both Hepplewhite and Sheraton styles.

Pembrokes were originally intended to be light, movable tables at which one could eat breakfast or take tea. When the table was not in use, its leaves could be lowered and the piece placed out of the way against a wall. Although we don't often eat at this Pembroke, Carol and I use it for innumerable other purposes. In fact, I wrote this book while sitting at this table.

Even in its closed position against the wall, this piece is an interesting and dynamic form. Its appeal results from a characteristic of Federal furniture to which I have referred again and again in this book: the creation of illusion.

This piece contains several examples of illusion, the first being its deceptively delicate appearance. The double-tapered leg makes the table appear to be perched on tip-toe. Like the leg on the gateleg table (p. 90), the Pembroke's leg is an ample 1%16 in. sq. at the top and tapers gently from the top on two sides. But unlike the leg on the gateleg, the Pembroke leg narrows at the ankle in an even steeper taper on all four sides. By comparison

with the gateleg, which is 1 in. sq. at the foot, the Pembroke leg is only ⅝ in. sq. at the bottom.

Besides creating an illusion, the double-tapered leg also presents a design problem. The sudden break from the first taper into the second could appear to be a mistake. A viewer might wonder if the steeper taper at the foot resulted from the cabinetmaker's inability to control his tools (did he allow the plane to roll as it neared the bottom of the leg?). Aware of this possible perception, the maker adopted a solution commonly used on double-tapered legs: a band of inlay at the point of transition, which announces that the second taper was expressly intended.

Another deceptive element found in the table involves the two ends of the skirt, which appear to be solid boards with an inlaid strip along the bottom edge. In reality, only one is a solid board, while the other is the front of a drawer running the width of the skirt. The drawer, which has no knobs, is pulled out by its bottom front edge, made accessible by the relieved front on the lower drawer rail. Many Pembroke tables have a drawer in one end, but it is not usually hidden. In fact, false drawers in Pembrokes are more common than real, hidden drawers.

The most striking illusion is the visual razzle-dazzle produced by the shape of the top. Like the double-tapered leg, the top's shape is not unique to Pembrokes. It was a common outline for the tops of Federal-period card tables, but on a card table it would have been bisected to fold in half. This symmetry meant that, even when folded, the card table's top could be easily imagined in full.

Visualizing the open tabletop on this Pembroke, when closed, is more difficult. The maker placed the rule joints that connect the fixed top and leaves about two-thirds of the way down the curve of the top's serpentine ends. When the leaves are lowered, the ends become elliptical, just like the sides. Thus, upon first seeing the closed table, one is likely to expect the open top to be circular. For the top's shape to be grasped, it must be seen with the leaves raised.

The original table is made of cherry, which time has turned a rich tobacco gold. The inlay on the ends of the skirt and running across the legs is made up of a strip of dark mahogany banding, outlined top and bottom by light-colored stringing, which is probably birch. The banding accents the edges of the skirt and the transition at the ankles without competing with the shape of the top.

If you copy this table, I recommend using the same simple banding. Doing so, however, limits the choice of primary wood to something of a medium color that would be lighter than the banding's core but darker than the stringing. Cherry or a light mahogany would work well.

The table's construction is fairly straightforward, and only several features require description. The first is the fly rail that holds each drop leaf in its raised position. This piece is a short extension of each side rail, attached to it with a wooden hinge like that on the gateleg table. This hinge is composed of a series of meshing wooden knuckles, pierced by a central hole and held together by a long, steel pin. (Instructions on making a wooden hinge can be found in the chapter on the gateleg table, on p. 94.) The hinge allows the fly rail to pivot at a right angle to the skirt and support the raised leaf. Note that this rail's shape differs from the profile of the adjacent skirt section, allowing the fly rail to be easily gripped. The back of the rail is also relieved to supply a fingerhold.

The fly rail requires that the skirt be constructed of two layers. On the original table the skirt's outer layer is cherry and the inner layer pine. After the fly rail and its hinge were made, the two layers of the skirt were jointed and glued together. The skirt was then treated as a single piece of wood. The tenon was laid out so that the glue joint ran right down its center, apparently in the interest of making a stronger skirt.

Another construction detail of note is found in the skirt end containing the hidden drawer. Normally a drawer is set between two visible, narrow, horizontal drawer rails, the upper one usually dovetailed into the top ends of the legs and the lower one mortise-and-tenoned. On this table the drawer rails are surprisingly wide: 3¾ in. for the upper rail and 3 in. for the lower one. This extra width allowed the maker sufficient room to cut a series of three dovetail pins on the upper rail, which prevents the skirt frame from racking out of square. The lower drawer rail is secured by two tenons, one joined to the side skirt and one to the leg.

Both these rails are set back to allow the drawer front to fit just behind the surface of the legs. The front of the drawer has a pronounced lip on both its upper and lower edges. These lips overhang the recessed rails and butt up against them when the drawer is closed. In this position, the drawer front effectively masquerades as a stationary part of the skirt.

I refinished the original table with three coats of 3-lb.-cut orange shellac. The color of the finish enhances the patina of the cherry, and together they produce the table's golden-tobacco color. If you make your table of the same wood, you can approximate this color by first staining the wood with a saturated solution of potassium permanganate. A layer of wax will protect the shellac from liquids.

Rule joints

The fixed top and hinged leaves on this Pembroke table and on the gateleg table are connected by rule joints. This joint is composed of a convex molding profile run on both edges of the fixed top, and a concave molding profile run on one edge of each leaf. I made these profiles with a pair of table-leaf planes. The plane shown on the left in the photo below is used to cut the convex molding. This plane has a fence but no depth stop. The plane shown on the right is used to cut the concave molding, and it has both a fence and a depth stop.

To begin the rule joints, joint the edges of the boards that will become the leaves and fixed top. Place one leaf in the front vise of your bench, with the underside of the leaf facing away from the bench. Set the fence of the plane shaping the concave profile against the outside surface of the leaf, gripping the plane with even pressure from behind and holding the fence against the outside of the leaf. This grip will make the plane cut a long, thin shaving, and at the same time keep it from wandering and cutting an incomplete profile. Be sure your hand doesn't interfere with chip ejection, or the plane will choke.

Each pass of the plane will form more of the molding, and each cut will produce a wider shaving. As the molding takes shape and the surface area with which the plane comes in contact increases, you'll find it progressively more difficult to cut. Try to make each cut without stalling, or you'll create a defect in the molding. Each new pass will remove a defect in the previous pass, but it's good to develop a clean, end-to-end cutting motion from the beginning. When the depth stop on the plane contacts the edge of the board, the plane will cease cutting.

After running the concave profiles on both leaves, place the fixed top in the front vise, with the underside of the top facing out. The plane used to shape the convex profile on both edges of the fixed top should be gripped like the other plane. Since it does not have a depth stop, however, it will cut indefinitely, and you should therefore simply stop cutting when the profile is completely formed. To cut the profile on the other edge of the fixed top, turn the piece over in the vise, again making sure the underside of the top faces out. When both sets of moldings are complete, lay them together to see how they nest.

Traditionally, rule joints are cut with a pair of table-leaf planes like these. The plane on the left shapes the convex edge of the joint and the one on the right the concave edge.

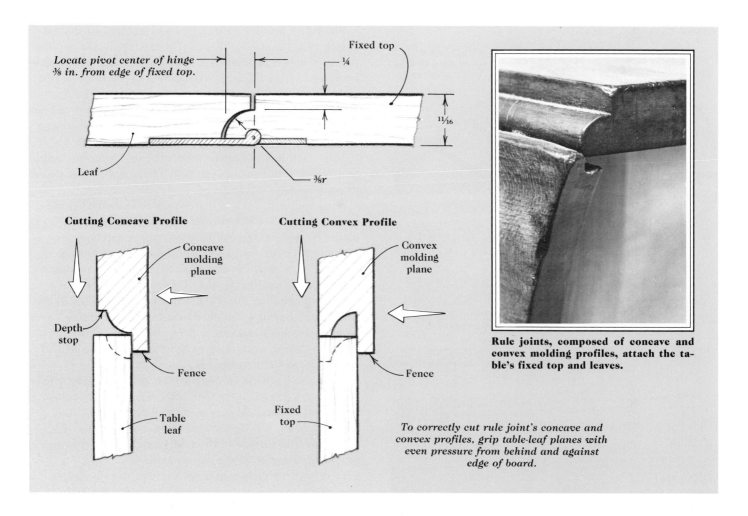

Locate pivot center of hinge ⅜ in. from edge of fixed top.

Fixed top

¼

11/16

Leaf

⅜r

Cutting Concave Profile

Concave molding plane

Depth stop

Fence

Table leaf

Cutting Convex Profile

Convex molding plane

Fence

Fixed top

Rule joints, composed of concave and convex molding profiles, attach the table's fixed top and leaves.

To correctly cut rule joint's concave and convex profiles, grip table-leaf planes with even pressure from behind and against edge of board.

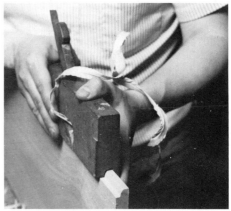

To cut the molding on the table's leaves and top, hold the pieces in the front vise of the workbench, with the underside facing away from the bench (above). Run the concave molding profile on one edge of each leaf (top right). In the photo, the plane has wandered slightly in the cut, but it will correct with subsequent passes. Run the convex molding profile on both edges of the fixed top (right).

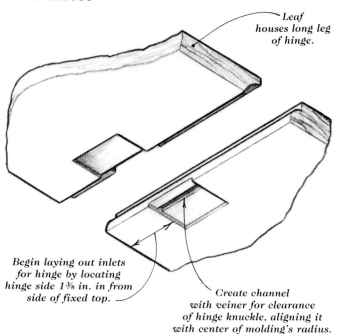

Leaf houses long leg of hinge.

Begin laying out inlets for hinge by locating hinge side 1⅜ in. in from side of fixed top.

Create channel with veiner for clearance of hinge knuckle, aligning it with center of molding's radius.

Nest the convex and concave molding profiles together to form the rule joint, leaving a slight gap between their upper edges to prevent binding with seasonal wood movement.

The design of table-leaf hinges, used to connect rule joints, has not changed in 200 years, as seen in the modern hinge above and its hand-forged, Federal-period counterpart.

The rule joints are held in place with a pair of special hinges called table-leaf hinges. These hinges have one leaf, or leg, longer than the other, which allows the screws to be placed below the concave molding of the rule joint.

To mount these hinges, lay out their position by first measuring on the underside of the fixed top 1⅜ in. in from each corner on the long sides. Use a square to draw lines locating the outside edges of the four hinges. With the hinges positioned on these lines, the hinge knuckles will be parallel to the edge of the leaf, allowing the table leaves to pivot without binding.

With the fixed top and leaves laid on the workbench, underside up, nest the two rule joints. Don't butt the leaves too tightly against the top; a slight gap between the upper edges of the top and the leaves will prevent the joints from binding. Now lay out the inlets for the hinges. Place a hinge just inside one of the squared lines you scribed. Locate the hinge's knuckle about ⅜ in. inside the edge of the fixed top (aligned with the center of the molding's radius) and scribe the outline of the hinge on the underside of both the top and the corresponding leaf. Repeat these steps to lay out all four hinges.

Cut these lines with a dovetail saw or score them with a broad butt chisel at least 1 in. wide. Then pare out the inlet for the hinge. Be sure to occasionally test-fit the hinge while working, since you want it to sit flush with, not below, the surface of the underside. Repeat this procedure for each of the eight inlets.

To mount the table-leaf hinges so that their knuckles are invisible, you need to undercut a groove for the knuckle in the underside of the fixed top. This step can be a bit tricky. Don't cut any deeper than necessary, or you may weaken the delicate edge. I used a *U*-shaped veiner and cleaned up the ends of this channel with a ¼-in. chisel.

To test the rule joint's function, drive a single screw into both legs of the two hinges along one joint. I started a pilot hole with a hand-held gimlet, but a brad awl will also work. Don't overtighten the screw, or you'll risk creating a dimple on the top surface. I'd suggest that you drive the screw in almost all the way, then back it out and grind off its point. This will eliminate the possibility of a dimple, while taking advantage of the screw's self-tapping ability.

With one screw in each hinge, you can carefully test the action of the rule joint. It should not bind. If it does, check to see that the hinges are flush. If they are and the joint still binds, you may have to slightly increase the gap between the leaf and the fixed top. To do this, remove one leg of each hinge and plug the screw hole with a wooden plug. Then attach the hinge in its new position. If the joint works well, back the screws out so that you can cut the top and leaves to their finished shapes. Finally, replace the hinges and drive all remaining screws.

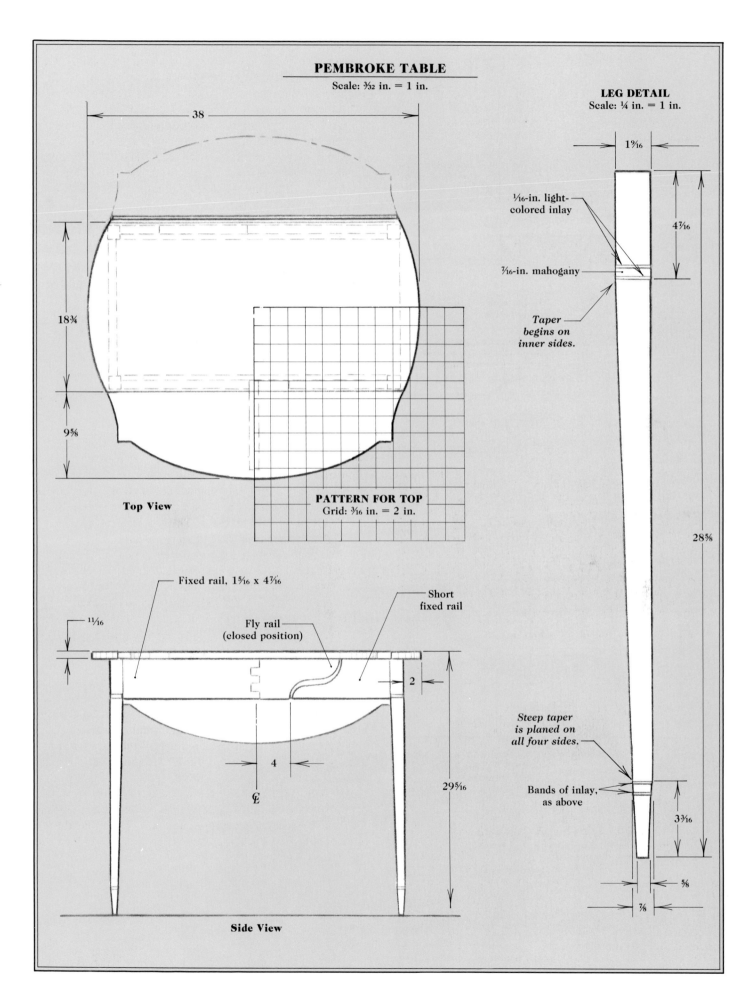

PEMBROKE TABLE
Scale: ³⁄₃₂ in. = 1 in.

LEG DETAIL
Scale: ¼ in. = 1 in.

38

1⁹⁄₁₆

¹⁄₁₆-in. light-colored inlay

4⁷⁄₁₆

⁷⁄₁₆-in. mahogany

18¾

Taper begins on inner sides.

9⅝

PATTERN FOR TOP
Grid: ³⁄₁₆ in. = 2 in.

Top View

28⅝

Fixed rail, 1⁵⁄₁₆ x 4⁷⁄₁₆

Short fixed rail

Fly rail (closed position)

11⁄₁₆

2

Steep taper is planed on all four sides.

4

Bands of inlay, as above

C̷L

29⁵⁄₁₆

3³⁄₁₆

⅝

⅞

Side View

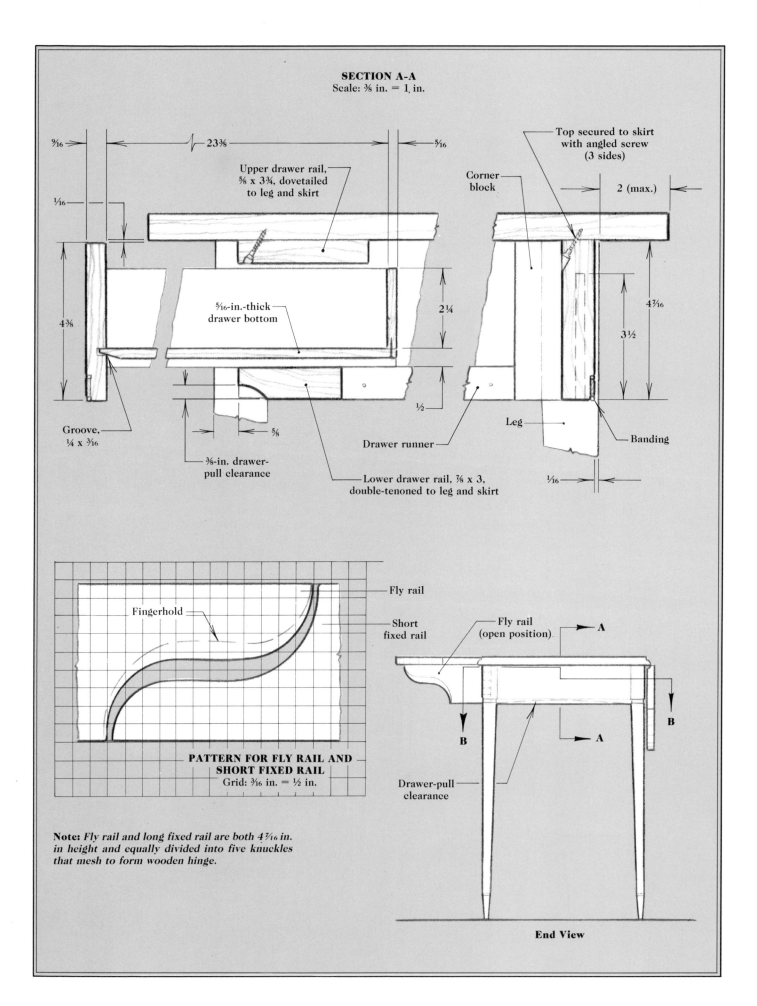

SECTION A-A
Scale: ⅜ in. = 1 in.

⁹⁄₁₆

23⅜

⁵⁄₁₆

Upper drawer rail,
⅝ x 3¾, dovetailed
to leg and skirt

Top secured to skirt
with angled screw
(3 sides)

Corner
block

2 (max.)

1⁄16

4⅜

⁵⁄₁₆-in.-thick
drawer bottom

2¼

4⁷⁄₁₆

3½

½

Groove,
¼ x ³⁄₁₆

⁵⁄₈

½

Leg

Banding

1⁄16

Drawer runner

⅜-in. drawer-
pull clearance

Lower drawer rail, ⅞ x 3,
double-tenoned to leg and skirt

Fly rail

Fingerhold

Short
fixed rail

**PATTERN FOR FLY RAIL AND
SHORT FIXED RAIL**
Grid: ³⁄₁₆ in. = ½ in.

Fly rail
(open position)

A

B

B

A

Drawer-pull
clearance

Note: *Fly rail and long fixed rail are both 4⁷⁄₁₆ in.
in height and equally divided into five knuckles
that mesh to form wooden hinge.*

End View

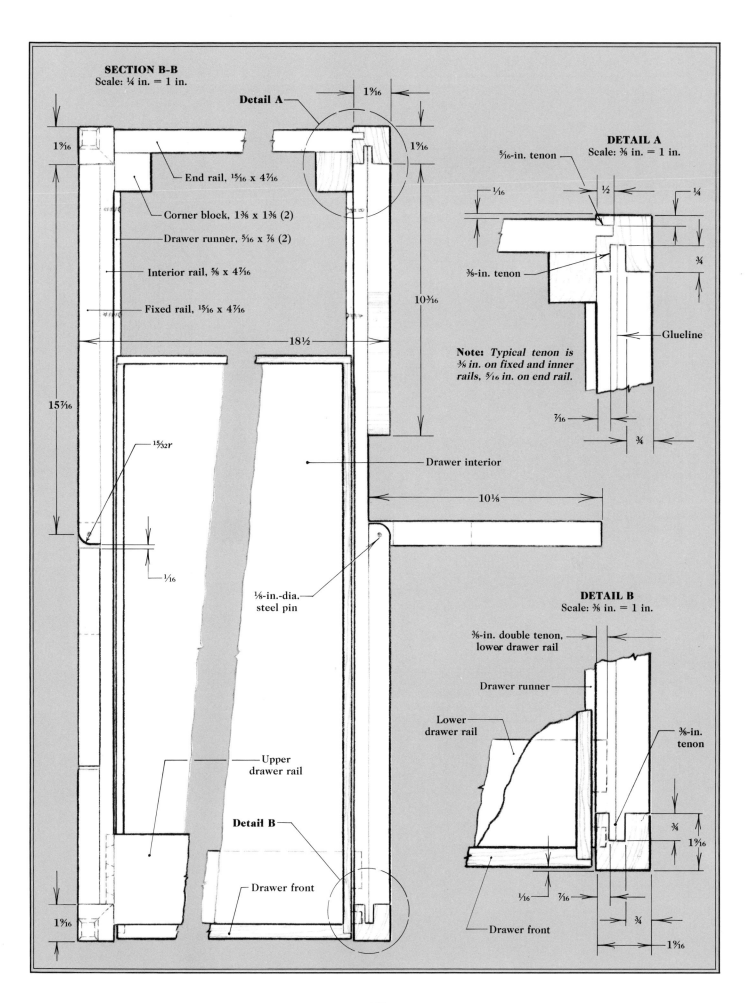

SECTION B-B
Scale: ¼ in. = 1 in.

Detail A

1⁹⁄₁₆

1⁹⁄₁₆

1⁹⁄₁₆

End rail, ¹⁵⁄₁₆ x 4⁷⁄₁₆

Corner block, 1⅜ x 1⅜ (2)

Drawer runner, ⁵⁄₁₆ x ⅞ (2)

Interior rail, ⅝ x 4⁷⁄₁₆

Fixed rail, ¹⁵⁄₁₆ x 4⁷⁄₁₆

10³⁄₁₆

18½

15⁷⁄₁₆

¹⁵⁄₃₂r

1⁄₁₆

⅛-in.-dia.
steel pin

Drawer interior

10⅛

Upper
drawer rail

Detail B

Drawer front

1⁹⁄₁₆

DETAIL A
Scale: ⅜ in. = 1 in.

⁵⁄₁₆-in. tenon

1⁄₁₆

½

¼

¾

⅜-in. tenon

Glueline

Note: *Typical tenon is
⅜ in. on fixed and inner
rails, ⁵⁄₁₆ in. on end rail.*

⁷⁄₁₆

¾

DETAIL B
Scale: ⅜ in. = 1 in.

⅜-in. double tenon,
lower drawer rail

Drawer runner

Lower
drawer rail

⅜-in.
tenon

¾

1⁹⁄₁₆

1⁄₁₆

⁷⁄₁₆

¾

Drawer front

1⁹⁄₁₆

Storage chests like this one were the Federal-period equivalent of cardboard boxes; yet unlike the many purely functional examples of such chests that have survived from the period, this piece is distinguished by its careful workmanship, graceful lines and pleasing bracket base. (Project: Rabbeted lid moldings, p. 166.)

Bracket-Base Blanket Chest

Chapter 19

Is it possible to ever have enough storage space in a house? It certainly wasn't in either the house I grew up in or the one I live in now. Since I suspect that most homes need more of such space, I decided to include this chest. It will provide almost 6 cu. ft. of additional storage area, and although mundane in function, this chest is aesthetically pleasing and successful.

Contemplate storage for a minute. We all have dozens of cardboard cartons in the attic and in closets, which are ideal for their purpose because they are broad and deep. In function there is little difference between those cardboard boxes and this chest: it is a deep box into which almost anything can be put. The fellow I bought it from raised basenjis and used it in the kennel to store the dogs' blankets. The chest's original owner probably stored household items in it, just as we now do.

The dilemma faced by the craftsman who made this chest was how to be innovative when the piece's function so emphatically dictated its form. With little room left for self-expression, he nonetheless managed to create an unusual and successful design. We can appreciate his talent by comparing this chest with others made during the Federal period for household storage. The latter are all quite large and sufficiently strong, but the quality of their workmanship is unimpressive. Most are simply rabbeted and nailed. None is ugly, but they are all quite plain and uninteresting to look at. They are what they were intended to be—the cardboard boxes of the Federal period. The reason I am so fond of this piece is that, unlike many other chests, it is well designed and well made, even though it need not be to perform its function.

The design feature that most distinguishes this chest from more common examples is its bracket base. This base does more than just lift the chest off the floor and allow a partial view underneath the piece. If these were the only functions of the base, it could easily have been designed with simpler bootjack ends. Instead, this bracket base is a logical aesthetic component of the piece, giving it a visual beginning and end. With this type of base, the chest becomes more than just a raised box for storage. It becomes a piece of furniture, elevated on feet like a table, chair or bed.

The base on this chest is restrained in comparison with the bracket base on the chest of drawers (p. 170); yet it is amply complex in its own right. The feet curve in on themselves just before reaching the floor, suggesting French feet, which are common on Hepplewhite-style case pieces and are used on the secretary (p. 58). The upper edge of the base is outlined by a stepped-cove molding. Here the concave shape starts as a narrow fillet, giving the illusion that the base is made of thinner stock than it really is. This reflects the concern of Federal-period cabinetmakers for creating the appearance of delicateness without sacrificing strength. The stepped cove works so well on this piece that I would hesitate to substitute another shape. The cove molding can be made with a molding plane or a shaper. While cutters for the cove itself are easy to find, finding one that can produce the stepped-cove profile is likely to be a problem. You might be tempted to leave the step out, but I would advise against it. Without that extra fillet, from above the molding would read as just a simple chamfer. If you can't find either a stepped-cove molding plane or a shaper cutter that is stepped, you can make the step by hand after the cove is cut. Clamp a fence on a rabbet plane, and adjust it for a very narrow cut, which should work nicely.

The lid employs a similar visual device. It is made from a 7/8-in.-thick board and has a 1/2-in.-deep by 3/4-in.-wide rabbet cut into the underside of the overhang. The rabbet reduces the visible outer edge to 3/8 in. and has set into it a molding with a steep ogee-and-astragal profile. This molding reinforces the illusion of thinness because it steps quickly back out of sight, and it also works as a cornice.

Cornices usually appear on tall pieces of furniture where they will be quite visible. Since this blanket chest is low, the hint of a cornice molding acts as a visual tease. It can be seen in its entirety only when the viewer is down on hands and knees or has opened the lid. Such subtlety, unusual even on elaborate pieces, is extremely rare in a simple storage chest. Although the ogee-and-astragal profile need not be used, you will want to choose a shape that steps back just as quickly. This will maintain the illusion of thinness and produce a molding that coyly hints at its presence.

This molding also serves a practical purpose. It is run out of ¾-in. stock and set in a ½-in.-deep rabbet. The extra ¼-in. overhang serves as a lip that fits down over three sides of the chest, keeping out dust and moths better than a simple flat top would.

Like the bracket base, the joinery in the body of the chest is pleasing to the eye. I cannot recall seeing elsewhere such precision in hand-cut dovetails. They are so perfect that if I did not know the age of this piece, I would suspect they were done by machine. The use of joinery as a design detail is characteristically modern and is particularly unusual in a Federal-period piece, where the details of construction were typically concealed. The pronounced pattern of the highly refined dovetailing undoubtedly accounts in part for the strong appeal of this chest for most people who see it.

If you are unable to cut such exacting dovetails by hand, you may want to use a router and a dovetail jig. To retain the flavor of this piece, I would recommend duplicating as closely as possible the spacing of the original dovetails. Whether you do the joinery by hand or with a router, use a marking gauge to scribe layout lines the depth of the tails and pins on all carcase sides. These layout lines set off the regular, precise pattern of the dovetails and prevent that pattern from being overshadowed by the wood's random, erratic figure.

The bottom of the chest fits inside the dovetailed carcase and is secured with 8d or 10d drawn or cut finish nails driven through the bottom edges of the four sides. This construction may seem crude and of questionable strength, but the nails are covered by the bracket base and their resistance to shear is very high. Consequently, a lot of weight can be safely stored in the chest. For added strength, there are diagonal braces supporting the rear feet, attached with drawn or cut finish nails driven through the feet and into the back of the chest.

The bracket base is nailed onto the chest with *T*-headed brads. The virtue of the *T*-headed brad is that, once it is set, the fibers of the wood spring back to partially, and sometimes completely, hide the head of the brad. (A source for *T*-headed brads—called headless brads by this supplier—is included in the sources of supply at the back of the book.) Always drive *T*-headed brads with the length of the head oriented in the same direction as the grain of the wood. Very little filler, if any, will be needed. The two front corners of the bracket base are mitered, and these should be glued and also nailed, in both directions, with two brads on each side.

This chest is made of walnut. The dark color gives it a serious appearance, and the hardness of the wood makes possible crisp details on the base and cornice—effects that would be difficult to achieve in pine or poplar. When making this piece, therefore, choose a hardwood, like walnut or mahogany, that works easily and will not lose detail with wear. The chest's broad surfaces will handsomely display the wood's figure, whereas if a more even-grained material like birch or maple were used, they would read as very plain. Be sure to hand-plane the boards to remove milling marks from a thickness planer on any of the visible surfaces. Don't oversand, or you'll risk rounding the crisp arrises on the chest's edges and corners.

There was a lock on the original blanket chest, but as usually occurs with old chests, that lock is now gone. I assume that at some point the key was lost, the lock jimmied and the damaged lock removed. If you want to add a lock, you can find one through one of the hardware suppliers listed in the appendices.

When selecting a finish, consider how you plan to use the chest. If it will be placed in a room where glasses or other vessels may be set on it, consider finishing it with varnish or lacquer. Shellac will mellow to a nice patina in a number of years; however, it will bloom, or turn white when exposed to most liquids. Oil and wax are water-resistant and, unlike shellac, are quick and easy to apply.

Rabbeted lid moldings

The ogee-and-astragal molding around the outer edge of the chest lid is set into a rabbet. This method of construction is stronger and neater than simply nailing the molding onto the lid's lower surface, and, as discussed on p. 165, the slim visible edge of the lid creates the illusion that the top is quite thin. If the top were actually that thin, it would be too fragile.

To cut the rabbet, I used a universal fillister plane. My fillister, made mostly of wood, was produced in Connecticut during the mid-19th century. Many tool companies sell metal fillister and rabbet planes.

The universal fillister adjusts in a similar manner to an adjustable plow plane (described in the chapter on the candle box on p. 132) and can cut rabbets of various depths and widths. To set the width of the rabbet (up to 1½ in.), loosen the two screws in the bottom of the fence, slide the fence to the desired width, then retighten the screws. The plane also has an adjustable stop that can be set to a maximum depth of ½ in. by means of a brass thumbscrew in the front of the stock.

Two features of this plane work together to produce a clean cut: the scribe and the skewed iron. The scribe is located just in front of the iron. When the plane is cutting across end grain, the scribe nicks the fibers in front of the cut to help eliminate tearout. The skewed iron is set so that the inside corner is forward and cleanly cuts the wood fibers first severed by the scribe. If tearout occurs somewhere across the width of the rabbet as the blade continues cutting, the split cannot run on and damage the shoulder; the inside edge of the rabbet will have already been cut by the forward corner of the skewed iron.

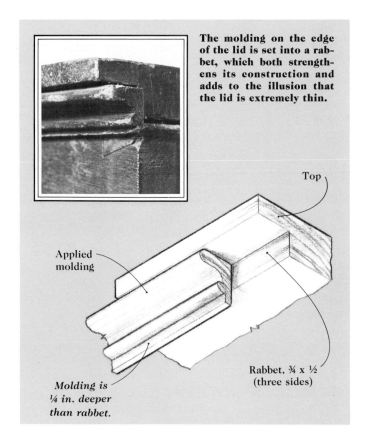

The molding on the edge of the lid is set into a rabbet, which both strengthens its construction and adds to the illusion that the lid is extremely thin.

Top

Applied molding

Molding is ¼ in. deeper than rabbet.

Rabbet, ¾ x ½ (three sides)

Set the fillister to make a rabbet ¾ in. wide by ½ in. deep, and work the two ends of the chest lid first. Clamp the lid, underside up, between benchdogs with a strip of waste on the far side, as shown in the photo below, to prevent chipping the corner. Hold the plane so that your hand does not cover the throat and cause the tool to choke. Apply pressure from behind and against the fence to keep the plane from wandering. Try to hold the plane square. If it should tip, no damage will be done, as the plane is self-correcting and will clean up square when it reaches the bottom of the cut.

After cutting rabbets in the two ends, rabbet the front edge. (No waste strip is needed to protect the end of this cut because the plane is cutting on edge grain.) If any of the rabbets have rough surfaces, they can be cleaned up with a metal rabbet plane. The one I'm using in the photograph is an old Bailey Patent No. 10, an early version of a metal rabbet plane made about 1900. A low-angled shoulder rabbet plane will also work. Both planes are available through catalog tool dealers.

When the rabbet has been cut, test-fit the molding. If the two surfaces of the rabbet are square with the surface of the chest lid and if the back two edges of the molding are square, the fit should be tight along the entire rabbet. If it's not, check to see whether the molding or the rabbet is out of square. Correct by planing the problem surface.

The universal fillister plane cuts rabbets of various depths and widths. The scribe, set in front of the skewed iron on the bottom of the plane, nicks the fibers ahead of the cut to eliminate tearout.

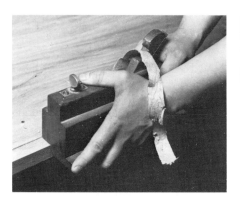

Run the end rabbets first. Clamp the lid between dogs, with a strip of waste on the side of the lid toward which you are running the plane (above). The strip will prevent chipping the corner. Making sure your hand does not cover the tool's throat, apply pressure from behind the plane and hold the fence tight against the edge to keep the cut straight (far left). Clean up any rough surfaces with a metal plane (left), such as the Bailey No. 10 rabbet plane, or a low-angled shoulder rabbet plane.

BRACKET-BASE BLANKET CHEST

Scale: ³⁄₃₂ in. = 1 in.

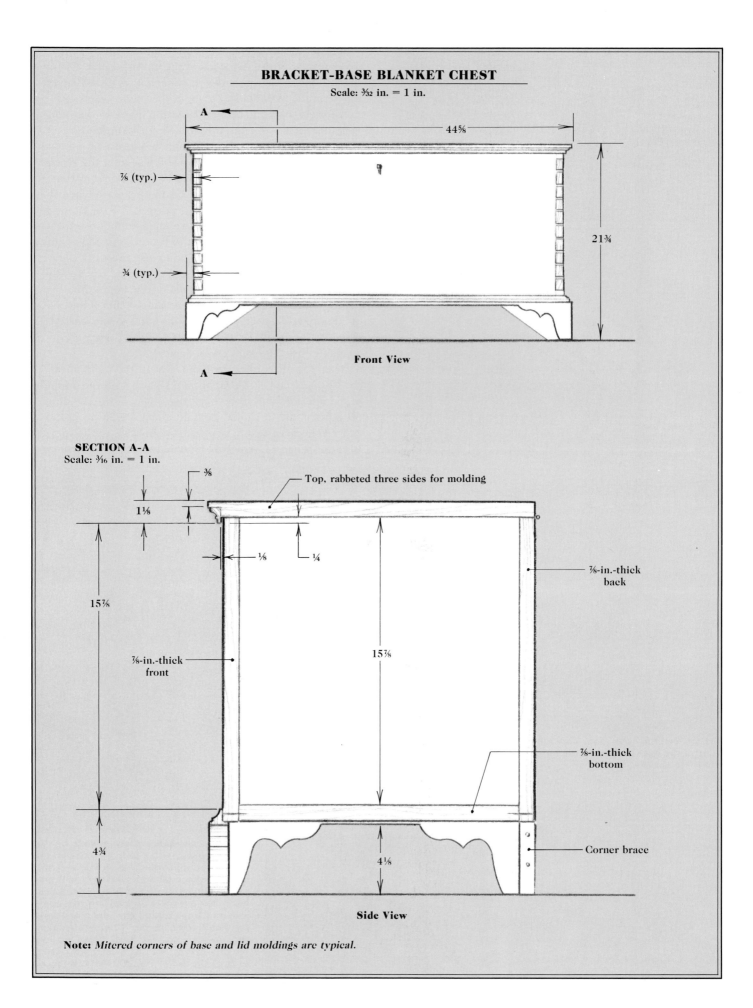

A

44⅝

⅞ (typ.)

21¾

¾ (typ.)

Front View

A

SECTION A-A
Scale: ³⁄₁₆ in. = 1 in.

⅜

Top, rabbeted three sides for molding

1⅛

⅛   ¼

⅞-in.-thick
back

15⅞

⅞-in.-thick
front

15⅞

⅞-in.-thick
bottom

4¾

Corner brace

4⅛

Side View

Note: *Mitered corners of base and lid moldings are typical.*

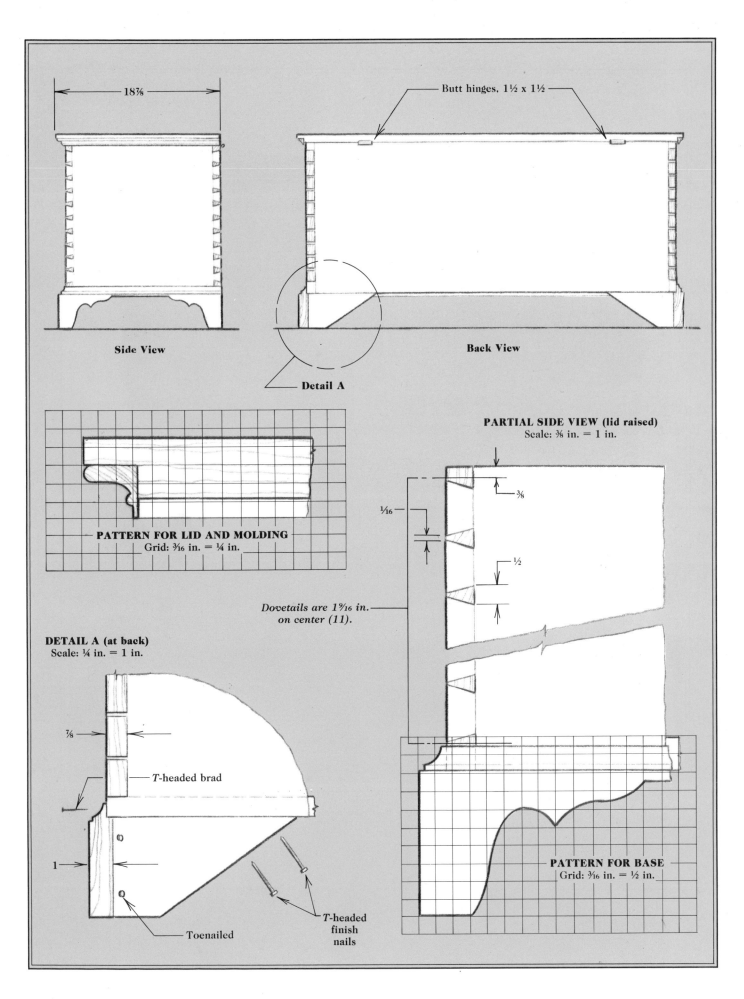

18⅞

Butt hinges, 1½ x 1½

Side View

Back View

Detail A

PATTERN FOR LID AND MOLDING
Grid: ³⁄₁₆ in. = ¼ in.

PARTIAL SIDE VIEW (lid raised)
Scale: ⅜ in. = 1 in.

³⁄₈

¹⁄₁₆

¹⁄₂

Dovetails are 1⁹⁄₁₆ in.
on center (11).

DETAIL A (at back)
Scale: ¼ in. = 1 in.

⁷⁄₈

T-headed brad

1

Toenailed

T-headed
finish
nails

PATTERN FOR BASE
Grid: ³⁄₁₆ in. = ½ in.

The elaborate curves of the base transform this simple, informal chest of drawers into a piece that is at once functional and quite visually pleasing. (Project: Simulated cock beading, p. 173.)

Chest of Drawers

Chapter 20

Chests of drawers are usually personal pieces of furniture. Unlike the blanket chest on p. 164, which has a deep well for storage, this chest has readily accessible drawers to hold clothing needed on a daily basis. Its top serves as a handy shelf for a mirror, brush, toiletries or other personal items that would not be stored in a drawer. My wife and I each have our own bureau, and anyone who sees them in our house can tell at a glance which is mine and which is hers by the things on top.

This chest, which is my personal bureau, is made of birch, a wood commonly used throughout northern New England for informal furniture in all early furniture periods. The top of the chest has a square, unmolded edge. The drawer fronts are very plain, embellished only with simulated cock beading, a half-round molding shape cut into the edges of the drawer fronts to help articulate the facade. It's difficult to determine if the wooden pulls are the originals, but even if they are not, they are in keeping with the plain facade. The only place elaborate ornamentation is found is on the bracket base, which is a riot of curves.

This chest of drawers is very simple in design, most likely because the craftsman was constrained by the customer's wish not to spend a lot of money on decorative, time-consuming features. But, as with many Federal-period pieces, ways were found to make this inexpensive, functional piece pleasing to look at. All distracting details, even brass escutcheons, which were almost always used on Federal chests of drawers, were eliminated from the facade of this chest. This total lack of ornament allows the viewer's eye to fall quickly to the elaborate curves of the base. Since the feet of the base are high enough to allow light underneath, these curves are not obscured by a shadowed background but are, in effect, backlighted, making their silhouette the dominant feature of the chest.

The joinery in this piece is uncomplicated and typical of Federal chest construction. The carcase bottom is dovetailed to the sides. A long dovetail tenon is cut on the upper end of each side, and the underside of the top has matching grooves to slide onto the tenons. The dovetails are stopped 1⅝ in. from the top's front edge. This sliding-dovetail joint prevents the wide surfaces of the top and sides from warping but allows for seasonal movement.

The drawer dividers also fit inside the carcase with sliding dovetails. This construction design has two important functions: it holds the dividers securely in place and it also prevents the carcase from racking.

Exposed dovetails were unusual in the Federal period. This was not an attempt to be secretive; cabinetmakers simply chose not to explain visually how a piece was put together, preferring instead to cover joints and other construction details. On this chest, a ¼-in. facing strip of birch covers the dovetails on the drawer dividers. This strip is set into a ¼-in. haunch cut into the dividers, so that their outer edges and the facing strip are flush. As a result, the drawer dividers appear to be simply butted against the sides of the carcase.

On most Federal chests of drawers, the backboards are nailed into a rabbet at the back edges of the sides. The maker of this chest chose instead to run two ¼-in.-wide by ⅜-in.-deep grooves ½ in. from the rear inside edges of the sides and floated the backboards in these grooves to keep their seasonal movement unconstrained.

The backboards themselves are wide pine boards butted together and left unglued. The upper board is 18¼ in. wide, and the lower one 15⅞ in. wide. Both are roughly planed to a thickness of about ½ in. and chamfered on their ends to slightly less than ¼ in. Before the invention of plywood, wide boards like these offered an easy and inexpensive way to cover broad surfaces. If you use plywood for the backboard, make the groove in which it is to sit as wide as the plywood is thick.

To assemble the carcase, first glue and attach the dovetails that join the sides to the bottom. Next insert the backboards. Then slide the top onto the two dovetailed tenons on the ends of the sides. Insert the drawer dividers without glue and nail on the ¼-in. facing strips. On the original chest, the drawer runners are attached with nails and are still secure after 170 years. Use screws if you prefer.

Cut out the bracket base with a bowsaw or a bandsaw, and then clean up the edges with a chisel or a spokeshave. Miter the ends of the front and sides of the base where they meet. Attach the base in the same manner as the method described for the walnut bracket-base blanket chest (p. 164).

Because this chest is large, you'll need to use glue blocks behind all four feet and along the front and sides of the bracket base. Glue blocks are commonly used to reinforce two surfaces that meet at a right angle. The blocks are placed in the back of a joint, glued to each surface and tacked into place. They make the base rigid and less liable to break if the chest is dragged on its feet. Here, the blocks are short lengths of pine, 1 in. sq. in cross section and about 4 in. long. (Glue blocks are made of scrapwood, and neither dimension is critical.) Apply glue to two adjacent sides of each block, then position it and tack it in place. After the blocks are attached, they can be chamfered to make them less visible.

If you can't find wooden drawer pulls, you can make them yourself. Turn them to the shape shown in the drawing on p. 175, and place them on the horizontal center of the drawer front. Secure them in place with a wood screw passed from the inside of the drawer.

Much furniture of the Federal period can be interpreted either formally or informally without major changes in design or construction. This informal chest, for example, can be transformed like a Cinderella with only superficial alterations. The possibilities are vast, and, for obvious reasons of space, they cannot all be given here. Instead I'll simply offer general suggestions for making a more sophisticated version of this chest and refer readers interested in such an interpretation to the survey books in the bibliography, which contain many examples of formal versions of this chest.

This chest could be made of mahogany or walnut. Both woods are dark and have a pronounced figure, which make these species more suitable for formal furniture. On a formal chest, the sides and front edges of the top would probably be molded. The shape typically used was a shallow reverse ogee, a survival feature from a Chippendale chest of drawers. To articulate its façade, each drawer front would have real, rather than simulated, cock beading (that is, a thin strip of wood with a half-round edge would be applied to the edges of the drawer front instead of this molding shape being cut directly into the drawer front). Brass drawer pulls would be almost obligatory. They probably would have been of the oval-backplate variety associated with the Hepplewhite style. Small oval escutcheons would be used with this type of pull.

The final alteration I would suggest would be to replace the simple ovolo molding on the edge of the base with a more sophisticated shape, such as a stepped cove. A stepped ogee would also be effective. Both the cove and the ogee are common Federal architectural and furniture molding profiles. When they are used on a bracket base, they are seen from above, a perspective that can make it difficult to discern the profile's shape. To help articulate these moldings, an additional step, or fillet, was often added to the upper edge. The detail is contained in the plane used to make the molding, and such planes were most often intended for furnituremakers rather than craftsmen in the building trades. These planes are distinguished from others that make the same shape without the step and are called stepped-cove planes or stepped-ogee planes.

Each of these formal details is a subtle addition. We cannot, however, add such details without paying attention to how they will relate to the base. On the original chest, the base is complex because the facade is so plain. Yet if the original base were to be retained on a formal version of the chest, the design would be overpowering and cease to be successful.

For the formal version, the base could be simplified by eliminating everything between the spurs on the feet. This would leave a straight line across most of the bottom edge of the skirt, both on the front and on the sides.

Many chests of this type are only 36 in. high, while this example is 41 in. The scale of this chest is appropriate for our bedroom, though, which is 14 ft. by 17 ft. with a 7-ft. ceiling. Another similar Federal chest we own has graduated drawers and is only 36 in. high, the difference being in the height of the drawer fronts, which are each 1¼ in. narrower than those on this chest. If you want to reduce the height of the chest you are making, you can do so in the same manner.

If you have made the chest in mahogany or walnut, use a clear finish to let the figure of the wood show through. Oil and wax are acceptable for an informal chest, but they're too flat for a formal interpretation. On a formal chest, I would suggest a harder finish, like varnish or lacquer, which will reflect highlights. I usually prefer the appearance of shellac, but it's easily dissolved and can be damaged by liquids kept on a chest top, such as nail-polish remover or aftershave.

The original chest was stained with a red wash. The selection of birch as the primary wood may have affected this choice of finish. Birch has almost no figure, so there is no reason to use a clear finish—there is nothing to see. On this chest, a more recent coat of red paint over the original wash has become quite worn, but I have not disturbed it because the antique market places a high value on old paint, and I would damage my investment if I stripped the chest.

Simulated cock beading

A bead is a simple, half-round molding shape cut into or added onto the edge of an architectural or furniture part. Cock beading consists of a separate piece of wood, usually a thin strip of edge-grain mahogany, glued into a shallow rabbet so that it projects slightly above the surface of the wood. The raised and rounded lip of the cock beading serves to enhance a flat, uniform facade and, when added to a veneered piece, like the secretary on p. 58, also helps protect the edges of the veneer from chipping.

Cock beading replaced the thumbnail molded lip commonly used in the Queen Anne and Chippendale periods on unveneered drawer fronts like those on the desk on frame (p. 138). Eventually it became a convention used by nearly all Federal-period cabinetmakers. Real cock beading often adorned formal furniture of the period, while simulated cock beading, cut into the edge of the piece, was frequently used on informal furniture. Unlike real cock beading, this incised beading is flush with the flat surface it decorates and is set off from it by a groove. If this groove has a flat bottom, called a quirk, the molding is known as a quirked bead. If the groove is V-shaped, the molding is called a bead and bevel.

On this chest it was not necessary to use cock beading to protect the edges of the drawers because they are solid birch, but the piece is so simple that some decoration was required to break up the plain front. Although the maker and the customer most likely wanted to avoid the extra work and expense of veneer and real cock beading, they would have undoubtedly been uncomfortable without the detail that was such a universal part of the Federal-furniture idiom. The compromise used on this chest was simulated cock beading in the form of a bead and bevel.

This molding shape is usually made with a molding plane, but a plane will leave intersecting lines crisscrossing at the corners of the drawer fronts. Therefore I made the simulated cock beading with a scratch tool. Although the tool seems primitive, the way it works is fairly sophisticated. I made mine from a block of tulipwood, ⅞ in. by 1¼ in. by 4⅞ in. The exact dimensions are not important, however. My tool was made from a piece of scrap, cut to fit my rather small hands.

The wood makes up the body, or stock, of the scratch tool and acts as both a handle and a fence. The cutting is done by the slot of a No. 16, 1½-in. wood screw, which is screwed into the block leaving about ¼ in. of the head exposed. To make the tool, drill a pilot hole ¾ in. from one end of the stock and drive in the screw. The scratch tool is similar to a universal plow plane, or moving fillister plane, in that the width of cut is adjustable. With the scratch tool, this adjustment is made by turning the screw to drive or retract it, thus enabling it to make beads of different widths.

For the tool to work properly, the three edges of the screw—the flat head, the beveled underside and the slot—must meet at a sharp point. I used a soft Arkansas stone to sharpen both the flat surface of the head and the beveled underside.

To help articulate the chest's plain facade, the drawer fronts are decorated with simulated cock beading, a half-round molding shape cut into the edges of the drawers.

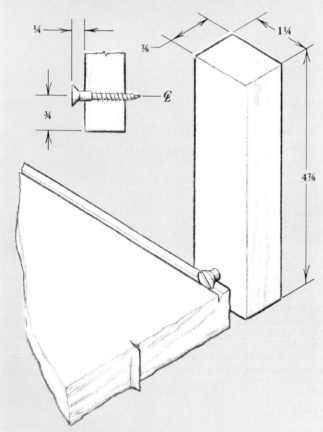

A simple scratch tool, made of a wooden block and a wood screw with a sharpened head, can be used to cut a V-grooved bead and bevel. A quirked bead must be produced with a molding plane.

Note: *Profile is completed by rounding arris with a block plane.*

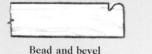

Bead and bevel

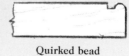

Quirked bead

PROPERLY ANGLING THE SCREW SLOT

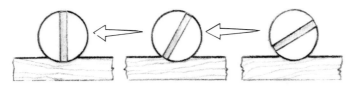

A. *With slot vertical, tool won't cut.*   **B.** *Correct slot angle to contact wood.*   **C.** *Too much angle, tool just scores line.*

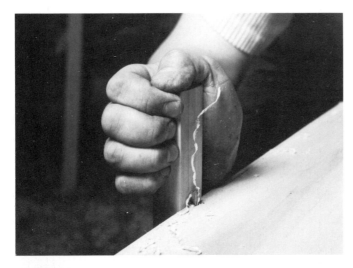

The body of the scratch tool acts as a handle and a fence (top). Push or pull the tool firmly against the edge of the drawer front. The slot in the screw will cut a narrow groove, about 1/16 in. deep, ejecting the chip as it creates the groove. Use a small parting tool to join the grooves at the corners (above). Then with a block plane, round the arris of each edge (right).

To use the tool, first place the block firmly against the edge of the drawer front with the edge of the screw head in contact with the wood's surface. Then turn the screw to the angle at which the slot cuts best, as shown in the drawing at left. If the slot is vertical, as in A, the tool won't cut. In B, the leading edge of the slot is raised so that the cut can be made by the edge that follows. Tilting the slot too much (C), however, raises the cutting point so that you merely score a line with the edge of the screw head without removing any wood.

Use the scratch tool to make a groove as deep as the tool will cut on each of the four edges of each drawer front. The tool works well on both the long edges and the short edges. On the latter, the chip will curl up into and be ejected by the screw slot, much like it would be in the throat of a molding plane. Try to make the grooves come as close together in the four corners as you can without overlapping them. You can use a small parting tool to join the grooves in the corners where the scratch tool will not reach.

These grooves establish the bevel part of the bead-and-bevel molding profile. Rounding the arris with a block plane will complete the rounded part of the profile. On the two ends of the drawer front, where there is end grain, you risk chipping the corners if you plane straight across them. Therefore plane from the corners toward the middle when working on the ends. After you're finished, use a scrap block of wood with 120-grit sandpaper wrapped around it to smooth away the faceted plane marks.

You can also use this scratch tool to cut beading on several other pieces shown in this book, such as the backs of the continuous-arm and oval-back Windsors on p. 120. The flat fence of this tool will not work on the inside edge of a piece of bent wood, though, such as on the bent backs of the Windsor chairs. To cut a bead on these curved surfaces, you'll have to make another tool with a rounded fence so that it can cut on the inside of a radius.

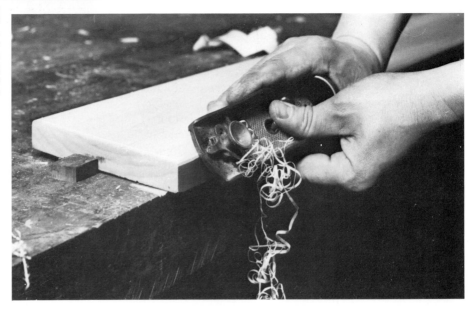

CHEST OF DRAWERS

Scale: ³⁄₃₂ in. = 1 in.

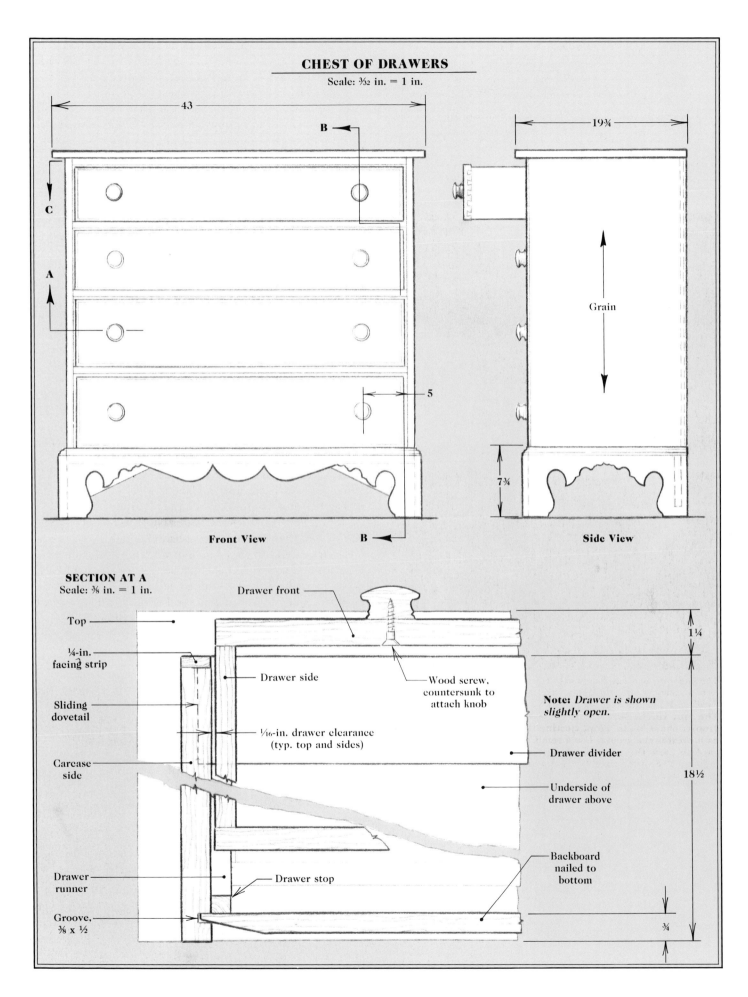

43

19¾

B

C

A

Grain

5

7¾

Front View

B

Side View

SECTION AT A
Scale: ⅜ in. = 1 in.

Drawer front

Top

¼-in.
facing strip

Drawer side

Wood screw,
countersunk to
attach knob

1¼

Sliding
dovetail

Note: *Drawer is shown
slightly open.*

¹⁄₁₆-in. drawer clearance
(typ. top and sides)

Drawer divider

Carcase
side

Underside of
drawer above

18½

Drawer
runner

Drawer stop

Backboard
nailed to
bottom

Groove,
⅜ x ½

¾

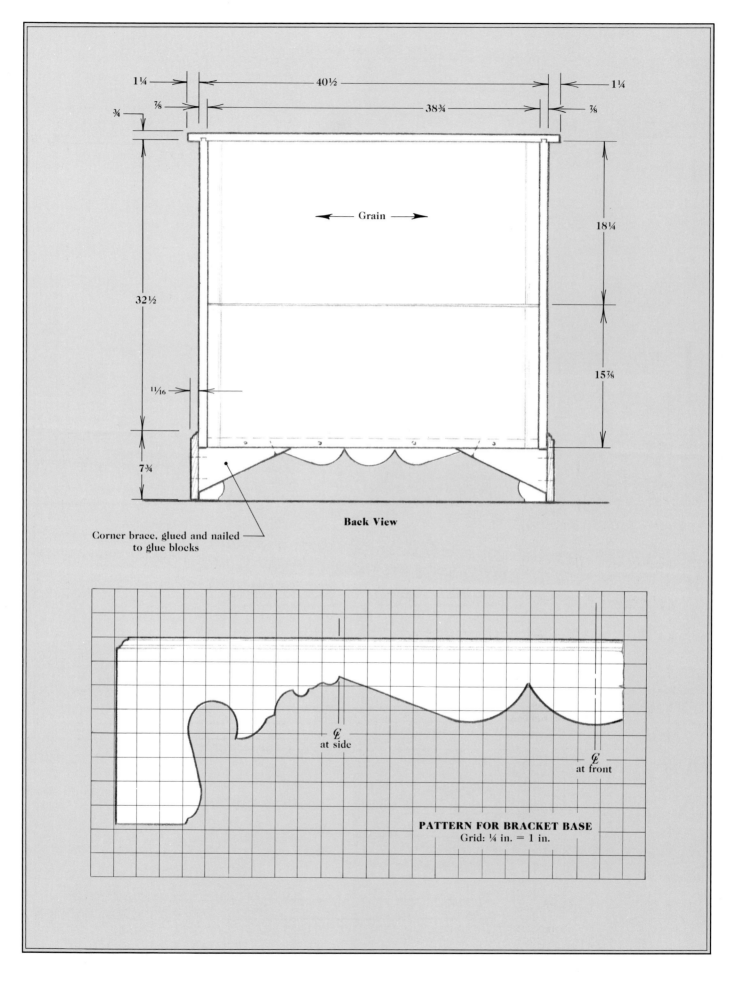

1¼ 40½ 1¼
⅞ 38¾ ⅞
¾
Grain
18¼
32½
15⅞
11/16
7¾

Back View

Corner brace, glued and nailed
to glue blocks

𝒞L
at side

𝒞L
at front

PATTERN FOR BRACKET BASE
Grid: ¼ in. = 1 in.

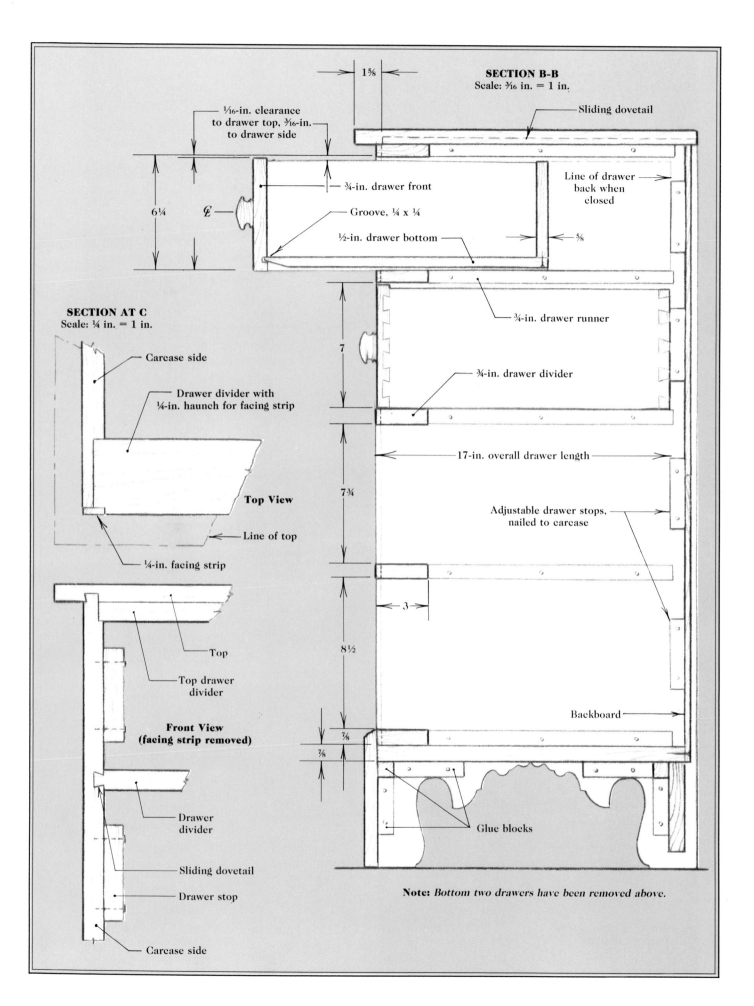

SECTION B-B
Scale: ³⁄₁₆ in. = 1 in.

1⁵⁄₈

¹⁄₁₆-in. clearance to drawer top, ³⁄₁₆-in. to drawer side

Sliding dovetail

¾-in. drawer front

Line of drawer back when closed

6¼

℄

Groove, ¼ x ¼

½-in. drawer bottom

⁵⁄₈

SECTION AT C
Scale: ¼ in. = 1 in.

Carcase side

Drawer divider with ¼-in. haunch for facing strip

7

¾-in. drawer runner

¾-in. drawer divider

Top View

Line of top

¼-in. facing strip

7¾

17-in. overall drawer length

Adjustable drawer stops, nailed to carcase

Top

Top drawer divider

Front View
(facing strip removed)

3

8½

Drawer divider

Sliding dovetail

Drawer stop

Carcase side

Backboard

⁷⁄₈

⁷⁄₈

Glue blocks

Note: *Bottom two drawers have been removed above.*

Sources of Supply

Finishes
Old Fashioned Milk Paint Company, Box 222, Groton, MA 01450

Hardware
Ball and Ball, 463 W. Lincoln Hwy., Exton, PA 19341

18th Century Hardware Company, 131 E. Third St., Derry, PA 15627

Horton Brasses, Nooks Hill Rd., Box 120MA, Cromwell, CT 06416

Tremont Nail Co., 8 Elm St., Box 111, Wareham, MA 02571

Reverse glass painting
Gilders Workshop, 7 Sheffield Rd., Winchester, MA 02890

Veneer and inlay
The Woodworker's Store, 21801 Industrial Blvd., Rogers, MN 55374

Constantine, 2050 Eastchester Rd., Bronx, NY 10461

Other sources of supply and information
For suppliers of rush, reproduction fabric and related products, see the advertisers in the following magazines:

Colonial Homes, The Hearst Corp., 1700 Broadway, New York, NY 10019

Early American Life, Historical Times, Inc., Box 8200, 2245 Kohn Rd., Harrisburg, PA 17105

The Magazine Antiques, Straight Enterprises, Inc., 551 Fifth Ave., New York, NY 10176

Yankee, Yankee Publishing, Inc., Dublin, NH 03444

Glossary

acanthus-leaf decoration Ornamentation resembling acanthus leaves used in classical architecture. Early in the Federal period, this motif was a common, carved decoration, accurately copied from classical sources; it later grew more and more stylized and eventually became purely textural carving.

apron See *skirt*.

architrave The lowest element of an entablature. Often used separately around door, window and fireplace openings in interior architecture.

astragal A projecting, half-round molding, often set off by a fillet on either side, which is frequently used in combination with other molding profiles, such as a cove or an ogee.

backband The molding applied to the outer or upper edge of an architrave.

ball-and-claw foot A decorative motif used with the Chippendale cabriole leg and carved in the shape of a bird's claw with three talons grasping a ball.

banding See *edge banding*.

bead An incised, half-round molding, commonly used in architecture and on furniture, sometimes simulating cock beading. Run on an edge of an architectural or furniture part, the bead is flush with the surface and set off by a *V*-groove (then called a bead and bevel) or by a flat-bottomed groove, or quirk (then called a quirked bead).

beading, cock A thin strip of wood with a rounded outer edge, which is often applied to the edges of veneered drawers for decoration and protection.

bed bolt A bolt with a flange around the bottom of the head, used to secure a heavy mortise-and-tenon joint such as that on a bed frame.

bed-bolt cover A decorative plate, usually made of stamped brass, tacked over the heads of bed bolts.

bootjack A cut-out shape resembling a bookjack (the device used to help remove high boots), which was sometimes used on the bottom of simple case pieces.

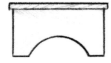 

bookmatched veneer Sheets of veneer from the same flitch, butted together to produce a pattern and its mirror image.

boss 1) On a pedestal table, the base of the pedestal into which the table's legs are joined. 2) A round, central, projecting ornament, which is usually applied.

bracket base The shaped boards applied to the base of a piece of case furniture to form the feet. More common in the 18th century, this base was largely replaced during the Federal period by French feet or turned legs.

bricklaid A method of strengthening curved surfaces, such as a table skirt, by gluing together two or more layers of wood with staggered joints, which resemble brickwork.

broken pediment See *pediment*.

cabriole leg See *leg, cabriole*.

canopy The cloth curtains suspended from the frame, or tester, of a high-post bed. In the late 19th century, a simplified canopy of cloth or knotted netting was often used as a purely decorative covering on the frame.

card-table hinge A special scissor hinge, used to attach the leaves of a card table.

casein paint An inexpensive alternative to oil paint for utilitarian purposes, which uses milk casein as a binder. Also called milk paint.

cavetto See *cove*.

Chippendale The furniture period introduced to America from England in the mid-18th century, which followed the Queen Anne period and preceded the Federal period. Characterized by robust, often ornately decorated furniture, which made frequent use of such rococo motifs as carved shells, the ball-and-claw foot and the *C*-scroll.

claw-and-ball foot See *ball-and-claw foot*.

cleat A thin, wooden batten, usually applied to the underside of a wide surface such as a tabletop or lid to minimize warpage. Cleats can be made to function mechanically as part of a hinge block.

clench nail A soft, wrought nail that turns back on itself when driven through wood and against a metal surface. Until machine-made wood screws were developed in the early 19th century, clench nails were commonly used to permanently secure two pieces of wood.

cock beading See *beading, cock*.

cornice The upper horizontal section of an entablature, consisting of one or more moldings and sometimes a row of dentils. Often separated from the entablature and used independently, for example, in architecture under an eave, or, in furniture, on the top of tall case pieces and some mirrors.

cove A concave quarter-round molding profile (*near right*). Also called a cavetto. When this molding is stepped, the profile is called a stepped cove (*far right*).

crest rail The horizontal member at the top of a chair back that connects the chair's two stiles.

crown glass Window or sheet glass commonly made until the early 19th century by spinning a large, flat wheel or disc of glass from which panes were then cut.

crown plank The board cut from the center of a log, which contains the pith, or heartwood. The wood on either side of the pith is desirable because it is exceptionally stable.

cyma curve An *S*-shaped double curve, which is often used as a molding profile and which is also called an ogee. When the top of the curve is concave, it is called a cyma recta or reverse ogee (*below left*). When the curve is convex on top, it is called a cyma reversa but is often simply referred to as an ogee (*below right*).

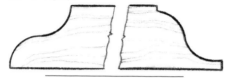

demi-lune A half-round shape. Many Federal-period card tables and pier tables, as well as some commodes, sideboards and chests of drawers, had demi-lune tops.

dentil, or denticulated, molding A molding, often used in a cornice, composed of a series of rectangular blocks resembling teeth.

drop-leaf table A table with a fixed top and hinged leaves that can be raised and lowered.

edge banding A narrow band or strip of vertical-grain veneer.

Empire The furniture period originating in Europe at the beginning of the 19th century, which became popular in America around 1815 and gradually brought the Federal period to a close. The period took its name from Napoleon Bonaparte's French Empire and was influenced by the archaeological finds at Greek and Egyptian sites. Empire furniture tended to be heavier than Federal furniture and was frequently ornamented with Greek and Egyptian motifs and with matching mahogany veneers.

engaged column A column that projects on the front but is flat on the back and attached to a wall or other surface.

entablature The architectural elements above the capitals of columns and below the pediment, consisting of the cornice, frieze and architrave.

escutcheon A plate, usually brass, applied over or inlaid around a keyhole.

false drawer A simulated drawer front.

false-graining A painting technique for simulating the figure and grain of real wood with two or more layers of paint. The effect produced can range in verisimilitude from trompe l'oeil to abstract. Also called, as in French, *faux-bois*.

Fancy chair A turned, Federal-period chair with a japanned finish, usually decorated with striping, stenciling or freehand painting. This inexpensive chair generally had a woven cane or rush seat.

fillet A narrow, flat surface used to set off a molding or to separate two moldings.

finial A turned element often used to surmount a post or a pediment.

flitch A sheaf of successive, or sister, cuts of veneer.

fluting A series of vertical and parallel, concave grooves carved on a surface. The opposite of reeding.

fly rail The movable part of the hinged skirt that supports a leaf on some drop-leaf tables.

foot, French A flared foot, associated with the Hepplewhite style and often used on case furniture.

foot, pad A shaped foot set on, or elevated by, a thin platform.

foot, spade A sharply tapered, nearly diamond-shaped foot, sometimes used on the tapered leg associated with the Hepplewhite style.

frieze The middle element of an entablature, which is found beneath the cornice and above the architrave.

gallery A raised edge often used on tabletops, chests of drawers, trays and other furniture, which can be solid or pierced.

gateleg table A drop-leaf table whose leaves are supported by hinged, swinging legs rather than by fly rails.

Georgian A style of architecture popular in England in the late 17th century, which coincided with the Chippendale period. Georgian architecture became fashionable in America throughout most of the 18th century and preceded Federal architecture.

gesso A paste made of whiting and either sizing or glue, used as a smooth base for gilding, japanning or painting.

gimlet A small tool with a threaded point, used to prebore a screw hole.

Gothic arch A pointed arch, borrowed from Gothic architecture, which has a joint at its apex rather than a keystone.

haircloth A tough fabric with a sheen like satin, whose warp is cotton, linen or wool and whose weft is hair from horse manes and tails. Often used as upholstery fabric during the Federal period.

Hepplewhite One interpretation of neoclassical furniture popularized by the 1788 publication in England of George Hepplewhite's pattern book, *The Cabinet-maker and Upholsterer's Guide*. Though Hepplewhite furniture typically incorporates such features as curved lines, tapered legs, and French or spade feet, it may also feature the squarer lines and turned legs generally associated with Sheraton furniture. These two contemporaneous furniture styles were actually very similar but were assigned somewhat arbitrary distinctions by late 19th-century and early 20th-century collectors.

hinge block The wooden block tenoned to the top of a tripod-table pedestal and attached to the cleats on which the tabletop pivots.

iron oxide A rust-colored pigment used to make red paint.

japanning A finishing process imitating oriental lacquerwork, consisting of several layers of varnish applied over a painted and often gilded surface. Japanning was popular on painted Federal furniture like Fancy chairs and on tinware of the period.

keeper A device to lock into position a latch bar or lock bolt securing a door, lid or top of a tip-top table.

leg, cabriole A curved leg with a projecting knee and an incurved ankle, which is associated with the Queen Anne and Chippendale periods. This leg can terminate in a variety of feet; for example, ball-and-claw, scroll or pad.

leg, turned A leg shaped on the lathe. Turned legs, with or without reeding, were often used on Sheraton and Empire furniture.

Marlborough leg A square leg, either plain or more commonly molded, that was popular during the Chippendale period.

milk paint See *casein paint*.

molding A narrow, continuous strip of wood used for decoration, generally shaped as a concave or convex profile, or a combination of the two, but which can also be flat.

mullion See *muntin*.

muntin A thin, wooden molding strip dividing the panes of glass in a window or door. Also called mullion or munnion. Though mullion actually refers to the vertical dividers, the terms are generally used interchangeably.

neoclassical The period in furniture and architecture originating in Europe in the mid-18th century, which followed the Chippendale period and became popular in America around 1790. Triggered by archaeological discoveries at classical sites, the revival of interest in classical Greek and Roman forms expressed itself in America in what is called Federal art and architecture.

ogee See *cyma curve.*

old red stain Antique dealers' term for an inexpensive, thin red paint, sometimes used to finish utilitarian woodwork. On formal mahogany furniture, the same stain was sometimes applied to light-colored secondary woods to lessen their contrast with the dark primary wood.

ormolu The cast-brass decoration on late Federal and Empire furniture, which was popularized by French cabinetmakers who immigrated to America fleeing the French Revolution.

ovolo A quarter-round molding profile, set off top and bottom by a fillet.

patera A small, ornamental disc, oval, round or square, applied to or inlaid on a flat surface.

patina Discoloration, usually a darkening, of a wooden surface due to age and use.

pattern books Books published from the mid-18th century through most of the 19th century by individual cabinetmakers or other members of the furniture trade, which were intended to familiarize cabinetmakers and their customers with the latest designs in furniture and interior decor.

pediment 1) The triangular space forming the gable of a pitched roof. 2) A device of the same or a similar shape used over doorways and windows, or to top some pieces of furniture. Sometimes a pediment is open at its apex and is then called a broken pediment.

Pembroke table A small drop-leaf table with a wide, fixed top and narrow leaves. Introduced in the Chippendale period as a portable table on which to have breakfast or tea, the Pembroke form became even more popular in the Federal period.

pier The space on a wall between two openings, whether doors or windows.

pilaster A flattened pillar, rectangular in cross section, that is applied to a wall or other surface and ornamented as a column.

plinth A square or rectangular block serving as the base for a column, pilaster, finial or even a statue.

pommel The elevated center in the front top edge of a Windsor chair seat, which fits between the sitter's legs.

primary wood The species of wood used on the visible surfaces of a piece of furniture.

Queen Anne Early 18th-century furniture period in England and America, which preceded the Chippendale period. Queen Anne furniture is delicate, restrained in its ornament and strongly curvilinear.

quirk A flat-bottomed groove used to set off a molding. Quirked moldings became stylish during the Federal period.

rail A horizontal member of a frame.

reeding A series of parallel, convex moldings used to decorate flat or curved surfaces. An ornament associated with the Sheraton style, reeding is the opposite of fluting.

Regency In England, the early 19th-century furniture period inspired by classical Greek and Egyptian forms and motifs, which corresponds to the early Empire period in America.

reverse ogee See *cyma curve.*

reverse painting Painting on the back side of glass or sometimes mica; a common Federal-period technique prized for its luminance and lifelike depth and quality.

riven wood Wood used for furniture, cooperage or construction that is split, rather than sawn, from the log.

rosette A disc ornamented with relieved, foliate decoration or concentric circles. Rosette drawer pulls are associated with Sheraton-style furniture and that of the early Empire period.

rule joint A hinged joint used on drop-leaf tables, composed of a concave edge on a drop leaf and a convex edge on the fixed top.

secondary wood An inexpensive, easy-to-work wood used to make furniture parts that are unseen; for example, drawer interiors, backboards and the core of a veneered panel.

Sheraton An interpretation of neoclassical furniture named for the English cabinetmaker Thomas Sheraton, whose pattern book, *The Cabinet-maker's and Upholsterer's Drawing-Book* (1791-93), spread the style first in England and then to America. Straight lines, turned legs and reeded decoration are generally associated with Sheraton furniture, but it also occasionally carries the curved lines, tapered legs and ornament considered characteristic of the contemporaneous Hepplewhite style.

skirt The horizontal frame beneath a table-top that joins the legs and may be plain or shaped. Also called an apron.

slip seat A padded and upholstered, removable seat that fits inside the seat rails of a chair.

spiral turning A rope-like detail, associated with the Empire period, that is carved on a piece that has been turned on a lathe.

splat The thin, vertical member filling the area in the back of a chair between the stiles. The design of splats varied from period to period and could be pierced, carved or veneered.

stile 1) A vertical member of a frame. 2) The sections of the rear legs above the seat rails, which frame a chair back and are connected at the top by the crest rail.

stretcher One of a system of members connecting the legs of a chair or table. Federal-period chairs were usually constructed with either box stretchers or *H*-stretchers.

string inlay Thin strips of wood contrasting in color (usually lighter) with the primary wood, laid in recessed inlets in the surface of a piece of furniture.

stringing See *string inlay.*

striping Thin, painted lines, usually of a contrasting color, simulating the string inlay used on some formal furniture. Striping often decorated Fancy chairs, Windsor chairs and other painted furniture both during and after the Federal period.

survival feature A feature characteristic of one furniture period that remains in use, or "survives," in succeeding periods.

table-leaf hinge A rectangular hinge with one leg longer than the other, designed for drop-leaf tables.

tester The wooden canopy frame on a high-post bed.

T-headed finish nail A cut or wrought nail with a thin, *T*-shaped head that is difficult to see when set because the wood fibers spring back to partially hide it. These nails range in size from brads to 16d flooring nails.

thumbnail molding A quarter-ellipse molding profile commonly used on Georgian interior woodwork and on the edge of drawers in the Queen Anne and Chippendale periods.

tip-top table A pedestal table whose top is hinged to allow it to be raised and lowered.

trifid support A three-legged iron plate, nailed to the bottom of the boss on tripod tables to strengthen the table-leg joints.

tripod table A pedestal table with three radiating legs that are usually dovetailed to the boss. Popular from the early 18th century, pedestal tables were produced in even greater quantity during the Federal period.

twist turning See *spiral turning.*

urn A classical vase shape with square, rather than round, shoulders and a square or round pedestal bottom. This was a popular motif in Federal furniture, often used in such places as tripod-table pedestals, finials and chair splats.

vase A common turning shape that is bulbous at the bottom and has round shoulders and a narrow, elongated neck.

Windsor chair An informal, painted chair made primarily of turned or whittled parts, with a solid-wood seat and usually some bent elements. Introduced in America in the mid-18th century, the Windsor reached the height of its popularity during the Federal period.

Bibliography

Blanchard, Roberta Ray. *How to Restore and Decorate Chairs.* New York: M. Barrows and Co., Inc., 1952.

Bogdonoff, Nancy Dick. *Handwoven Textiles of New England: The Legacy of a Rural People.* Harrisburg, Penn.: Stackpole Books, 1975.

Brazer, Esther. *Early American Decoration.* 1947. Reprinted, New York: AMS Press.

Comstock, Helen. *The Looking Glass in America, 1700-1825.* New York: The Studio Publications, Inc., 1968.

Comstock, Ruth B. *Rush Seats for Chairs* (pamphlet). Ithica: Cornell University Press, 1968.

Crafton, John Seville. *The London Upholsterer's Companion.* London, 1834.

Dunbar, Michael. *Antique Woodworking Tools.* New York: Hastings House, Inc., 1977.

———. *Make a Windsor Chair with Michael Dunbar.* Newtown, Conn.: The Taunton Press, 1984.

Garrett, Elisabeth Donaghy. "The American home, Part I." *The Magazine Antiques* 123 (January 1983): 214-25.

———. "The American home, Part II." *The Magazine Antiques* 123 (February 1983): 408-17.

———. "The American home, Part III." *The Magazine Antiques* 123 (March 1983): 612-25.

———. "The American home, Part IV." *The Magazine Antiques* 126 (October 1984): 910-22.

———. "The American home, Part V." *The Magazine Antiques* 128 (August 1985): 259-65.

———. "The American home, Part VI." *The Magazine Antiques* 128 (December 1985): 1210-23.

Hepplewhite, George. *The Cabinet-Maker and Upholsterer's Guide.* New York: Dover Publications, Inc., 1969.

Hewitt, Benhamin A., Patricia E. Kane, and Gerald W.R. Ward. *The Work of Many Hands: Card Tables in Federal America 1790-1820.* New Haven: Yale University Art Gallery, 1982.

Hummel, Charles F. *With Hammer in Hand.* Charlottesville: University Press of Virginia, 1968.

Kane, Patricia E. *300 Years of American Seating Furniture.* Boston: New York Graphic Society, 1976.

Lea, Zilla Rider, ed. *The Ornamented Chair: Its Development in America (1700-1890).* Rutland, Vt.: Charles E. Tuttle Co., 1960.

Montgomery, Charles F. *American Furniture, The Federal Period, in the Henry Francis du Pont Winterthur Museum.* London: Thames and Hudson, Ltd., 1966.

Morse, John D., ed. *Country Cabinetwork and Simple City Furniture.* Charlottesville: University Press of Virginia, 1970.

Nutting, Wallace. *Furniture Treasury.* New York: Macmillan Publishing Co., Inc., 1928.

———. *A Windsor Handbook.* Rutland, Vt.: Charles E. Tuttle Co., 1973.

Ormsbee, Thomas H. *The Windsor Chair.* Great Neck, N.Y.: Deerfield Books, Inc., 1962.

Peterson, Harold L. *American Interiors from Colonial Times to the Late Victorians, A Pictorial Sourcebook.* 1971. Reprinted, New York: Charles Scribner's Sons, 1978.

Sack, Albert. *Fine Points of Furniture: Early American.* New York: Crown Publishers, Inc., 1950.

Santore, Charles. *The Windsor Style in America.* Philadelphia: Running Press, 1981.

Sheraton, Thomas. *The Cabinet-Maker and Upholsterer's Drawing-Book.* New York: Dover Publications, Inc., 1972.

Publisher, Books: Leslie Carola
Associate Editors: Deborah Cannarella, Scott Landis, Christine Timmons
Design Director: Roger Barnes
Associate Art Director: Heather Brine Lambert
Copy/Production Editor: Nancy Stabile
Illustrations: Brian Gulick, Heather Brine Lambert
Manager of Production Services: Gary Mancini
Coordinator of Production Services: Dave DeFeo
System Operator: Claudia Blake Applegate
Production Assistants: Deborah Cooper, Dinah George
Pasteup: Marty Higham, Deb Rives-Skiles, Barbara Snyder

Typeface: Caslon Book, 9½ point
Printer and Binder: Aarhuus Stiftsbogtrykkerie, Arhus, Denmark